THE ENCYCLOPEDIA OF THE
YELLOW JERSEY

TEXT AND STATISTICS
PHILIPPE BOUVET AND FRÉDÉRIQUE GALAMETZ

ILLUSTRATIONS
GREG

CONTENTS

THE ENCYCLOPEDIA OF THE YELLOW JERSEY

Fausto Coppi,
1952 Parc des Princes.

I REMEMBER...

BY EDDY MERCKX

I remember Charly Gaul, in yellow, in 1958.

I remember that in 1969 the yellow jersey's sleeves were printed with the initials HD.

I remember that in 1969 Rudi Altig beat me in the prologue in Roubaix because I had not been competing since my exclusion from the Giro.

I remember the Virlux branding, the first real sponsor of the yellow jersey.

I remember putting on my first yellow jersey in Belgium, thanks to time bonuses, after the team time trial in Woluwe-Saint-Pierre. But it was only on the Ballon d'Alsace that I really felt it belonged to me.

I remember Joaquim Galera on the Ballon d'Alsace and Joaquim Agostinho on Mont Ventoux.

I remember wearing yellow as I passed Tervuren, where I used to live, and there being a huge crowd.

I remember Guillaume Driessens telling me to be careful on the road to Mourenx.

I remember how hot it was in the Pyrenees that day.

I remember the yellow jersey was made of wool.

I remember Julien Stevens and Italo Zilioli, two team mates in yellow.

I remember that at Mont Ventoux I was wearing a black mourning ribbon in memory of Vincenzo Giacotto, the manager of Faema who died during the Tour.

I remember having exaggerated my illness at the top of Ventoux to get down the other side more quickly… in an ambulance.

I remember that the yellow jersey went much better with my colouring, as opposed to the pink jersey of the Giro.

I remember that my critics were always saying that I would never win the Tour because I could not tolerate the heat.

I remember winning in 1969, a full 30 years after Sylvère Maes.

I remember that for the journalists, I lost every time I did not win.

I remember when Antoine Blondin compared me with the Attila the Hun.

I remember the thrill of entering the Cipale (velodrome) in front of 25,000 people.

I remember that it was Christian Raymond, of the Peugeot team, who nicknamed me 'The Cannibal'.

I remember the storm on the Col de Menté in 1971, a torrent of black mud, and my own crash on the bend, but not that of Luis Ocaña.

I remember that some journalists wrote that Ocaña could have continued the next day.

I remember people were spitting at me at the Col du Portillon after Ocaña's crash.

I remember that the morning after the Menté stage, I was so stiff and sore that I rode up Peyresourde as a warm-up.

I remember that I went over to ask Lucien Van Impe to take it easy.

I remember Jacques Goddet's colonial outfits.

I remember that in 1971, in the Alps, Félix Levitan had caught up with the 'two Ks' and their leader José Manuel Fuente, who went on to win two stages.

I remember that everything was arranged so that Merckx would not win.

I remember that I was wearing a Rodania watch.

I remember that sometimes we slept in gymnasiums.

I remember Giorgio Albani, my team manager.

I remember that during the Tour I was sent threatening letters from French spectators who did not want me to equal the record of Jacques Anquetil.

I remember crashing behind the derny, with the yellow jersey, in September 1969 at the Critérium de Blois, and never being quite the same again.

I remember the ease and skill with which I came down the Col d'Allos in 1975.

I remember…nothing at all about going up Pra-Loup.

I remember that in 1975 the entire peloton was united against me.

I remember that Francesco Moser was assisting Bernard Thévenet down the descent of Col de la Madeleine, and without his intervention I have no doubt I would have retaken the yellow jersey.

I remember having worn it for 97 days, and only having one or two left at my house.

100 YEARS LATER

BY PHILIPPE BRUNEL

It is now 100 years since the yellow jersey was born. Invented with the simple mission of identifying the race leader in the peloton, over the past century it has taken on a legendary status, becoming a symbol of the Tour de France, and recognized the world over. Something of its power can be seen in how we use the very words themselves: the yellow jersey is an object, a prize, but when the jersey is worn, it becomes the cyclist – the rider who is race leader IS the yellow jersey.

Events of the last two decades have not helped the image of competitive cycling, the Tour itself, nor indeed, at times, the image of the yellow jersey. These days, the jersey can look like a relic of more innocent times, when the race was simply about human endeavour: the cyclist fighting his mental and physical battles with his rivals over the endless kilometres for days on end. Back in the day, we might venture to hope, the influence of money and the pressure of doping were not part of the picture.

While it is tempting to try to idealize the Tour, it is misplaced. Each summer, the Tour unfolds like a kind of intense three-week human drama. There are acts of aggression, betrayals, revenge and repentance, bitterness and rancour, heroism, bravery, self-sacrifice. As spectators, we get drawn into the drama, with our sense of the good guys and the bad guys, we pick our winners, savour their victories and suffer with them when it all goes wrong.

There has been a darker side to the Tour since the very early days. The first indications of this came in 1924 when the Pélissier brothers decided to abandon the Tour halfway through a stage in Coutances in Normandy. In an interview with journalist Albert Londres (who met them in Coutances), the brothers complained about the punishing regime of the race, and how they felt subjugated by the organizers. 'You have no idea,' said Henri Pélissier, 'what kind of an ordeal – what kind of a martyrdom – this Tour really is.' Warming to his theme, he told Londres how they were doped up with stimulants with the single aim of getting them to Paris, and emptied a bag onto the table in front of Londres: 'Here, look, cocaine for the eyes, chloroform for the gums…' While Albert Londres's subsequent report was aimed as a challenge to the Tour founder Henri Desgrange, there is little evidence that anything really changed, and the Tour became even more popular at the time. But what became clear was that a multi-stage road race across thousands of kilometres did not come without a price.

The symbolic power of the yellow jersey persists to this day. Those who wear it can experience a rare moment, becoming part of something totally unique, overwhelming and fulfilling all at the same time. Little wonder that so many tough-minded professional cyclists find themselves moved to tears on receiving the jersey. This book is packed with examples of battling adversity to realize a dream, and often, to see that dream evaporate soon afterwards. There are stories of self-sacrifice, such as that of René Vietto who, in 1934, climbed back up a mountain to give his wheel to his team leader Antonin Magne, just so that Magne could keep the yellow jersey. There are betrayals too, such as that suffered by Raphaël Géminiani: 'Judas' was how he described his compatriots Gilbert Bauvin and Louison Bobet in 1958, guilty, he claimed, of offering him no support against the attacks of Charly Gaul in the Chartreuse mountains. ■ ■ ■

Eugène Christophe: in 1919, he became the first man ever to wear the yellow jersey. At the time, nobody imagined that this simple piece of cycling kit would eventually take on such iconic status.

whole of France watching. He went on and on, over 140km on the hot slopes of the Col du Tourmalet. It was an act of pure bravura. Among his many jerseys, there was one that Merckx refused to wear, gained in Luchon in 1971 when his great rival Luis Ocaña crashed out while descending the Col de Menté. For while one route to the yellow jersey is through bitter struggle, the other is simply through someone else's misfortune.

Merckx had misfortune of his own four years later, as the mood among some Tour spectators seemed to have turned against him. The race leader was climbing the Puy du Dôme, when a man emerged from the crowd and punched him in the kidney. Merckx was unable to recover the stage, and apparently weakened by painkillers he collapsed during the climb of Pra-Loup while Frenchman Bernard Thévenet took the yellow jersey. 'We were all so used to his total domination that I had trouble believing that I had actually beaten him,' recalled Thévenet many years later. 'That night I saw the yellow jersey folded over the back of a chair, and I said to myself: "What the hell am I doing in Eddy's room?"'

Some jerseys are lost under the most extraordinary circumstances. Fiorenzo Magni was race leader when the entire Italian team quit the Tour in 1950 on the orders of Gino Bartali. He packed it into his case and took the train back to Italy. Michel Pollentier wore the jersey on the Alpe d'Huez in 1978 before being discovered trying to cheat the doping test that evening, and was ejected from the race. Bjarne Riis, who toppled Miguel Indurain in 1996, took the winner's jersey but effectively lost it, buried in a cardboard box in his garage after admitting to doping offences. And in a similar way countless jerseys were presented over the years to Lance Armstrong, who was later stripped of his titles for drugs cheating.

More recently, the jersey has been passing mainly between the members of Team Sky (known as Ineos from 2019 when the sponsorship changed), from Sir Bradley Wiggins to Chris Froome and Geraint Thomas. Ice-cool climbing specialist Chris Froome is a far cry from the saints, sinners and martyrs of the Tour's history and more in the mould of 21st-century athletes from many other sporting disciplines, subject to tightly controlled training regimes aimed at maximizing marginal gains across a range of areas. In 2013 he seemed to shrug off the effects of gravity during the climb of Mont Ventoux, past the memorial of Tom Simpson's death in 1967, on the same climb where Merckx, on the edge of consciousness, appeared to be wrestling his way up the slope in 1970. Froome pedalled on steadily, showing no signs of suffering, his rhythm relentless.

As this book demonstrates, the yellow jersey can be a fleeting experience of just a few hours, or it can add up to years of dominance on the Tour de France. While it is easy to look back on the stars of the past, we have yet to discover how today's riders will be seen by future generations. All we know is that the time will come, inevitably, to hand on the torch. ∎

■■■

There is crushing disappointment, epitomized by Laurent Fignon who saw his 50-second lead evaporate in the Paris time trial in 1989, ultimately losing by just eight seconds to Greg LeMond in a nail-biting final stage. And there is the constant threat of serious injury or even death. Wim Van Est was defending his yellow jersey when he fell into a ravine while descending the Col d'Aubisque, narrowly missing two huge boulders and miraculously escaping unscathed.

Yellow jersey riders face inevitable judgement by press and public. Some were lucky: the 'beautiful' and 'charming' Hugo Koblet in 1951 made his attacks look effortless on the road to Albi. Others were less fortunate. Roger Walkowiak was harshly judged for what was seen as a 'calculating approach' or a lack of 'panache'. Jacques Anquetil, the first five-time winner, suffered similar criticism and was even mocked for his short stature in 1961 by Tour director Jacques Goddet – no doubt forced to eat his words later as Anquetil led the race from the first to the final day.

In something of a 'rags to riches' theme, rank-and-file team members have also known the rare pleasure of putting on the yellow jersey, though usually with permission of the team. Winning the jersey was a cause of some anxiety for Andrea Carrea, the modest 'gregario' of team Bianchi (and of the great Fausto Coppi). Plenty of other team riders also got their moments of glory: Jean Robic, Jacques Marinelli, Georges Groussard, Felice Gimondi, Raymond Delisle, Richard Virenque, Thomas Voeckler and many, many more.

And then, of course, there was the phenomenon that is Eddy Merckx, the man who was awarded the yellow jersey an incredible 111 times during his career. Merckx came on the scene at the same time as the televised races, so his lone breakaway to Mourenx in 1969 had the

" **That night I saw the yellow jersey folded over the back of a chair, and I said to myself: 'What the hell am I doing in Eddy's room?'** "

Bernard Thévenet after Stage 15, from Nice to Pra-Loup, of the 1975 Tour.

HALL OF FAME

Multiple victories, dozens of yellow jerseys, millions of fans: a select few are guaranteed a special place in Tour de France history.

Jacques Anquetil, the first five-times Tour winner, made the yellow jersey his own.

ANQUETIL
A MAN OF QUIET EFFICIENCY

Pragmatic and perfectionist, Jacques Anquetil became the first five-times winner of the Tour de France.

Anquetil sets the pace on the Belgian cobbles.

1961

An all-rounder who could hold his own in the mountains too.

1962

"You need to have seen THAT, at least once in your entire life, to understand what perfection in cycling actually means."

Pierre Chany in *L'Équipe*.

Jacques Anquetil's name will always be synonymous with the Tour de France. A brilliant champion, he was never the most flamboyant, nor the most popular of the yellow jerseys. In fact, he took a lot of criticism for being something of a racing machine: perhaps back in the 1950s he was a man ahead of his time. Never a great crowd-pleaser, he simply gave exactly what was required to win. But he could also push himself to the limits like no other.

His Tour debut in 1957 felt like the start of a new era. Louison Bobet, triple winner of the Tour de France from 1953 to 1955, was beginning to feel his age. Heckled during his gruelling Giro ordeal earlier in that year in Italy, Bobet admitted he was 'not ready' to take part in the Tour de France. 'I'm 32,' he said. 'Time for younger riders to step up.'

Anquetil needed no further encouragement. Four years earlier, as a skinny teenager, he had won his first Grand Prix des Nations at 19 years old. Now aged 23, he was about to make his debut on the Tour de France, and win it first time. He began his campaign early, winning Stage 3 in Rouen, and then two days later putting on the yellow jersey for the first time in Charleroi. Anquetil had made a decisive breakaway shortly after the stage had begun in Roubaix. 'Jacques really started to ride, and left everyone behind', recalled Gilbert Bauvin, a France national team rider who won the stage that day. The mountains were still an unknown territory for Anquetil, and this would play on his mind on the Col d'Aubisque in the Pyrenees. 'I had to fight like never before,' he said in Pau, where the Belgian Marcel Janssens, had cut 2'38"

from Anquetil's lead. 'I was starving, and I was very inexperienced. After that I got my act together. I was learning – at my own cost – how to race the Tour.'

It took only a short time for Anquetil to establish his total dominance on the Tour. The climbers (Gaul and Bahamontes) took the 1958 and 1959 Tours, as the France team struggled with internal rivalries. Anquetil tasted his first Giro victory in 1960. Then, from 1961, he made the Tour his own. As Tour director Jacques Goddet said at the time: 'The yellow jersey was, for him, a second skin.' But his seemingly inevitable wins in the following years drew criticism too: the Tour had become less exciting to watch. ■■■

1963

The year that Anquetil performed brilliantly in the mountain stages.

A time trial from Bourgoin to Lyon: Jacques Anquetil catches up with Raymond Poulidor, who had set off before him. Poulidor would just have to watch him go past.

The Tour de France 1957, when the young Anquetil rode to his first Tour victory.

Anquetil versus Poulidor: on the Puy de Dôme that day, cycling became a contact sport.

1961: YELLOW (ALMOST) FROM START TO FINISH

Huge talent sometimes looks like arrogance. But what else was Anquetil supposed to do with a time trial around Versailles, other than win it? 'It was mine for the taking,' said Anquetil, already a winner of the world's premier time trial, the Grand Prix des Nations.

In fact, despite winning the Stage 1 time trial, Anquetil would not be the exclusive wearer of the yellow jersey on the 1961 Tour: there was the little matter of a half-stage on the first morning, from Rouen to Versailles, which was won by André Darrigade, who wore the jersey for half a day.

Anquetil's success did not win him much love from the public, who found his attitude rather cold and calculating. 'I got the yellow jersey on the first night, which is something you don't turn down. So I'm looking forward to defending it,' he declared in Versailles. For Anquetil, it wasn't about PR, it was about winning. The following year, his star status was evident from the start, but became linked with the most heroic of his (unsuccessful) rivals: the much-loved Raymond Poulidor. Ominously, Poulidor started the 1962 Tour with a wrist in plaster, and bad luck seemed to follow him round. Fortune, though, smiled on Anquetil, and it was on a Friday 13th, two days from the finish in Parc des Princes, that Anquetil finally wowed the crowds – in his own typical way. The Bourgoin–Lyon time trial became a kind of cycling exhibition. 'You need to have seen THAT at least once in your life to understand the meaning of perfection in cycling,' wrote journalist Pierre Chany in L'Équipe. Antonin Magne, the former Tour winner who became the sporting director of Mercier, was watching as Anquetil, who had started three minutes

behind Raymond Poulidor, began to overhaul him halfway through the race: 'Move over, Raymond,' he shouted. 'There's an express coming through!'

Joining him by the podium, the ever-popular Louison Bobet congratulated Jacques Anquetil on the turf of the Parc des Princes, perhaps underlining how much the crowd still loved Bobet and failed to engage with Anquetil. Tellingly, the organizers cut back on the number of time trials for the following year's Tour, only to see Anquetil start to excel in the mountain stages as well. On the 17th stage of the 1963 Tour (from Val d'Isère to Chamonix) the world's best time trialist took on the climbers. 'I would have been so disappointed if I'd had to wait for a time trial before taking the yellow jersey,' he admitted, after beating Federico Bahamontes in a final head-to-head at Chamonix.

That Tour win of 1963 was, for Anquetil in every sense, a summit. But the best of all the yellow jerseys would come the following year. In 1964 Anquetil had a lot on his plate. Still feeling the physical effects of winning the Giro, he did not excel on the way up the Port d'Envalira in the Pyrenees, and had a mental battle on the vertiginous descent (prior to the race, a celebrity astrologist had predicted that he would die in a crash). Most famously, he rode elbow-to-elbow against Raymond Poulidor at the Puy de Dôme before snatching victory, and only managed to secure his Tour victory in the final Versailles to Paris time trial. 'I had to really surpass myself to beat this great champion, Poulidor,' he admitted at the Parc des Princes, receiving his 51st yellow jersey. It was the last, and perhaps, ultimately, the most brilliant jersey of his career.■

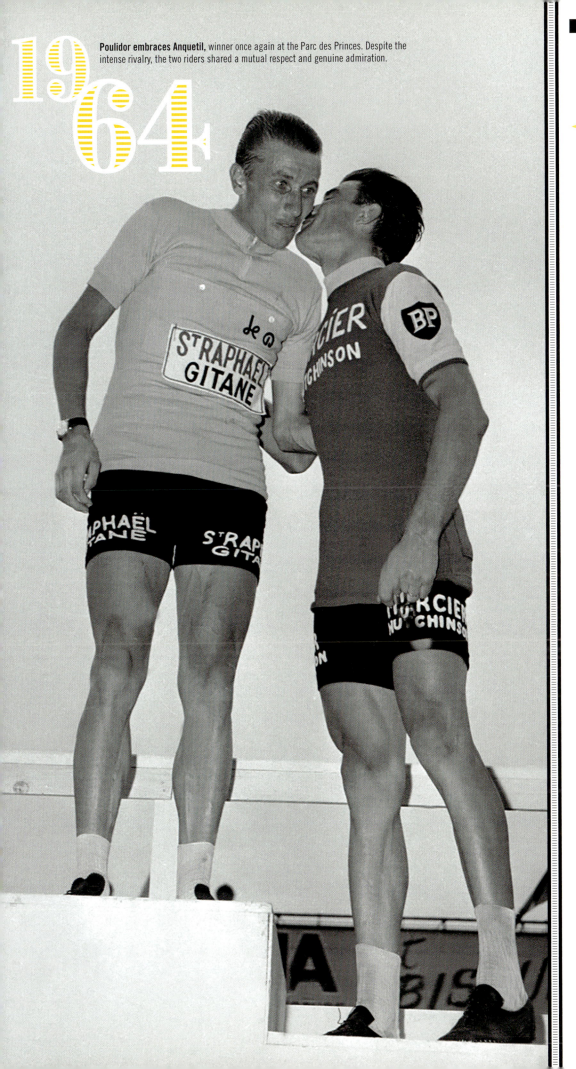

1964

Poulidor embraces Anquetil, winner once again at the Parc des Princes. Despite the intense rivalry, the two riders shared a mutual respect and genuine admiration.

Eddy Merckx in the Virlux yellow jersey in 1969, one of the most cherished of the 111 that he collected over his Tour career.

MERCKX

IN HIS SUMMER
GEAR

The Belgian champion and five-times Tour winner spent more than three months of his life wearing the yellow jersey.

Eddy Merckx nears Mourenx during his scintillating breakaway.

Eddy Merckx recalls with some emotion his childhood years, when he used to cycle around the streets of Woluwe-Saint-Pierre, a Brussels suburb. He had a little bike with fat tyres, and locals, with extraordinary foresight, used to nickname him 'Tour de France'.

His cycling career extends way beyond the Tour de France, given the vast extent of his professional wins over the decades. But it is perhaps in the Tour, a race he won five times from 1969 to 1974, that he experienced the very best moments of his career.

Eddy Merckx first laid eyes on the yellow jersey at the age of 13, on the day of the Tour's arrival in 1958 (when it was won by Charly Gaul) during a carnival near Brussels. 'A kid was dressed up in a yellow cycling jersey and I wanted one,' Merckx recalled. As an adult, that boyhood wish was granted beyond his wildest dreams: he spent an astonishing 97 days in the yellow jersey: more than three months of his life. It was as if the yellow jersey was nothing more than Merckx's summer cycling outfit. He won more yellows than anyone else in the world – 111 jerseys in total, counting all the part-stages that have featured across the years on the Tour maps.

In an interview at his home in Meise, on the outskirts of Brussels, he admitted he had very few jerseys remaining. 'How many have I got left, Claudine?' he asked his wife. 'Maybe one or two,' he guesses. 'I've donated them to charities, to sponsors, to kids. And then, at the end of the Tour, we give them away to team mates and staff. So I've got hardly any.'

Among the rare yellow jerseys carefully wrapped on the first floor of his home is one particularly cherished. 'The 1969 jersey, the Virlux [a brand of butter, the first sponsor's name to appear on a yellow jersey]. I've kept that one – it was the best moment of my career. A childhood dream come true.' ■ ■ ■

Local hero: Merckx takes **the yellow jersey** in his home town of Woluwe-Saint-Pierre, with team manager Guillaume Driessens (front, right).

On Mont Ventoux, 'The Cannibal' digs deep to dominate the rest of the field.

19
70

It was the incredible breakaway at the Col du Tourmalet – with Merckx riding alone for 140km. His Tour victory was already in the bag. So it was an act of pure audacity.

■■■

Eddy Merckx began the 1969 Tour inauspiciously, losing the prologue stage in Roubaix, 7 seconds behind Rudi Altig. But the disappointment was short-lived. The first yellow jersey of his career was waiting for him the next day, at the end of a team time trial, won by his Faema team on the streets of Woluwe where Merckx had grown up. 'It was absolutely unforgettable. The next day, I was wearing yellow, at the front of the peloton, at Tervuren where I was living at the time. Of course, at the end of that day I had to give up the jersey to a team mate [Julien Stevens], because that's how the race is – you can't try to chase down everybody. Anyhow, the most important yellow jersey of all is the one you get in Paris.' Merckz recovered the jersey four days later during Stage 6 from Mulhouse to Belfort, crossing the Ballon d'Alsace. 'There, I really did go for it. It was basically mine for the taking. This was the big one – my first "real" yellow jersey.'

Traditionally, riders 'defend' the yellow jersey. Merckx, however, went on the attack. It was Stage 17, from Luchon to Mourenx, and Merckx made a superb breakaway as he passed the summit of the Col du Tourmalet, riding 140km alone. His Tour was already in the bag, but he added eight minutes on Pingeon and Poulidor in the following group. It was an act of pure audacity. It was perhaps 'the' moment of his career – even if, with Merckx, extraordinary moments are almost commonplace. He also felt that after that win, and a crash later in the year at a Criterium track race in Blois, he never again found quite the same level of skill in the mountain stages. 'At 24, normally, you are not at your physical peak,' he said, 'but over the following years I was winning each Tour with a reduced lead.'*

Even so, there were to be plenty more of Merckx's attacks in yellow during the seasons to come: at Mont Ventoux in 1970, for example, or in the closing moments of the penultimate stage (from Vouvray to Orleans) in 1974, during a humdrum morning semi-stage ahead of the final time trial later that day. 'There, too, I did do something,' admitted Merckx. 'Everyone was attacking from all sides, and so to clean it all up a bit, I took off. They were riding at 60km/h behind me, and I gained a minute [1'25" in fact]. It did cost me the time trial in the afternoon, though'. (He was beaten by Michel Pollentier.)

The yellow jersey had almost become Merckx's everyday cycling gear, and had become part of a ritual. 'In the evening,' he said, 'I would put my race number over it, the 51 [the number which was assigned to him in 1969 before the '1' became the norm]. I got all my things ready the night before. I put the jersey, shorts, gloves and socks on the chair.' In 1970, he had a chance to wear yellow from start to finish of the Tour, but he let it go – with good grace – to his Faema team mate Italo Zilioli. 'I was happy for him. All I wanted was to wear the jersey in Paris.'

'I thought I looked pretty good in the yellow jersey.'

Merckx would be the first to say that no two yellow jerseys are ever quite the same. In 1971 Merckx won a stage but had little interest in the jersey after Tour leader Ocaña crashed out of the race. At the ■■■

Visiting Luis Ocaña who had to drop out following a crash. Merckx would have preferred to take race leadership under rather different circumstances.

1972

Cyrille Guimard, the green jersey, takes on Merckx. But it's a one-sided fight.

■■■

podium in Luchon, at the end of a long day that had seen Ocaña badly injured on the Col de Menté, he waved it away. 'No, it's not for me,' he said, and asked the race organizers to allow him not to wear the jersey for the following day's Stage 15 to Superbagnères. His request was granted. Merckx had, in his own way, paid homage to his great rival, but more to the point, the circumstances did not match up to what he felt the yellow jersey was all about. 'I really would have preferred to finish in second place and really have to battle for it,' he insisted. Speaking nearly 50 years later, he had not changed his view. At the moment of Luis Ocaña's crash, the Spaniard had a lead of more than seven minutes. Ocaña was the better rider, Merckx believes, but the Tour was not a done deal. 'He would have still had to fight some battles to win it,' he said. Merckx himself had been hit in the face at Orcières during Stage 11, where Ocaña left him nearly nine minutes behind. 'I was nearly knocked out,' he said. 'But a boxer gets back on his feet. I felt myself battered and beaten up right through to the final day.' Nonetheless, Merckx did go on to win the 1971 Tour that year, his third consecutive win, though he found the return route towards Paris to be 'dull' without Ocaña in the race, even though Zoetemelk and Van Impe were providing some threat. 'Frankly, I think Luis could probably have carried on,' said Merkx. 'He was back on his feet the next day, and I think he got scared. If he was really so sure of winning, why take the risk of following me so closely?' Merckx also got injured, crashing on the Col de Menté, but was able to go on. 'The handlebar went into my groin and I really

didn't know if I would be able to carry on the next day. The following morning, I had to climb halfway up Peyresourde just to warm up and see if I could do it. I even asked Van Impe not to do anything crazy at the start.'

If we try to point to when exactly the reign of Eddy Merckx finally came to a close, it would have to be on Stage 15 (from Nice to Pra-Loup) of the 1975 Tour, with the Belgian on the attack in the yellow jersey. 'I had made an impressive descent from the Col d'Allos. And going up Pra-Loup, in any case, is not really that difficult. But I got the feeling I was losing my power, that I could no longer keep in gear,' he recalled. It was Bernard Thévenet who turned it all upside down. 'Gimondi caught up with me first. That surprised me, but I could sense I was in trouble. Gimondi dropped me, and then Thévenet went past me, though I can't picture it so well now. I felt so tight. I had been punched [by a spectator] in the Puy du Dôme and I think that whatever nonsense the doctor had given me to thin my blood was reacting with me.' After this day, there would be no more yellow jerseys for Eddy Merckx, except those seen in the photographs of his glorious past. 'Yes, I thought I looked pretty good in the yellow jersey,' he said with mischievous smile. 'I had dark hair, so it suited me. I looked the part.' Which is the least anyone can say. ■

* 1969 : 17'54" on Pingeon ; 1970 : 12'41" on Zoetemelk ; 1971 : 9'51" on Zoetemelk ; 1972 : 10'41" on Gimondi ; 1974 : 8'04" on Poulidor.

1975

Bernard Thévenet: the man who brought down Merckx.

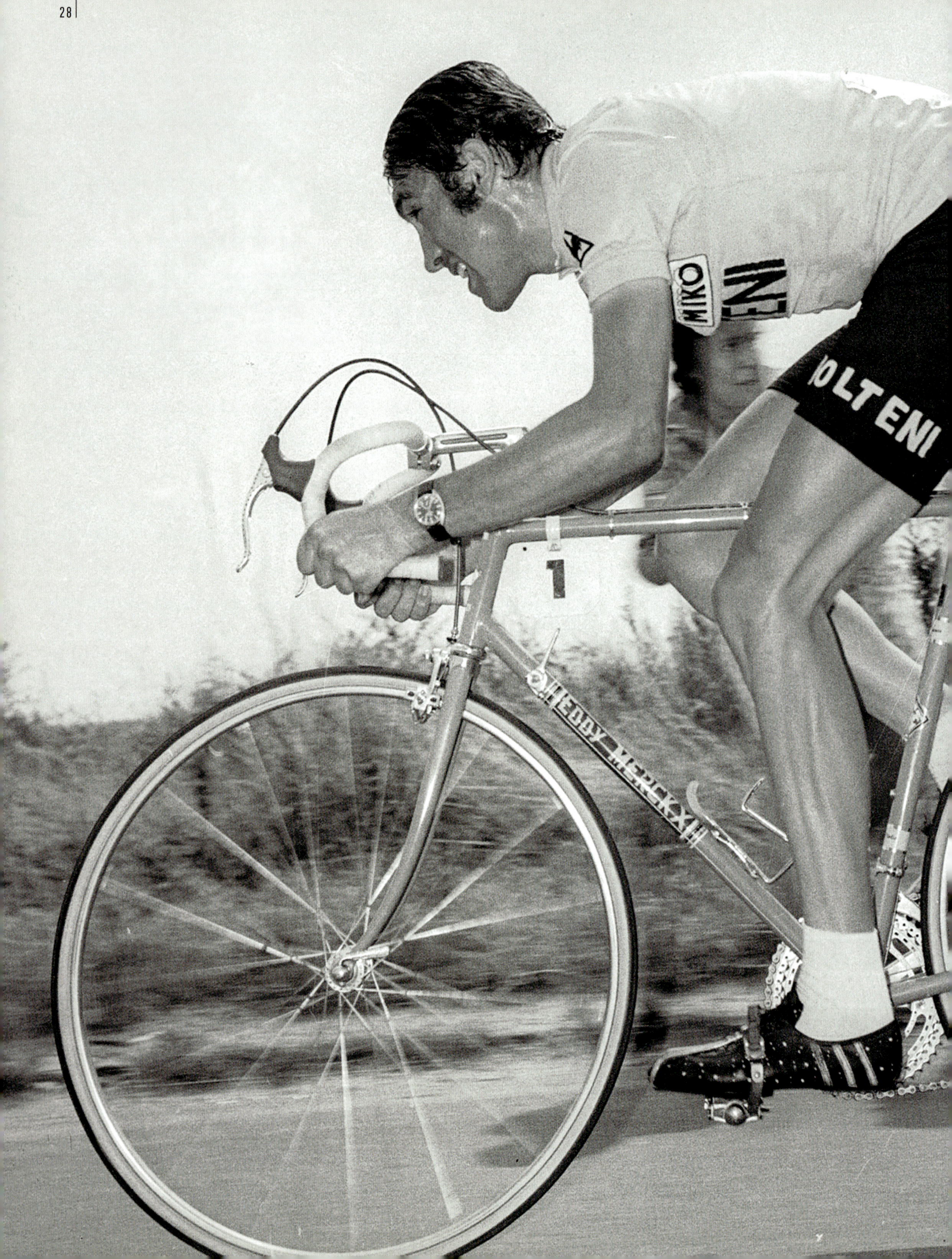
MIKO
OLTENI
1
EDDY MERCKX

Eddy the King: pure class.

Bernard Hinault was not so obsessed with titles and trophies, and raced for the love of racing. He took pleasure in battling with his rivals.

HINAULT

PURE ENJOYMENT

Nobody, not even Eddy Merckx, had ever worn the yellow jersey on eight different Tours de France. Bernard Hinault won five, dropped out of one, and fought his most epic battles in the two Tours that he lost.

A fitting reward:
one of many.

1979

It was Hinault's first ever yellow jersey, just 72 hours away from the finishing line on the Champs-Élysées. Did he let the pressure get to him? No. He took a nap instead.

'm here to win it.' Bernard Hinault showed up for the 1978 Tour with steely determination. Aged 23, and with three years already on the professional circuit, he was sure of himself and what he could do. Even the prospect of taking his first ever yellow jersey did not faze him, and as he waited to start Stage 20, the individual time trial from Metz to Nancy, he even took a nap. Renault's team trainer remembers the moment well: 'He was sitting in the back of the car, sunk down into the seat, his legs streteched out, cap pulled down over his eyes.' Cyrille Guimard had to shake him awake, just four minutes before his departure time, while Joop Zoetemelk (yellow jersey since the Alpe-d'Huez four days earlier) was returning from his warm-up.

'I can remember well those 14 seconds that I had to win back,' said Hinault in a later interview. 'I was completely relaxed. I knew I was going to take the jersey.'

Like Jacques Anquetil and Eddy Merckx before him, Hinault had the honour of winning his debut Tour de France. The following year his grip on the 1979 Tour was even stronger. The route was unusual, starting in the Pyrenees, promoting speculation that Hinault might be planning to wear the yellow jersey from start to finish. That plan was nixed early on by the Dutch rider Gerrie Knetemann who won the Fleurance prologue. No matter. Hinault got himself back in yellow by Stage 2. The only hitch after that was in Stage 9 (from Amiens to Roubaix) on the cobblestones that Hinault detested. A puncture at the start of the stage, followed by an all-out chase with a pack of passive followers on his back, then another puncture 10km from Roubaix: enough trouble for

Hinault to lose the yellow jersey and give Zoetemelk a lead of more than three minutes. Jacques Anquetil later praised Hinault for his gutsy damage limitation. 'He could have lost the Tour that day,' Anquetil reflected, 'but instead, he won it.'

Having lost the jersey in Roubaix, Hinault then embarked on a kind of guerilla warfare, jumping straight onto any and every sprint. Then, on the Avoriaz time trial (on Stage 15) he crushed the opposition and retook race leadership in what became one of the highlights of the Tour. ■■■

With Joop Zoetemelk, runner up, on the Champs-Élysées, at the height of his powers.

Knee trouble: Hinault's pain worsened, and he was forced to quit the Tour.

With his rivals left scattered, 'The Badger' took control, with 19 days in yellow out of a possible 25. Lucien Van Impe finished in second place in Paris, more than 14 minutes behind Hinault.

1981

1982

1985

On the winner's podium with his wife Martine and sports minister Edwige Avice. Also pictured, from the left: Johan Van der Velde (third) Joop Zoetemelk (second) Phil Anderson (best young rider), Sean Kelly (green jersey) and Bernard Vallet (King of the Mountains).

Black eyes at Saint-Étienne, but Hinault will press on.

■■■

Aptly enough, Hinault's Tour victory was won with a bitter head-to-head duel between himself and his only credible opponent, Joop Zoetemelk, , who mounted his attack on the slopes of the Chevreuse valley on the final stage into Paris. 'I thought maybe a few other riders would go with me,' the Dutchman said, 'but I never imagined I would find myself out there alone with Hinault.' For a moment, he hoped the Frenchman would allow him the consolation prize of a stage win, but Hinault, in full domination of the Tour, was not feeling quite so generous. Some people thought that the drama and excitement of the final stage duel had been stage-managed, a claim that Hinault later denied: 'Nothing had been pre-planned, and there was nothing irregular,' he said.

Hinault's reign was interrupted by a knee injury in 1980 which forced him to quit a Tour that he seemed destined to win. After that, in 1981 and 1982, it was a simple story of total domination, albeit against a field of riders who had become rather resigned to their fate.

'The Tour is all yours'

Hinault's absence from the 1983 Tour (for a knee operation) probably contributed to the rise of the youthful Laurent Fignon who won that year, and who dominated again in 1984. That year, Hinault got the yellow jersey only once, in the prologue of a Tour which would be largely dominated by Fignon. In a sense, Hinault had the last word, because in 1985 it was Fignon himself who missed the Tour to get surgery, during which time Hinault came back with a vengeance to win his fifth Tour – despite crashing on the Cours Fauriel Boulevard at Saint-Étienne. Above all though, his 1985 Tour is marked by a promise he

made to his talented young team mate Greg LeMond: 'Next year,' he told the American, 'the Tour is all yours. I'll be there, but simply to support your campaign.' Effectively, Hinault had chosen his successor. Or had he? When the 1986 Tour got going, Hinault found himself in excellent shape, tempted by the prospect of a record-breaking sixth Tour win, and probably regretting the vow he had made to LeMond. He made a blistering attack at the stage to Pau, where his series of offensives on the rolling Basque hills gave him a lead of nearly five minutes. The next day he did the same again, this time on the descent from the Col du Tourmalet, and then back on the attack on the slopes of the Col d'Aspin. Hinault seemed intoxicated by his speed and power, but ran out of juice later in the day. As he approached Superbagnères he squandered

almost all the gains he had made the previous day, and LeMond was now just 40 seconds behind. A few days later the American took the yellow jersey. The image of the two riders arriving at the Alpe d'Huez hand in hand, beaming, became a symbol of the new order of things. LeMond let Hinault win the stage, but LeMond would go on to win the Tour. Bernard Hinault had managed to appear to quit while he was winning. But the question on everyone's mind was whether he had blown his chance of a sixth Tour victory. Jacques Anquetil thinks he did: 'If it was me, with a lead of five minutes, I would have blocked the race,' he said. 'If I had been where Bernard was at Pau, I think I would have won my sixth Tour.' For Hinault, though, there are no regrets: 'I did everything I had to do, and that's it. And I had a good time doing it.' ∎

At the Alpe d'Huez, with Greg LeMond on his wing, Hinault bows out of the leadership race.

1986

A little greedy: Hinault could have defended his yellow jersey in the Pyrenees, but instead, he chose to attack

Miguel Indurain had only one nickname.
They called him 'The Big Guy'.

INDURAIN

FIVE YEARS, FIVE WINS

The Spaniard was one of the greatest road racers of all time. And the first ever to conquer the Tour five times in a row.

With Claudio Chiappucci (right) heading for Val Louron. The Indurain era had begun.

He had to bide his time in the shadow of Pedro Delgado (right). But this time, Indurain's turn had come.

Indurain did just enough to keep ahead of his rivals (including, pictured from left, Tony Rominger, Álvaro Mejía and Andy Hampsten) even on the major Alpine stages where the Spaniard was at the summit of his powers.

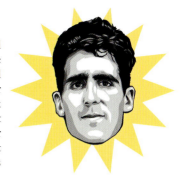

From his rural origins, Miguel Indurain had acquired a certain quiet strength, and he had also learned to be patient. He would need to be. Unlike those five-times Tour winners Jacques Anquetil, Eddy Merckx and Bernard Hinault, Indurain was not someone who tasted victory on his Tour debut. Far from it. In fact, of all the multiple Tour winners, it was Indurain who took the longest time to get his campaign going.

Miguel Indurain made his Tour debut in 1985, at the age of just 21, but dropped out before the mountain stages during his first two Tours. 'Miguel is a diamond that needs time to be cut into shape,' said José Miguel Echavarri, his coach in the Reynolds (and later the Banesto) team, which was also home to the 1988 Tour winner, Pedro Delgado.

By the time of the 1991 Tour, the diamond Indurain was well and truly in brilliant form. He was 27, on his seventh Tour, and he made his mark on the final kilometre of the route up the Col du Tourmalet. First he dropped Greg LeMond, and then he went head-to-head after the summit with Claudio Chiappucci – heralding a whole new era of Tour rivalry. The Italian won the stage at Val Louron, and the Spaniard took the yellow jersey. There would be 59 more for him during his Tour career.

The Indurain era had begun. The big, imposing Spaniard (1.88m and 80kg) dominated in the mountains, and especially in the Pyrenees, which was his own backyard (he came from Navarre). He won only two 'regular' Tour de France stages (as opposed to time trials) and both were in the Pyrenees: one in Cauterets in 1989 and the other in Luz-Ardiden in 1990. Despite jibes about lack of style or flair, for Indurain it was all about the clock: during his long reign he won only on stages with a time trial. Five times out of five, he won the first major time trial of the Tour, a hallmark of his quality: Alençon in 1991; Luxembourg in 1992; Madine in 1993; Bergerac in 1994 and Seraing in 1995. More often than not, he did the same again with the final time trial too. But he was also one of the two or three greatest road racers of all time, easily on a par with both Anquetil and Hinault. ■ ■ ■

1994

Richard Virenque (left) and Luc Leblanc mount an attack, but the yellow jersey powers on steadily.

1993

**Miguel is
a diamond
that needs
time to
be cut to
shape.**

José Miguel Echavarri,
Reynolds team coach

1995

Miguel Indurain laid the foundations for his fifth Tour victory in Belgium, in the kind of scintillating finish normally seen in the likes of the Liège–Bastogne–Liège Classic.

Who needs to attack, anyway?

A highpoint of Indurain's Tour career came during the so-called multi-country 'European' Tour de France of 1992, which set off almost on his home patch of Saint-Sébastien in the Spanish Basque country. Later, in Luxembourg, he put in an incredible time trial performance, finishing a full three minutes ahead of his second-placed team mate Armand De Las Cuevas – giving Indurain the biggest time trial lead ever recorded in the history of the Tour. Fifth-placed LeMond was more than four minutes back at the finish.

However, all these comfortable time trial wins meant that Miguel Indurain took much of the drama out of the Tour as a spectator sport. It played to his strongest suit, and he simply had no need to mount audacious attacks to win the Tour. Instead, he controlled his rivals in the mountain stages where, despite his height and weight, he was also a world-class climber. So rather like Jacques Anquetil, he did what was necessary, and no more. But he was generous too. In 1993 he could have taken two of the major Alpine stages for himself, but he let them go to his rival Tony Rominger. And when he did go on one of his rare attacks (in the Ardennes in 1995) he allowed the stage win to go to Johan Bruyneel in Liège. (There was, however, a time trial scheduled for the very next day.)

The tactics worked, and Indurain was impregnable in defence. In each of his five Tour victories, he beat five different rivals into second place, starting with Gianni Bugno, then Claudio Chiappucci, Tony Rominger, Piotr Ugrumov and Alex Zülle, with none being able to offer any real threat to Indurain's supremacy.

Indurain retired after the 1996 Tour where he took a respectable 11th place in Paris – although he still looked worthy of a much higher ranking. In fact he had lost the Tour which passed right in front of his family's farm in Villava, 2km from Pamplona. Even though he arrived there buried in the back of the third peloton, he got a huge reception from a crowd that loved him not just because he was a winner, but because of who he was.

'I did feel I still had it in me to take a sixth Tour de France,' he said when he retired. But perhaps that sixth Tour win should have been nearer the beginning, rather than the end of his career. Team manager José Miguel Echavarri probably picked the wrong leader in 1990 in the form of the hugely popular Pedro Delgado (supported by Indurain, who turned out to be the faster rider of the two).

Following Indurain's rise to power, the PDM affair – the strange sickness which forced the entire Dutch PDM team to withdraw – could be seen as an omen of the pervasive use of medications that was about to come. Five years on, the situation had worsened, and Bjarne Riis had to do little more than just get up off his seat to drop Indurain with consummate ease. Times had changed. Indurain had to choose between the hope of winning a sixth Tour, and the real risk of competing one time too many. Wisely, he quit while he was on top. ∎

Indurain found the ascent towards Hautacam a gruelling ordeal. The end of his brilliant career was closing in.

AND HERE COME THE BRITS

It took no less than 99 years of the Tour de France before a British rider finally won it. But with the victory of Sir Bradley Wiggins, Chris Froome and Welshman Geraint Thomas, the Brits have made the Tour their own.

Why did it take so long for a British rider to win the Tour? Probably because, until recently, competitive cycling in Britain was never really a part of the national culture. By the time the Tour de France was launched in 1903, competitive road racing in Britain had already been banned for ten years. A law passed in 1894 made competitive road races in Britain illegal, following years of disputes and accidents involving cyclists and members of the public. Cyclists were seen by many people – including the police – as mad, bad and dangerous. And it would stay that way until the end of the Second World War. In the meantime, cycling in Britain was limited to time trials only: these were hugely popular at their peak, but lacked the vast public spectacle that major road racing would provide.

This small reminder of cycling history may go some way to explaining those 99 years that elapsed without a Tour de France win going to a British cyclist, even while the rest of the English-speaking world was beginning to be represented on the podium in Paris. The American Greg LeMond got there in 1986, the Irish racer Stephen Roche claimed victory in 1987, while the Australian Cadel Evans won in 2011.

Six out of seven Tours

'The target is for a British winner of the Tour de France within five years,' announced Dave Brailsford, team principal of the newly formed Sky team in 2009. Brailsford was a resolute Welshman who had enjoyed remarkable success at the head of the GB Olympic track cycling team. His new set-up involved putting in some serious resources, and it took just three years for his plan to come to fruition. Bradley Wiggins, already an iconic track cyclist, would become the first British winner of the Tour. At first sight, he was not the obvious candidate. Yes, he was great in pursuit, and an exceptional time trialist too. But not only did Wiggins take the yellow jersey in Paris in 2012, he did it with a fellow Brit in second place – his team mate Chris Froome, suggesting that he was perhaps already riding faster than his team leader in that year.

In any case, for Wiggins, the Tour was a one-off. He was already 32 years old, and he felt little desire to sign up once again to the gruelling regime – notably in terms of body weight – that he had needed to go through in preparation for the 2012 Tour. Also, he had not relished all the publicity and celebrity status that came in the wake of his Tour win. For Wiggins, it was job done. For Team Sky, though, the job was far from over, and they went on to write a substantial chapter of Tour history from 2012 onwards, with an incredible six Tour wins out of seven.

If Wiggins gave the impression of being something of a free spirit, his successor Chris Froome could be seen more as an an 'employee' of the team. Born in Nairobi to British parents, Froome began his cycling career training in South Africa, and is almost as good a racer on the flat as he is a climber – or vice versa. The total domination of the race that he displayed at Mont Ventoux in the 2013 Tour sparked a certain amount of resentment, particularly in France, ■ ■ ■

Bradley Wiggins (right) is led to victory in the 2012 Tour by a young prodigy called Chris Froome.

48

Mont Ventoux, 14 July 2013: Chris Froome
asserts his dominance over the Tour.

■ ■ ■

with plenty of speculation over the cumulative effects of the marginal gains that Team Sky was trying to create across every aspect of the race and in the lives of the riders themselves: in preparation, materials, equipment, diet and nutrition. At the same time, with memories of the devastation caused by Lance Armstrong still fresh in most minds, the yellow jersey had become, in a sense, systematically suspect.

At the same time, there is no disputing the quality of the Sky teams during this period. Often it appeared as though each team member seemed to be as strong as the leader of any of the rival teams. Between 2012 and 2018, Sky locked down the Tour and lost only one edition, that of 2014. In that year Froome crashed out of the race, allowing Vincenzo Nibali to become the first Italian winner since Marco Pantani in 1998. Froome was back with a vengeance the following year (it is likely that it was only the crash that denied him a win in 2014) and he then won faultlessly in 2015, again in 2016 (despite having to run, on foot, part-way to the finish line after his bike was damaged in a pile-up) and again in 2017. During that race, his lead was being eroded, but his performance in the time trials continued to make all the difference.

Fancy Bear and the Jiffy Bag affair

Sir Bradley Wiggins never rejoined the Tour after his win in 2012, but when he retired from competitive cycling in 2016 he found himself the subject of a doping investigation. A group of Russian hackers, calling themselves 'Fancy Bear' revealed that he had been granted authorization for the therapeutic use of a cortico-steroid between 2011 and 2013.

Team boss Sir Dave Brailsford (knighted in 2013) was summoned before a British Parliamentary Committee to explain the 'Jiffy Bag' affair, relating to a mystery package that Wiggins was alleged to have received on the final day of the Critérium du Dauphiné race. No evidence was uncovered of any wrongdoing.

Meanwhile, Chris Froome has had his share of scrutiny too. An anti-doping test on the Vuelta race in 2017 recorded an abnormally high level of salbutamol in his urine (twice the limit permitted to treat his asthma). The issue was resolved with the involvement of experts and lawyers, with his participation in the 2018 Tour hanging in the balance until the very last moment. He was cleared to take part, but nonetheless had to put up with a hostile public and the ill effects of the distractions of the previous months. He finished the Tour in third place.

Sky, though, was never short of leaders, and Welshman Geraint Thomas stepped up, proving himself to be the best of all in 2018. Thomas's Tour de France triumph meant that British riders won all three Grand Tours in the same year: Chris Froome took the Giro, while Simon Yates, a fellow Brit on an Australian team, won the Spanish Vuelta. But while Froome is still in the running to join the exclusive club of five-times winners of the Tour, the British media group Sky announced – predictably enough after nine years – that it would terminate its team sponsorship in 2019. The team name changed to Ineos, and with the new name, new investment. ■

The moment that Geraint Thomas realizes victory in the 2018 Tour will be his. He has just won the time trial from Saint-Pée-sur-Nivelle to Espelette.

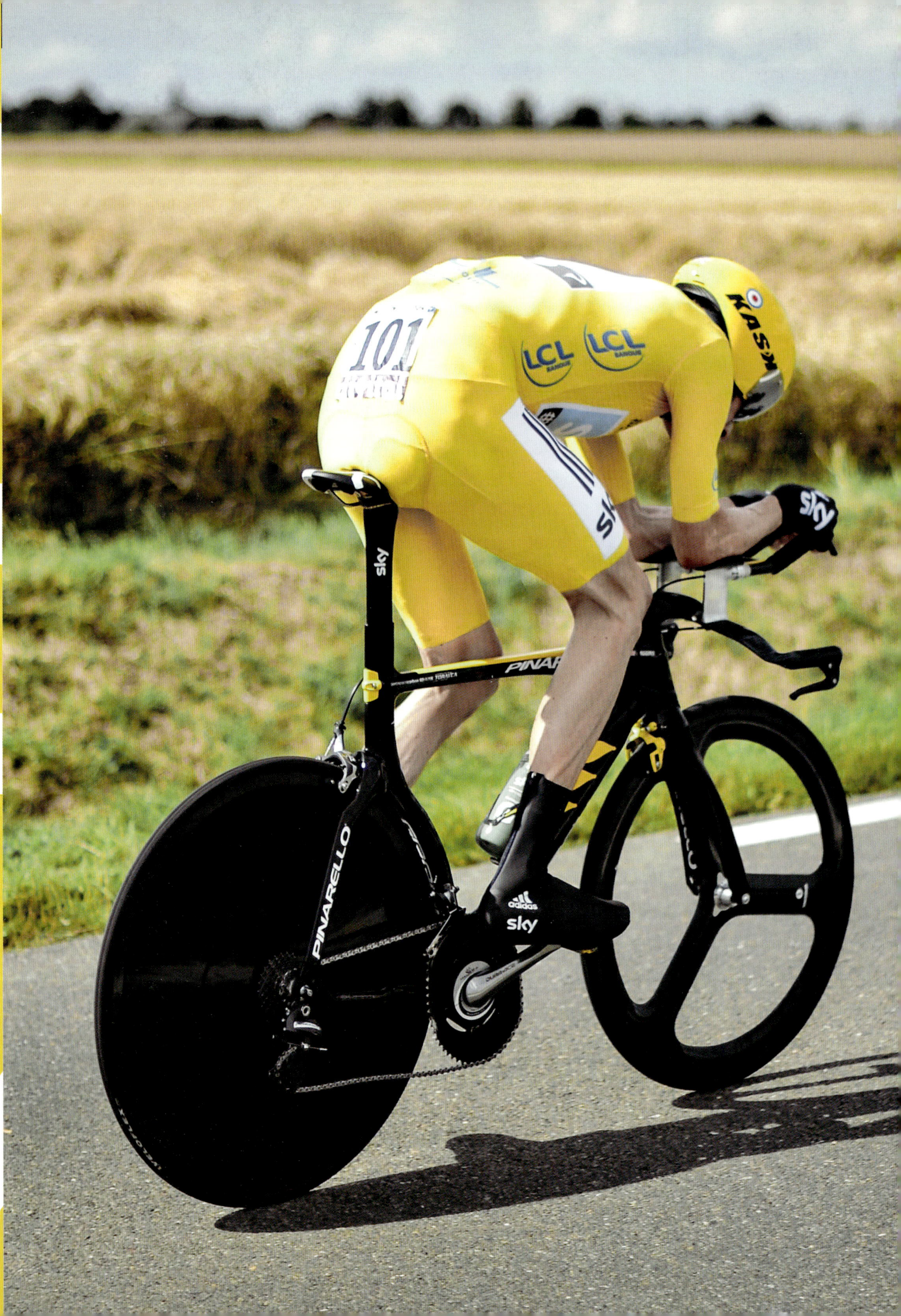
101
LCL
LCL
KASK
sky
sky
sky
PINAR
PINARELLO
adidas
sky

Bradley Wiggins gives it everything between Bonneval and Chartres in 2012, becoming the first Briton to win the Tour.

Yvette Horner, the official and immensely popular accordionist of the Tour de France, congratulates Louison Bobet. A golden era.

BOBET
THREE IN A ROW

Louison Bobet was the first to win three Tours in a row. The Breton was bold, brave and determined to succeed.

On hot July afternoons in the Breton village of Saint-Méen-le-Grand, a crowd of locals would gather outside the boulangerie - not to buy bread, but to listen to coverage of the Tour de France on the radio, blasting out from the Bobet family's kitchen. On 3 July 1939, however, there was a particular excitement in the air, as local rider Jean Fontenay from nearby Saint-Servan had just taken the yellow jersey at Rennes. The next day, the Tour would pass just 10km from Bobet's boulangerie, and so Bobet senior took the whole family by car to watch. All, that is, except for his son Louison, aged 14, who would make his own way to the Tour on the treasured Stella cycle he had been given for passing his exams. Riding with ease up the hillside of Saint-Jouan-de-l'Isle, Louison Bobet joined the huge crowd, and it was there that he glimpsed the yellow jersey for the very first time. In the eyes of this teenage cycling nut, it was a dazzling sight.

While seeing local hero Jean Fontenay in the yellow jersey was a big moment, Bobet's real idol, René Vietto, had sped past in the blur of the passing peloton on his way to taking the yellow jersey 24 hours later in Lorient. But Bobet and Vietto would meet again eight years later. When the Tour ■■■

19 39

In the final Tour before the war, Breton rider Jean Fontenay became race leader. This was the first yellow jersey that the young Louison Bobet ever laid eyes on, and the experience reinforced his determination to ride with the Tour.

In Nantes, **Guy Lapébie** (left) took the bouquet for stage winner, and Bobet put on his very first yellow jersey. Lapébie was an immensely popular rider in the post-war years, but Bobet was setting out to become a cycling icon.

19 48

Louison had to learn patience. It would be five whole years before he wore the yellow jersey again. But when he did, it would be on the winner's podium in Paris.

■■■

resumed in 1947 after the war, this same René Vietto was there to welcome Bobet to the French national team for his Tour debut, albeit with little ceremony: 'What is it with all these riders on the French team who do not shave their legs?' moaned Vietto in his trademark Southern accent.

Bobet dropped out of his debut Tour in the Alpine stages, but before then he got to see Vietto in the yellow jersey on this first post-war Tour (eventually won by Jean Robic). The following year Bobet himself picked up his first yellow jersey on Stage 3 (from Dinard to Nantes). He lost it the following day to Roger Lambrecht, but recovered it on Stage 6 (from Bordeaux to Biarritz) and kept it for the next eight days before passing it on to Gino Bartali who would go on to win his second Tour de France. The Italian team boss Alfredo Binda felt Bobet had missed a chance: 'If I'd been managing Bobet,' he bragged, 'he would have won.' In reality, it was less clear cut. At 23 years old, Bobet was still maturing, and above all, he needed to learn patience. He would have to wait a full five years before wearing the yellow jersey again, but when he did finally get it, in 1953, he had it for keeps. Bobet waited until Stage 18 to mount his attack, on the road from Gap to Briançon in the Guil valley. His team mate Adolphe Deledda pushed himself to the limit to help build an unassailable gap for Bobet, who stormed the Col d'Izoard and won in Briançon with a five-minute lead. He won the stage, the yellow jersey, and his very first Tour de France a few days later. ■■■

19 53

Louison Bobet in a time trial from Lyon to Saint-Étienne, on his way to his first Tour victory.

19 53

A victory lap around the Parc des Princes to mark the first 50 years of the Tour de France. More of those would follow.

■ ■ ■

At 28 years old, Bobet had found cycling glory but had somehow failed to connect with the crowds. Fellow Breton Jean Malléjac of the France West regional team wore the yellow for five days in 1953 and came second (to Bobet), but it was Malléjac who got the biggest cheer from the crowd at the Critérium de Châteaulin race in Brittany that same year. It was the same story in the 1954 Tour. Bobet rode through Brittany wearing yellow, but for the regional press and the watching public, it was all about Malléjac in the white jersey of the France West team. Even so, winning the 1954 Tour and the World Championships in Solingen the same year was a career highlight for Bobet. 'It was his happiest year ever on a bike,' according to his brother Jean, also a professional cyclist who accompanied his brother throughout his career.

In 1954 Bobet was on peak form. Even so, the competition in the 1954 Tour was intense. During Stage 6 (from Saint-Brieuc to Brest) the 'Two Ks' of Swiss cycing – Ferdi Kubler and Hugo Koblet – mounted a spirited attack at the Morlaix feed zone. Bobet fought back on the road to Saint-Thégonnec, and said later that he saw defeat written all over Koblet's face as he passed him. Bobet thus retained his yellow jersey at Brest. In Saint-Brieuc the previous evening, however, he had managed to 'lose' the jersey rather differently. His sister Madeleine had paid him a visit and he gave the jersey to her as a gift, not realizing race organizers were only handing out a new jersey to the lead rider every other day. Luckily, Bobet's good friend and cycling trainer Raymond Le Bert lived nearby, so prior to the next day's departure, Bobet dropped in on him to grab the yellow jersey he had sent Le Bert the previous year as a gift. That

jersey had shrunk so much that Bobet had to ask a heavyweight boxer to put it on briefly to stretch it out, before finally returning, properly attired, to start Stage 6.

1954 was also the year of Bobet's storming victory on the Col d'Izoard (he took the stage at Briançon with a two-minute lead over Ferdi Kubler), making it very much Bobet's favourite climb. His bother Jean said Louison seemed inspired by the surroundings: 'I think Louison needed a kind of backdrop, something really theatrical.'

The 1955 Tour was more of an ordeal. 'It was a case of just trying to hang on in there,' Bobet said of his third successive Tour win. Once again, he suffered saddle sores, a recurrent injury that was a constant impediment to his career. 'He basically did the entire Pau to Paris section out of the saddle,' commented his brother, describing Louison as 'mentally tough, determined to deliver on his ambitions.'

Wherever he went, Bobet had become an ambassador for French cycling, and exuded a kind of star quality (he even flew his own plane). During the 1970s he started a business running upmarket sea water health spas. His brother Jean worked alongside him: 'I kept it all running, as Louison wasn't cut out for that kind of stuff. But when he turned up for the important meetings, you could see the effect he had as soon as he walked into a room. He drew everyone to him.'

His popularity had been huge, and his influence, not just on the cycling world, had been considerable. ■

19 54

Bobet rides through the moon-like landscape of the Casse Déserte, on the approaches to the Col d'Izoard, to the delight of his fans.

The **Number 1** rider of the 1950s: Bobet was hugely popular and knew how to work the crowds.

19 55

II

ALL THE AMAZING STORIES

Since its creation in 1919, the yellow jersey has become an essential part of the legendary history of the Tour de France.

1919: THE BIRTH OF THE YELLOW JERSEY

The Tour de France was already in its 13th year when the idea of the yellow jersey was born. It was first awarded at Grenoble on 19 July 1919, midway through the Tour, and the first man ever to wear it was the Frenchman Eugène Christophe.

HOW TO SPOT THE LEADER

It was an inspired idea. On the morning of 10 July 1919, as the race (now in its 13th year) was making its way through the Pyrenees, a small news item appeared in the columns of *L'Auto*, the newspaper that organized the Tour de France. The short headline said it all: 'How To Recognize The Leader.' There were just 11 lines of text: 'A great idea from our editor in chief! To allow sportsmen to look at the peloton and instantly recognize the leader of our great race, our editor in chief, Henri Desgrange, has just decided that from now on, the racer who is placed first in the general classification will wear a special jersey.'

IT HAD TO BE YELLOW

Why yellow? The distinctive jersey, which would from then on be attributed to the leader of the Tour, corresponded with the colour of the pages of the newspaper, *L'Auto*. So not only was yellow easy to see in the peloton, it could also help to sell newspapers. However, Henri Desgrange, the creator of the Tour, may also have been inspired by an idea from Alphonse Baugé, who was sporting director of a consortium called *La Sportive*, which supplied medics, trainers and catering staff for the Tour. They all wore yellow, to be more easily identifiable by the riders, especially at night during the pre-dawn starts of some of the first Tours de France. The yellow jersey was thus one of the earliest examples of 'high viz'.

Eugène Christophe negotiates the slopes of the Col de Port in the Pyrenees on 7 July 1922. He had already lost the yellow jersey to Jean Alavoine, and would never wear it again.

Eugène Christophe, Léon Scieur, Jean Alavoine and Firmin Lambot (from right to left) on the morning of Stage 11 of the 1919 Tour, from Grenoble to Geneva. They all wanted the same thing: that newly minted yellow jersey.

The newspaper *L'Auto*, which created the Tour de France in 1903, was published daily on yellow paper. The jersey for the race leader would therefore take the same colour.

A CAFÉ IN GRENOBLE

The hugely popular Eugène Christophe was already race leader from the end of Stage 4 at Les Sables-d'Olonne, but it was only when the Tour paused at Grenoble, just before Stage 11, that Christophe received the very first yellow jersey ever presented on the Tour. Many years later, in a recorded interview, he recalled exactly what had taken place: 'In Les Sables d'Olonne, Baugé had been talking to Desgrange. "Look," he was saying, "people are trying to see who's in first place, but there's no way of picking him out. It's crazy. The leader ought to wear a special jersey. But how could we do that – a special jersey? Maybe a jersey like *L'Auto* – like the newspaper!" Then Desgrange said to Baugé: "You're right! So get onto it – order me some yellow jerseys." That evening, Baugé telephoned a supplier in Paris to start manufacturing. But by the time they were finished and sent off, I was already in Grenoble. So that's where I received a fine package of six jerseys.'

This time, there was a short news item of eight lines in the 'Echoes' section of the newspaper. 'This morning I presented Christophe with a superb yellow jersey. You already know that our director [note how Desgrange wrote himself into the story!] decided that the man at the head of the general classification will wear a jersey in the colours of *L'Auto*. There will be hard-fought battles ahead for possession of the jersey!'

Without much ceremony, the presentation was made at the Cafe de l'Ascenseur, on Cours Gambetta in Grenoble. The next day Christophe set out at dawn on 19 July, to attack the Grenoble to Geneva stage via the Col du Galibier. He was wearing the first ever yellow jersey.

EUGÈNE CHRISTOPHE

EUGÈNE CHRISTOPHE: THE FORKS GUY

'No racer deserves it more than he does,' wrote Tour director Desgrange. Christophe was already one of the Tour's heroes from before the Great War, and it seemed a fitting reward. Even so, it did not bring him much luck and he failed to take it all the way to Paris. As in 1913, when Christophe had to repair his broken front forks at a blacksmith's forge in Sainte-Marie-de-Campan, he was again the victim of a forks failure on the rough cobbles at Haisnes, on the penultimate stage from Metz to Dunkirk across a landscape ravaged by the war. He was only 30 minutes ahead of the Belgian Firmin Lambot in the general classification, but it took him an hour to repair his bike. The yellow jersey had already begun to weave its own folklore, somewhere between tragedy and glory. Christophe himself, though, was unsentimental, and did not keep any of his six jerseys: "I ended up using them as cleaning cloths," he admitted later.

NOT ONE WORD

Oddly enough, apart from the two brief articles that announced the creation of the yellow jersey in *L'Auto* (the organizers' newspaper) there would be no further talk of the yellow jersey during the 1919 Tour. Not a mention, then, when Eugène Christophe's front forks broke leading him to lose the jersey to Lambot, nor when Lambot himself became the first to receive the yellow jersey at the Parc des Princes. The yellow jersey had not yet entered into the vocabulary of the Tour. Symbols take time to get established. The legend, though, had already begun. ∎

The Tour de France had always been popular, but the creation of the yellow jersey sharpened public interest in the race and provided a focus for the news coverage.

Firmin Lambot (pictured here in 1913) took part in ten Tours de France. He won two (in 1919 and 1922) but only wore the yellow jersey for five days.

Ottavio Bottecchia, the first Italian to win the Tour, in 1924, was also the winner of two stages in the Pyrenees the same year. His all-round talent was undeniable.

OTTAVIO
BOTTECCHIA

Nicolas Frantz was not content simply to lead the 1928 Tour from start through to the finish: he also won five stages (the 1st, 6th, 12th, 18th and the final stage). And he did all this while fighting off one of his toughest and most committed rivals, André Leducq.

FROM THE FIRST DAY TO THE LAST DAY

Just three riders have worn the yellow jersey from one end of the race to the other. And all three finished the Tour in style, taking the final stage win in Paris

It may not be a total coincidence that Ottavio Bottecchia, Nicolas Frantz and Romain Maes all managed to lead the race from start to finish during the Tour's inter-war era. The state of the roads and racing conditions in general during this time could lead to just one strong rider getting an unassailable lead right from the start.

In the mid-1920s, Italian rider Ottavio Bottecchia dominated the climbing stages, but for his 1924 Tour victory, he took the lead on the first stage from Paris to Le Havre. Bottecchia's undoubted strength may have been a factor in the decision of his main rivals to quit the race: Henri Pélissier, his brother Francis, and team mate Maurice Ville all dropped out in Coutances (and later met up with journalist Albert Londres, prompting him to write his famous critique of the Tour called 'The Prisoners of the Road').

Normandy – this time in Caen – was also where the Luxembourger Nicolas Frantz won the first stage of the 1928 Tour. He had already won the Tour the previous year, and once he had the yellow jersey on his back, he was intent on keeping it there.

The extraordinary performances of Bottecchia and Frantz would be joined in 1935 by that of Romain Maes. The Belgian was lucky enough to slip through a level crossing just before the barrier came down, leaving the peloton fuming as Maes made his escape. He picked up the yellow at Lille that evening. Maes was only 22 and had dropped out of his debut Tour the year before, so nobody expected him to keep the yellow for a second day. But he gave no ground over the coming three weeks. He would only ever finish one Tour in his cycling career but he was, as the saying goes, in it to win it.

All three riders, Bottecchia, Frantz and Maes, were stage winners on the first day as well as on the final day, and wore the yellow jersey throughout the race, riding into the Parc des Princes, and into posterity too. ∎

ANQUETIL'S MORNING OFF
Many cycling buffs will tell you that Jacques Anquetil wore the yellow jersey from one end of the Tour to the other during the 1961 race. This is almost, but not quite true. The first day was split into two part-stages, with André Darrigade winning the morning session from Rouen to Versailles, so he wore yellow for the afternoon. As for Anquetil, he took over at the end of the day, after the individual time trial around Versailles. Anquetil did indeed wear the yellow jersey from the first to the last day. But he was not the only wearer of the yellow on the 1961 Tour.

SHARING THE GLORY

Just three times during the Tour's history, in 1920, 1929 and 1931, spectators had the curious sight of more than one 'race leader' on the road at the same time.

1920

THYS - MOTTIAT - ROSSIUS - MASSON - GOETHALS

TOO MANY LEADERS BUT NO JERSEYS!

The early stages of the 1920 Tour progressed at a rather leisurely pace, with the result that at the end of Stage 2 from Le Havre to Cherbourg there were no fewer than five riders who crossed the line in a dead heat. Four Belgian riders – Philippe Thys, Louis Mottiat, Jean Rossius and Émile Masson, along with Frenchman Félix Goethals all recorded an identical time of 30 hours, 8 minutes and 31 seconds. Mottiat dropped away the next day in Brest, and things settled down towards Les Sables-d'Olonne, where only Thys and Masson crossed the line on equal points. When the race hit the Pyrenees on Stage 6 (from Bayonne to Luchon) it was Masson's turn to capitulate, allowing Philippe Thys to build up a solid lead. However, there would be no yellow jersey for Thys until three days later, as the jersey suppliers were running late, and had yet to despatch them to the Tour. Not that anyone was making much of a fuss over all this, as the yellow jersey had only been 'invented' the previous year. In 1920 it was still seen as a bit of a gimmick for spotting the leader, rather than as an iconic part of Tour de France culture. Nobody even mentioned its absence during the race commentaries. ■

PHILIPPE THYS

Nicolas Frantz (left) snatches victory in front of
Antonin Magne in Bordeaux in 1929. But he still had
to share his yellow jersey that day.

Three of a kind: Nicolas Frantz, Victor Fontan and André Leducq (from left to right) all wear the yellow jersey in the 1929 Tour between Bordeaux and Bayonne.

1929

LEDUCQ - FONTAN - FRANTZ

THREE IN ONE!

What were the odds of this happening? At the end of Stage 7 from Les Sables-d'Olonne to Bordeaux, three riders (André Leducq, Victor Fontan and Nicolas Frantz) all recorded identical times in the general classification. Who would get the yellow jersey? Tour director Henri Desgrange looked up article 29 of the regulations, which stipulated, rather unhelpfully, that 'the first placed rider in the general classification will wear the yellow jersey.' So he gave a jersey to all three.

'Of course,' wrote Desgrange in his column in *L'Auto* that day, 'the stage wins that Frantz took (in Bordeaux) and that Leducq won (in Calais) give them a slight advantage over Fontan. But Fontan still has the right to follow whatever race tactic he wants, and the rules are clear enough. So tomorrow, there will be three yellow jerseys in the race.' ∎

Raffaele Di Paco was desperate to win the yellow jersey, but in the face of Antonin Magne's stranglehold on the Tour, he was lucky to pick up a stage win (here, Stage 19 from Évian to Belfort).

1931

DI PACO - CHARLES PÉLISSIER

THE SPRINT DOUBLE

The 1931 Tour was the first where sprinters really made their mark. The Italian Raffaele Di Paco and Frenchman Charles Pélissier would each take five stages each. But from the start in Paris through to the Pyrenees, the general classification took time to settle down. A pack of 12 riders were on equal points behind the leader, Di Paco, after Stage 4 from Brest to Vannes. Pélissier's win on Stage 5 from Vannes to Les Sables d'Olonne then put the Frenchman on equal points with the Italian. So on the following day's ride to Bordeaux there were two yellow jerseys on the road.

Di Paco was the quickest to Bordeaux, and so got some time alone with the yellow jersey for a couple of stages afterwards, only to lose it to Pélissier again on Stage 8 from Bayonne to Pau. In the mountain stages that followed, it was the turn of Antonin Magne to show what he could do.

Eddy Merckx (here, riding alongside Désiré Letort) was the first rider ever to refuse to wear the yellow jersey, out of respect for his rival Luis Ocaña, forced to abandon the 1971 Tour after a crash.

4

CONSPICUOUS BY ITS ABSENCE

Sometimes there would be no yellow jersey in the peloton, often as a result of a dramatic exit.

1971

EDDY MERCKX

A SPORTING GESTURE

Luis Ocaña had held the yellow jersey since the start of the mountain stages and was having a great Tour. Then he crashed out on Stage 14 from Revel to Luchon, on the Col de Menté. That evening in Luchon Eddy Merckx, who had been 7'24" behind the Spanish rider in the general classification, turned down the yellow jersey at the podium ceremony. 'No, it's not for me,' he said sadly. Nor did he wear it the following day, on Stage 15 from Luchon to Superbagnères, having spoken with the race organizers. 'Just do me the favour of not having a yellow jersey in the peloton for this stage,' he asked them. His request was granted.

1978

JAN RAAS

JUSTICE WAS DONE

It had been raining constantly in the Netherlands, and the cobblestones of Leiden, on the outskirts of The Hague, were soaked and slippery. The Tour prologue of 1978 became a washout, with dozens of riders crashing out. As a result, Tour bosses decided not to count the prologue times in the general classification, which suited most riders – except, notably, Jan Raas who had recorded the best time of the day and would be denied the yellow jersey. This was all the more disappointing for Raas as the route was going to pass through his home town, Sint-Willebrord, on the way to Brussels. 'I was gutted that they would not give me the yellow jersey,' complained the road and sprint specialist, 'but that just added to my

motivation.' Jan Raas took the next morning's half-stage from Leiden to Sint-Willebrord, and finally received the yellow jersey in Brussels that evening, wearing it the next day on the Tour's return across the border into France. Justice had been done.

Jan Raas got no reward for his efforts in the prologue of the 1978 Tour. But he got his revenge the following day.

The 1980 Tour. Joop Zoetemelk would wait for the arrival in Luchon to put on the yellow jersey.

1980

LEADER FROM MIDNIGHT

By Stage 12 of the 1980 Tour (from Agen to Pau) Bernard Hinault was suffering from acute tendonitis in his knee, which forced him to drop out of the Tour on the evening of 9 July, (slipping discreetly out of his hotel via the kitchen door at the back). Second-placed Joop Zoetemelk duly woke up the following morning to find himself the new Tour leader. Given the circumstances, Zoetemelk chose not to wear 'Hinault's' yellow jersey on Stage 13 to Luchon. That evening, though, having held on to his lead, he took the yellow – and went on to keep it all the way to Paris.

1991

RESPECT TO SÖRENSEN

When Danish racer Rolf Sörensen crashed out on Stage 5 (from Reims to Valenciennes), fracturing his collarbone and making it impossible to continue on to Arras the following day, Greg LeMond, in second, declined to wear the jersey in his place. Stage 6 was thus run without a yellow jersey, and that evening, it would be handed to Thierry Marie, thanks to a mass breakaway that he had orchestrated. Unlike both Merckx and Zoetemelk, who had declined the jersey in previous Tours and then been rewarded with another one the following evening, Greg LeMond had to wait a couple more days, eventually getting hold of the yellow at Alençon after the time trial on Stage 8. He would not hold it for long, however, as Indurain was closing in.

2007

CONTADOR'S FIRST

Alberto Contador had never worn a yellow jersey. But after finishing Stage 17 between Pau and Castelsarrasin, his time had finally come. The previous evening, the Danish rider Michael Rasmussen (who had led the Tour since Stage 8 in the Alps) had been disqualified for misleading anti-doping authorities. Contador could have worn the leader's yellow on Stage 18 but, under the circumstances, he turned it down. Four days later he won his first Tour de France.

In a chaotic 2007 Tour which sees the race leader excluded, **Alberto Contador** inherited the yellow jersey in the evening but rode the following day without it.

Greg LeMond would get his final day in the yellow jersey in 1991, but won't wear it when his rival crashes out.

1949

NORBERT CALLENS: A VERY UNLUCKY MAN

It was the unfortunate destiny of Norbert Callens to face endless frustration in his quest to wear the yellow jersey. In 1949 he was part of the Belgian national team, and his compatriot Roger Lambrecht had just won Stage 2 (from Reims to Brussels) and was wearing yellow. On Stage 3, an early breakaway was set up as the riders headed for Boulogne-sur-Mer. Callens was riding with another Belgian, Florent Mathieu, and former French champion César Marcellak. The gap opened up to nine minutes, and at the finishing line Callens crossed first, winning the stage and, to his immense delight, the yellow jersey. But wait: somehow, the box of yellow jerseys was already in a supply truck that had left earlier that afternoon for the next stage departure. A disaster for Callens! Luckily, a Belgian journalist, Albert Van Laethem, happened to be wearing a yellow sweater of his own that day, and was kind enough to hand it to Callens. Sadly, though, Callens would never get his hands on the real thing – as the race lead passed on to Jacques Marinelli at the end of Stage 4. That, however, was not the end of the story. Some 45 years later (in 1994), during a Tour stage that arrived in Boulogne-sur-Mer, the French TV journalist Jean-Paul Ollivier presented Callens, at long last, with a 'genuine' yellow jersey. ■

At the finish in Boulogne-sur-Mer, there is no official yellow jersey available. Norbert Callens manages to borrow somebody's yellow shirt for the ceremony.

Norbert Callens fought hard for his victory, but at the end of the stage there was no yellow jersey to reward his efforts. This disappointment for the Belgian rider was only made up some 45 years later, when he was presented with the real thing.

Building his brand: André Darrigade receives the yellow jersey from celebrity accordionist Yvette Horner, after his successful first stage of the 1956 Tour from Reims to Liège (see photo opposite). Louison Bobet was sitting out the 1956 Tour, and can be seen (left) in the main picture.

5

VICTORY ON DAY ONE

**Some riders made it their mission to win the first yellow jersey of the Tour.
Here are some tales of the quick starters.**

1956-1961

DARRIGADE'S DAYS OF GLORY

Road and sprint specialist André Darrigade managed to win the Stage 1 yellow jersey an incredible five times out of his six Tours from 1956 to 1961.

André Darrigade was as powerful a sprinter as he was a road racer, the kind of all-rounder that is rarely seen these days. He was capable of scintillating acceleration, winning the World Championships in 1959. But he was also a canny and courageous tactician, keen to join and sometimes to initiate breakaways, and showing a generosity of spirit that was often reciprocated by other riders. 'Before finding the right breakaway, I needed to go along with some of the others, because nobody really wanted to ride with me!' he recalls, smiling. 'But I wasn't just going to sit on their wheels, I was working perhaps even harder than the other riders, and that seemed to work out.'

He used this technique to win his very first yellow jersey. No fewer than five times in all he picked up the yellow on the first stage of the Tour, with four consecutive first-stage victories from 1956 to 1959, and then once again in 1961 on the morning half-stage from Rouen to Versailles (thus denying Jacques Anquetil's 'start-to-finish' yellow jersey during that year.) What was the secret to Darrigade's success rate? 'I don't know if there is any particular reason,' he muses. 'Or rather, I approached each of the first stages as I would a [one-day] Classic.' Darrigade's thirst for victory and his love for the Tour seemed to fire him up more than any other competitive race. As team manager Guillaume Driessens put it: 'Darrigade, on the Tour? He is totally unrecognizable!'

THE GREEN JERSEY WAS MORE HIS STYLE

While Darrigade may not be a household name to many, his personal stats rank him high among Tour racers. Among those who have not won the Tour, he is in fifth place* in terms of the highest number of days in the yellow jersey (16½) and only Bernard Hinault has won as often on the first day, mainly through his performance on the prologues. ■ ■ ■

STAGE 1 WINNERS

★★★★★ 5 TIMES

André DARRIGADE (FRA) : 1956 (Liège) ; 1957 (Granville) ; 1958 (Gand) ; 1959 (Metz) ; 1961 (Versailles).

Bernard HINAULT (FRA) : 1980 (Frankfurt, prologue) ; 1981 (Nice, prologue) ; 1982 (Bâle, prologue) ; 1984 (Montreuil, prologue) ; 1985 (Plumelec, prologue).

Fabian CANCELLARA (SUI) : 2004 (Liège, prologue) ; 2007 (London, prologue) ; 2009 (Monaco, time trial) ; 2010 (Rotterdam, prologue) ; 2012 (Liège, prologue).

★★★★ 4 TIMES

Eddy MERCKX (BEL) : 1970 (Limoges, prologue) ; 1971 (Mulhouse, team time trial) ; 1972 (Angers, prologue) ; 1974 (Brest, prologue).

★★★ 3 TIMES

Rudi ALTIG (GER) : 1962 (Spa) ; 1966 (Charleville) ; 1969 (Roubaix, prologue).

Thierry MARIE (FRA) : 1986 (Boulogne-Billancourt, prologue) ; 1990 (Futuroscope, prologue) ; 1991 (Lyon, prologue).

Chris BOARDMAN (GBR) : 1994 (Lille, prologue) ; 1997 (Rouen, prologue) ; 1998 (Dublin, prologue).

★★ TWICE

Louis MOTTIAT (BEL) : 1920 (Le Havre) ; 1921 (Le Havre).

Robert JACQUINOT (FRA) : 1922 (Le Havre) ; 1923 (Le Havre).

Ottavio BOTTECCHIA (ITA) : 1924 (Le Havre) ; 1925 (Le Havre).

Miguel INDURAIN (ESP) : 1992 (Saint-Sébastien, prologue) ; 1993 (Puy du Fou, prologue).

Marcel KITTEL (GER) : 2013 (Bastia) ; 2014 (Harrogate).

PROLOGUE SPECIALISTS

Among the day one winners, several have been winners of the prologue, introduced in 1967.

★★★★★ **Bernard HINAULT** (FRA) : 5 times.

★★★★★ **Fabian CANCELLARA** (SUI) : 5 times (in 2009 in Monaco, this involved a Stage 1 individual time trial over a greater distance).

★★★★ **Eddy MERCKX** (BEL) : 4 times, of which one is a team event.

★★★ **Thierry MARIE** : 3 times.

★★ **Miguel INDURAIN** (ESP) : Twice.

ALTIG: PICK N' MIX

Only Rudi Altig got the first yellow jersey as a result of regular stages (1962, 1966) and a prologue time trial (1969).

■■■

During the Tours of the late 1950s, André Darrigade seemed capable of snatching Stage 1 victories again and again without fail. 'Maybe it was also a bit easier for me at that stage because the general classification was not yet established,' he said later. 'Mind you, riding in the breakaways I also had to avoid giving away any advantage to the rivals of [Darrigade's team mates] Bobet, Anquetil or Rivière,' he said. In fact, Darrigade was a key player in the France national team, and his influence on the race did not finish at the end of Stage 1 (and he won some yellow jerseys during later stages too). Even so, his job as road captain meant he frequently had to put his own ambitions to one side and occasionally drop back to help bring other riders – including Anquetil – out of the pack.

As a sprinter, though, the green jersey was a familiar sight on Darrigade's back. 'Perhaps I was more attached to the green jersey, because I was able to win it in Paris [in 1959 and 1961]. Whereas when I had the yellow, I was racing hard to keep it as long as possible. I wanted to chase everything that moved, and I certainly lost quite a few stages in my attempts to keep it. And during all this, the France team was racing to support its leader, not just for my own benefit.' This was never so evident as when Darrigade (wearing yellow) had a puncture 10km from Toulouse in the 1956 Tour. He was left to change the inner tube and pump the tyre himself, while team manager Marcel Bidot cruised by in the car, following closely behind team leader Gilbert Bauvin.

Darrigade was no climber, but he still managed to win the yellow jersey at Pau in 1956, at the end of a stage that included the ascent of the Aubisque. Statistically speaking, his achievement of being Tour leader over six different years was beaten only by Hinault (who could count eight Tours as leader) and was matched only by Fabian Cancellara. And the most treasured of his yellow jerseys? Perhaps the one he would wear in his home town of Dax during the mid-stage of the 1958 Tour. The rapturous reception he got at the finishing line prompted Jacques Goddet to write in *L'Équipe*: 'Darrigade Wins Half The Tour!' Joking apart, Darrigade did nothing by halves. ■

* Behind Cancellara, Vietto, Voeckler and Altig, according to rankings at the end of the 2018 Tour.

26 June 1958: raising his arm in triumph at the end of the first stage from Brussels to Ghent (right), André Darrigade knows that tomorrow will be a yellow jersey day.
7 July 1958: as he lobs his bouquet into the crowds in Dax (below), the Pyrenees stages are approaching. So he won't keep the yellow for long.

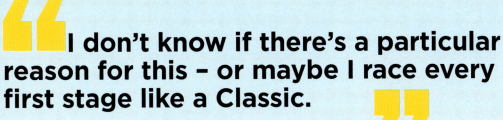

" I don't know if there's a particular reason for this – or maybe I race every first stage like a Classic. "

André Darrigade

IT'S DARRIGADE! AGAIN...

André Darrigade wore the yellow jersey over six different Tours (1956, 1957, 1958, 1959, 1961 and 1962). He also won it three times during the course of the 1956 Tour, in Liège for two days, Caen for three further days, and then in Pau for a final day. In all he recorded ten stage wins while wearing the yellow jersey, placing him third after Merckx (who recorded 14 wins in yellow) and Hinault (13 wins), which goes to show something of Darrigade's significance in Tour history.

DOWN TO THE WIRE: MASTERS OF SUSPENSE

On the morning of the final stage, they were still trailing the race leader. But by the same evening, they would become the victors of the Tour. For grit and determination, read on.

Jean Robic storms into the Parc des Princes ahead of Lucien Teisseire and Édouard Flachleitner, having saved his decisive attack, on the Côte de Bonsecours, for the very last stage – snatching a famous victory in the 1947 Tour.

HEROES OF THE FINAL DAY

Jean ROBIC (FRA)
Stage 21 of the 1947 Tour

Positions at Caen
1. Brambilla
2. Ronconi, 53"
3. Robic 2'58"

Positions at Parc des Princes
1. Robic
2. Fachleitner, 3'58"
3. Brambilla, 10'07"

Jan JANSSEN (HOL)
Stage 22 of the 1968 Tour
(individual time trial)

Positions at Melun
1. Van Springel
2. San Miguel, 12"
3. Janssen, 16"

Positions at La Cipale
1. Janssen
2. Van Springel, 38"

Greg LEMOND (USA)
Stage 21 of the 1989 Tour
(individual time trial)

Positions at Versailles
1. Fignon
2. LeMond, 50"

Positions at Champs-Elysées
1. LeMond
2. Fignon, 8"

Jean Robic on the Col du Tourmalet between
Luchon and Pau.

- 1947 -

JEAN ROBIC, LAST DAY HERO

**In 1947 the yellow jersey eluded Robic for the entire Tour.
But he would go on to win the first Tour de France of the post-war era.**

It was the most famous reversal in the history of competitive cycling, commemorated to this day by a memorial just outside Rouen. 'On 20th July 1947,' reads the inscription, 'Jean Robic made a breakaway on this hill and won the first Tour de France after the war.'

It was dawn, on the 1947 Tour's final stage from Caen to Paris, and Pierre Brambilla, the French superstar (of Italian parentage), looked set to become champion. He had held the yellow jersey for two days, and had a lead over third-placed Robic of just under three minutes. But Robic (nicknamed 'the kid' – as in a young goat) mounted an all-out attack on the slopes of Bonsecours, the hill that rises above Rouen.

His France national team mate Édouard Fachleitner went with him, but Brambilla, the yellow jersey, was caught off guard and quickly found himself dropped.

There were 140km left to the Parc des Princes and with Robic and Fachleitner working together, Brambilla's chances were fading fast. Robic was said to have proposed a deal to Fachleitner: 'You won't be able to win as I'll never let you get away,' said Robic. 'But if you stay with me…' It is uncertain whether Fachtleitner let himself be 'bought' into supporting Robic as his chances of winning seemed fairly slim. But supporting Robic is what he did.

At the Parc des Princes, Jean Robic finished seven minutes behind the stage winner Briek Schotte, but a full 13 minutes ahead of the hapless Brambilla. Robic won the Tour, with Fachleitner second, and Brambilla having to make do with third place. Only Jan Janssen, (thanks to a final stage time trial in 1968) and Greg LeMond (coming back to beat Laurent Fignon in 1989) would manage to pull off such dramatic last day reversals. ■

Jean Robic leaves Paris after the Tour de France, enjoying his celebrity status.

LE MIROIR DES
SPORTS

3f

LEJEUNE

L'ÉTOURDISSANT FINAL DE JAN JANSSEN

– 1968 –

VICTORY LAP FOR JANSSEN

On Sunday 21 July at noon, Herman Van Springel was race leader. By the evening of the same day, Jan Janssen had become champion.

The final stage of the 1968 Tour was a 55km time trial in the afternoon finishing in Paris. The field still looked wide open, with the top of the general classification much more tightly packed than usual, after what had been a slightly less arduous route that year. It was, after all, just one year since the tragic death of British rider Tom Simpson on Mont Ventoux.

By midday, at the end of the first half-stage from Auxerre to Melun, Belgian rider Herman Van Springel was defending the yellow jersey. Just 12 seconds behind was Miguel Indurain, though not much of a threat in a time trial. Jan Janssen was 16 seconds off the leader, but the betting odds were with Ferdinand Bracke. Although trailing by 50 seconds, he was a specialist time trialist and holder of the one-hour distance record. Ultimately, the competition was too much for Van Springel, and it was Jan Janssen who came through to win the Tour.

Janssen won by just 38 seconds, the slimmest margin of victory ever recorded (until another decisive time trial 21 years later with the famous duel between Greg LeMond and Laurent Fignon). Crossing the finish line on the municipal velodrome at Bois de Vincennes, the defeated Van Springel, normally rather undemonstrative, flung his bike to the ground in frustration and broke down in tears. Janssen also had to remove his glasses and wipe his eyes, overcome with the emotion of victory. 'I saw my chance, and I took it!' exclaimed the first Dutch winner of the Tour. 'I can't quite believe what has just happened.' And nor could Van Springel. The two rivals remained close friends over the coming years. 'For this Tour, I lost it, but you deserved it,' the Belgian rider told Janssen a few years later. Van Springel picked up plenty of second places as his career continued, but none so cruel a defeat as this one.■

Between Melun and Paris, Jan Janssen pushes on towards the yellow jersey.

Jan Janssen celebrates with a victory lap on his team car after winning the Tour in 1968.
He crossed the line at the Cipale with a winning margin of just 38 seconds!

The moment of truth: when Greg LeMond set off on the final time trial of the Tour, he faced a monumental
challenge with a slim chance of victory. In the Champs-Élysées, his dream came true.

– 1989 –

LEMOND WINS BY EIGHT SECONDS!

The American won the Tour three times, but it is his 1989 victory that remains his most extraordinary. He beat Laurent Fignon by the narrowest margin in Tour history.

Greg LeMond scored three impressive Tour victories. And he may have picked up even more, had he not been accidentally shot in a hunting accident, forcing him to sit out the 1987 and 1988 Tours as he recuperated. In his first (pre-accident) victory in 1986 he beat Bernard Hinault and gained instant fame as the first ever non-European to win the Tour. For his third victory, in 1990, he spent most of the Tour working to grind down the ten-minute lead accumulated by Claudio Chiapucci after a gruelling breakaway (along with Bauer, Pensec and Maassen) early in the Tour. But LeMond's most celebrated win of all time was his spectacular second Tour victory. The headline in *L'Équipe* the day after his win on the Champs-Élysées described it with just one word: 'Unforgettable'. No one who watched it would argue with that.

The gap was eight seconds: the closest winning margin ever recorded in the Tour de France. Unlike Jean Robic and Jan Janssen, Greg LeMond had already worn the yellow jersey before the finishing stage of the 1989 Tour. From the Stage 5 time trial from Dinard to Rennes, the race became an ongoing duel between LeMond and Laurent Fignon, who was race leader on the eve of the time trial on the final day's ride into Paris. The French racer had a substantial lead of 50 seconds over the American. So against one of the world's best time trial specialists, LeMond would need to gain slightly more than two seconds for each of the 24.5km that separated Versailles from the Champs-Élysées – a seemingly impossible task.

82 METRES IN FRONT

Greg LeMond was the incarnation of American technological innovation in cycling. But Laurent Fignon was decidedly old-school. While LeMond wore an aero helmet, Fignon cycled bare-headed into the wind. LeMond had also been experimenting in a wind tunnel with aerobars, which were starting to appear in the emerging discipline of triathlon. The impact of these had probably been underestimated when the American used them in Rennes to win the first major time trial of that same Tour, and the Tour rules neither explicitly allowed nor disallowed their use. Cyrille Guimard, Fignon's team manager who was well versed in Tour procedures, admitted that before the Dinard to Rennes time trial, he 'didn't know that LeMond had new handlebars' and was probably kicking himself for not spotting this innovation earlier. But he did not challenge their use, reluctant to set off any possible counter-challenge against his own team's methods.

When the morning of the final time trial arrived, LeMond could see the enormity of the task ahead. 'How about I win by just one second?' he thought to himself.

Unknown to LeMond, Laurent Fignon was also suffering from an invisible handicap. A saddle injury had opened up after Fignon's storming performance in the Alpine stages, though the wound had been a carefully guarded secret to avoid giving any kind of morale boost to LeMond. Fignon had obvious discomfort sitting on the saddle, and skipped the initial warm-up session.

As the race got underway, the split times said it all: just after the midway point, Fignon had conceded 24 seconds. After 18km, it was 35 seconds. But LeMond was not watching the clock. 'I didn't care about the split times, I just gave it everything I had,' he said later.

There had rarely been such incredible suspense on a final day of the Tour, and when LeMond crossed the line, the nail-biting wait for Fignon began. The American had started two minutes ahead of Fignon, and was standing on tip-toes scanning the horizon through the crowds. Finally, a small dot of yellow was visible in front of the Arc de Triomphe*. Fignon was racing hard down to the finish, but in vain. When he crossed the line he had given up 58 seconds to LeMond from a 50-second lead at the start. LeMond therefore had won by just eight seconds. In terms of distance cycled over a course of 3,285km, he had won by a miniscule 82m! ∎

*In 1989, the finishing line for the time trial was at the 'downhill' end of the Champs-Élysées.

1983-1984-1989

FIGNON: DON'T TALK TO ME ABOUT 1989

Laurent Fignon won two Tours de France (in 1983 and 1984) and lost one in 1989, under the cruellest of conditions. Here's the story.

Laurent Fignon pushes to the limit
on the Champs-Élysées.

1983
THE YOUNG CHAMP

Ambitious and talented, Laurent Fignon may have hoped to join the 1983 Tour as the man who toppled Bernard Hinault. No such luck, as Hinault was out of the race getting knee surgery. This left the field looking open, though to say that Fignon was therefore favourite to win, or even to become leader of the Renault-Gitane team, was pushing things a bit far. In the Pyrenees, Pascal Simon had built up a solid lead of 4'22" on the rookie Fignon, who had nonetheless done enough to pick up the white jersey for best young rider. The next day, however, would be decisive in accelerating Fignon's rise to the top. Pascal Simon had barely put on the yellow jersey at Bagnères-de-Luchon when he crashed out the following day near Montréjeau, breaking his shoulder blade. Simon then persisted with six further agonizing days of racing until he was eventually forced to drop out. Fignon seized his chance at the Alpe d'Huez to take the yellow (where he would also gain race leadership in 1984 and 1989). Young, blond and bespectacled, Fignon won his first Tour at just 23 year old, with all the swagger of a young champion.

1984: Bernard Hinault had been consistently outclassed by the young Laurent Fignon, most notably on the Alpe d'Huez. On the final day of the Tour, the two rivals managed to share a joke about it all.

1984
GILDED YOUTH

There was something all-powerful in the pedal strokes of Laurent Fignon in the 1984 Tour. He won five stages in all, of which three were in the Alps (Stage 16, Les Échelles to La Ruchère-en-Chartreuse time trial; Stage 18, Bourg-d'Oisans to La Plagne; Stage 20, Morzine to Crans-Montana). There was also a certain youthful lack of deference towards his elders and betters: 'I had a good laugh,' he said of Bernard Hinault, whom he was able to drop on the way up the Alpe d'Huez. Fignon looked to be an established part of Tour stardom. His solo breakaways at La Plagne, and then at Crans-Montana, wearing yellow on both days, created an aura of a kind of gilded youth.

1989
CRUEL DEFEAT

Laurent Fignon lost the 1989 Tour in the final moments of the final day. And he lost by just eight seconds. The event has passed into Tour folklore. As the yellow jersey pounded his way down the Champs-Élysées to the finish line, lungs bursting, his hopes of victory were hanging by a thread. Handicapped by a saddle sore, and lacking the triathlon-style aerobars that gave Greg LeMond more leverage, Laurent Fignon sensed, with mounting confusion, that something big was about to happen. 'What can I say?' he gasped, shortly after crossing the finishing line, grappling to comprehend the scale of his disappointment. In the hysteria that followed, nobody told him he had lost, but he sensed it. As he put it later: 'I don't really think that I lost the Tour in the Champs-Élysées, even if the cobblestones were agony. These eight seconds… I should have just picked them up elsewhere. There are a thousand different places where I lost the Tour.'

According to team manager Cyrille Guimard, Fignon never really recovered from this defeat. 'On that day, something got broken inside him. And nothing was ever the same again,' Guimard said in an interview for *L'Équipe*. Fignon found that whenever he talked about his career, someone always raised the subject of the 'eight seconds' and brought the whole sorry tale flooding back. For the rest of his life (Fignon died in 2010), he would always make a detour rather than have to pass the spot on the Champs-Élysées where that bitter defeat took place. ∎

Laurent Fignon would never forget his defeat on the Champs-Élysées. He missed out on becoming a triple winner of the Tour by just eight seconds.

1983: The public witness a new star of the Tour. Laurent Fignon drops
Peter Winnen during the Alpine stage from Bourg-d'Oisan to Morzine.

In 2018 at Fontenay le Comte, Fernando Gaviria
triumphs in the first sprint of his Tour career to take
both a stage win and the yellow jersey.

7

SPRINTING FOR YELLOW

**Sprinters already have their own jersey: the green one.
But quite a few of the great sprinters have worn the yellow too.**

The Tour's green jersey (for the highest number of points won) is generally seen as 'the sprinter's jersey'. But in fact, sprinters can and do also win the yellow. André Darrigade, for instance, won 19 yellow jerseys during his Tour career, partly because he was not only a sprinter but a great attacking stage racer too. History tells us that sprinters tend not to win the Tour de France, but there are some notable exceptions: André Leducq (who won the Tour in 1930 and 1932) was a die-hard sprinter who went on to become a great all-round racer. Jan Janssen (who won the Tour in 1968) was also seen initially as a pure sprinter, but he too widened his repertoire – and expanded his collection of yellow jerseys.

Sprint specialist Cyrille Guimard was electrifying on the finish line, and took on Eddy Merckx during the 1972 Tour. He claimed the yellow jersey early on from Saint-Brieuc through to the start of the Pyrenees stages, and then fought a bitter duel with Merckx that continued into the Alps, all the while suffering from intense pain in his knees which eventually forced him to withdraw just two days from Paris. Merckx therefore went on to win the green jersey, but out of respect for his fierce competitor, he gave it to Guimard.

There is a long list of sprinters who have found themselves with (albeit temporary) leadership of the Tour, from Charles Pélissier's rivalry with Raffaele Di Paco in the 1930s through to Marcel Kittel or Fernando Gavira. It has become more marked since the 1990s, when the system of bonus seconds given to the quickest racers through intermediate stages (as well as on the finishing line) has given sprinters more traction

in the general classification over the first part of the Tour. The 1999 Tour was in fact something of a sprint-fest, with sprint finishes at the end of each of the first seven stages. The Estonian Jaan Kirsipuu won one of these, Belgian Tom Steels took two, and Italian sprint ace Mario Cipollini won four in a row. However it was Kirsipuu who was able to make the most of all this, with six days wearing the yellow jersey thanks to the solid lead he gained on Stage 1, plus the various bonus seconds he picked up as the race went on.

There are other notable yellow jersey sprinters, such as the German Erik Zabel and Slovakian Peter Sagan, both six-times winners of the green jersey. Similarly, Mark Cavendish, one of the greatest sprint phenomenons of all time, finally won his yellow jersey alongside the famous Utah Beach in Normandy, one of the most successful winning sprints of his Tour career (and there are 30 of them in all!). ∎

1962: Raymond Poulidor had already won Stage 19 from Briançon to Aix-les-Bains, but André Darrigade (pictured right) took the sprint at the front of the peloton, ahead of Émile Daems. No yellow jersey for Darrigade this time (though he wore it for 16½ days during his career).

YELLOW JERSEY SPRINTERS

André Leducq (FRA), 1929, 1930, 1932, 1938
Charles Pélissier (FRA), 1930, 1931
Raffaele Di Paco (ITA), 1931
Rik Van Steenbergen (BEL), 1952
Miguel Poblet (ESP), 1955
André Darrigade (FRA), 1956, 1957, 1958, 1959, 1961, 1962
Cyrille Guimard (FRA), 1972
Patrick Sercu (BEL), 1974
Gerben Karstens (NED), 1974
Freddy Maertens (BEL), 1976
Sean Kelly (IRL), 1983
Wilfried Nelissen (BEL), 1993
Mario Cipollini (ITA), 1993, 1997
Johan Museeuw (BEL), 1993, 1994
Laurent Jalabert (FRA), 1995, 2000
Frédéric Moncassin (FRA), 1996
Jaan Kirsipuu (EST), 1999
Erik Zabel (GER), 1998, 2002
Jean-Patrick Nazon (FRA), 2003
Robbie McEwen (AUS), 2004
Thor Hushovd (NOR), 2004, 2006, 2011
Marcel Kittel (GER), 2013, 2014
Mark Cavendish (GBR), 2016
Fernando Gaviria (COL), 2018

HEIGHTS OF AMBITION

Climbers have always had a special place in the history of the Tour, and some set their sights on an even higher goal: the yellow jersey, or victory in Paris.

1939: René Vietto makes a determined attempt on the slopes of the Iseran during Stage 16 from Bonneval to Bourg-Saint-Maurice, but it feels like a lost cause. The previous day he had given up 17 minutes and lost the yellow jersey, and by the end of Stage 16 he will have lost a further ten minutes.

You have to be able to climb to win the Tour, but being able to climb is not enough on its own. In the post-war period, from Jean Robic (1947) through to Marco Pantani (1998), and including of course Charly Gaul (1958), Federico Bahamontes (1959) and Lucien Van Impe (1976), there have been just a handful of pure mountain climbers who have gone on to win the Tour. Mostly the Tour is won by talented all-rounders, and climbers often have weak points in other Tour disciplines – such as time trials or even on the descent from the summit. Even so, climbers have left their indelible mark on the history of the Tour, and have also had their part in the history of the yellow jersey.

Richard Virenque, the archetypal climbing specialist, won the Tour's King of the Mountains category a record seven times, and picked up the yellow jersey twice in his long career. 'Frankly, I would prefer the polka dot jersey any day to the yellow,' he said. Whatever value they attach to the yellow jersey, most climbers never get the chance of wearing it. Julio Jimenez, for example, three-times King of the Mountains (from 1965 to 1967), or the Colombian Luis Herrera, who won King of the Mountains in 1985 and was without doubt one of the greatest ever climbers, could both find themselves fading on the flat stages, and so never made it to the head of the general classification. Having said all that, there are some climbers who did manage it. Here are some of the most famous:

RENÉ VIETTO

YELLOW JERSEY IN 1939 AND 1947

Vietto began his cycling career in Cannes while working as a bell boy at a hotel in Nice – and quickly established himself as a brilliant, naturally gifted young climber on his first Tour in 1934 at just 20 years old. Vietto looked set to take yellow after team leader Antonin Magne crashed, but instead Vietto sacrificed his own chances and gave Magne his bike, allowing Magne to go on to win the Tour. Vietto had another shot at glory after the war on the 1947 Tour, but was eclipsed by Jean Robic in a time trial just two days from the finish.

1947: A stage victory at Digne gives René Vietto the yellow jersey. Unfortunately, he will lose it just three days from the finish.

1948: The previous evening, Gino Bartali had won the stage, while Louison Bobet managed to hold on to the yellow jersey. But not for long. The next day, between Briançon and Aix-les-Bains, Gino Bartali took the yellow and kept it all the way to Paris.

JEAN ROBIC

TOUR WINNER IN 1947, YELLOW JERSEY IN 1953

Standing in a crowd, Robic cut a rather diminutive figure. But on his bike, up in the mountains, he was a giant. And it was in 1947 that Robic made his own piece of history, leading the race across all the famous cols of the Pyrenees during Stage 15 from Luchon to Pau, and picking up time bonuses as he did so. By the time he reached Tourmalet, he already had a four and a half minute lead over Pierre Brambilla, and 12 minutes on René Vietto. 'With that, I'll go all the way to Brittany,' he vowed, pointing to his two water bottles containing some maximum strength coffee. He left it to the very last day, from Rouen to Paris, to clinch the first Tour victory of the post-war era.

1947: While Robic's last stage victory in Paris captured the public imagination, he had also been brilliant on the mountain stages too.

GINO BARTALI

WINNER IN 1938 AND 1948, YELLOW JERSEY IN 1937 AND 1949

If the Alps belonged to anyone, they belonged to Gino Bartali. In 1948 he won the three Alpine stages in a row in Briançon, Aix-les-Bains and Lausanne. His pedalling action was distinctive, with his shoes jabbing like the needle of a sewing machine, and just the slightest of pauses every ten strokes.

1954: Federico Bahamontes, the first Spaniard to win the Tour (in 1954) seemed to make light work of the mountain stages, including, here, the Col du Tourmalet.

1959: Bahamontes has the yellow jersey, but Charly Gaul won't let him get away.

CHARLY GAUL

WINNER IN 1958

Charly Gaul was responsible for one of the most extraordinary feats of cycling in the history of the Tour. It all happened on Stage 21 of the 1958 Tour in the Chartreuse mountains from Briançon to Aix-les-Bains. In previous days Gaul had been held back by equipment failure and a crash, giving up close to 15 minutes. So on Stage 21, in heavy rain and atrocious road conditions, the Luxembourg climber felt he had nothing to lose. He attacked on the Luitel Col and took back 14 minutes at the finish. It was only at the end of the final time trial (from Besançon to Dijon) that he got to wear the yellow jersey, on the eve of the finish in Paris.

FEDERICO BAHAMONTES

WINNER IN 1959, YELLOW JERSEY IN 1963

Federico Bahamontes is typical of the legendary climbers on the Tour. He would often end up giving away all the time he gained on the ascents by his relatively slow descents. And sometimes he even got off his bike at the summit, as he did in 1954 on the Col de Romeyère, where he picked up his points for the King of the Mountains and then took time to enjoy an ice cream. He was King of the Mountains six times between 1954 and 1964, and thanks to a certain amount of infighting within the French national team, he even managed to win the Tour in 1959.

LUCIEN VAN IMPE

WINNER IN 1976

Van Impe's ambitions were always focused on King of the Mountains, and after 1975 the introduction of the polka dot jersey gave a new sense of identity to this competition. He won it six times in all between 1971 and 1983. In 1976 the new boss of the Renault-Gitane team, Cyrille Guimard, convinced Van Impe that he had a serious chance of becoming Tour winner that year. Helped on by Luis Ocaña who gave his support to Van Impe in the Pyrenees, the Belgian did indeed go on to take the yellow jersey in Paris.

More used to wearing the polka dot jersey, Lucien Van Impe doubted he could win the Tour.

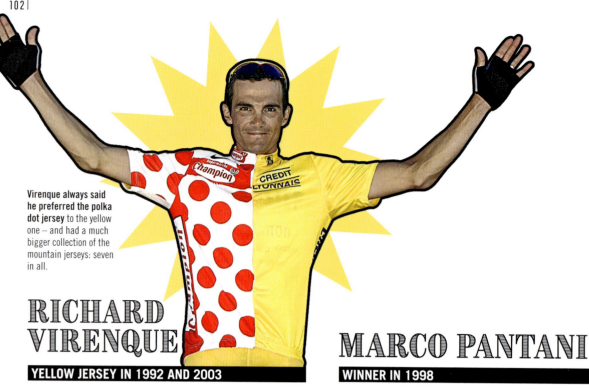

Virenque always said he preferred the polka dot jersey to the yellow one – and had a much bigger collection of the mountain jerseys: seven in all.

RICHARD VIRENQUE

YELLOW JERSEY IN 1992 AND 2003

Virenque holds the record for winning the mountains category no less than seven times between 1994 and 2004. However, it is thanks to the yellow jersey that he made a name for himself on his Tour debut in 1992. He led a successful attack on Stage 2 from Saint-Sébastien to Pau, with the stage won by his breakaway companion, Javier Murguialday. Virenque wore the yellow for just one day, and would only have the jersey again in 2003 after his victory in Stage 7 from Lyon to Morzine. Along with Gino Bartali, he is the only racer in the Tour's history to have won another yellow jersey after such a long interval – 11 years in total.

MARCO PANTANI

WINNER IN 1998

The first half of the 1990s were marked by the Tour dominance of Miguel Indurain, one of the greatest riders of all time. Marco Pantani, however was about to win it back for the climbers. In 1998 he won the Giro, and went on to win the Tour, mounting a decisive attack on Stage 15 from Grenoble to Les Deux Alpes and putting more than nine minutes into the struggling Jan Ullrich. Sadly, Pantani died tragically less than six years after his win, and the 1998 Tour is remembered more for the Festina affair and a series of doping scandals, somewhat tarnishing what was a great victory for the Italian climber.

2003: A big day for Virenque, as he climbs the Alpe d'Huez in the yellow jersey during the Centenary Tour de France. The next day though, Lance Armstrong would be in yellow.

1998: Marco Pantani wins Stage 15 at the Deux Alpes to take the yellow jersey, which he then keeps all the way through to Paris. He was the first Italian to win the Tour since Felice Gimondi in 1965.

FORCE QUIT: THE RACE IS OVER

It may well be the stuff of legends, but the yellow jersey provides its wearers with zero protection against pure bad luck. And there's nothing worse than having to drop out while you're winning.

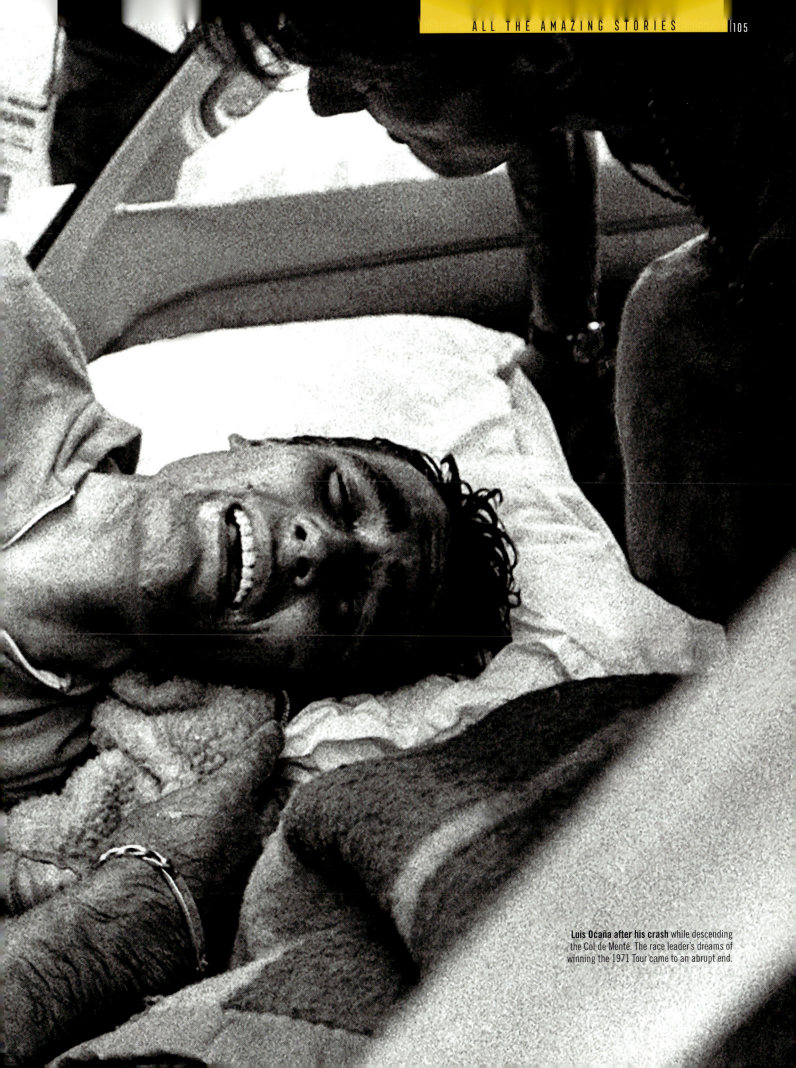

Luis Ocaña after his crash while descending the Col de Menté. The race leader's dreams of winning the 1971 Tour came to an abrupt end.

16 WHO QUIT WEARING YELLOW

Francis PÉLISSIER (FRA)
1927, Stage 6 Dinan–Brest : sick.

Victor FONTAN (FRA)
1929, Stage 10 Luchon–Perpignan : broken forks.

Gino BARTALI (ITA)
1937, Stage 12 Marseille–Nîmes : crashed out.

Sylvère MAES (BEL)
1937, Stage 17 Bordeaux–Royan : Maes and the Belgian team quit the race in protest over a series of escalating disputes over rivalry with Roger Lapébie.

Fiorenzo MAGNI (ITA)
1950, Stage 11 Pau–Saint-Gaudens : Italian riders dropped out of the race.

Wim VAN EST (NED)
1951, Stage 13 Dax–Tarbes : crash during descent of the Aubisque.

Bernard VAN DE KERCKHOVE (BEL)
1965, Stage 9 Dax–Bagnères-de-Bigorre : sun stroke on the Aubisque.

Luis OCAÑA (ESP)
1971, Stage 14 Revel–Luchon : crash during descent of the Col de Menté.

Michel POLLENTIER (BEL)
1978, Stage 16 Saint-Étienne–L'Alpe-d'Huez : disqualified after breaking rules on anti–doping controls.

Bernard HINAULT (FRA)
1980, Stage 12 Agen–Pau : left race that evening because of severe knee pain.

Pascal SIMON (FRA)
1983, Stage 17 La Tour-du-Pin–L'Alpe-d'Huez : broken shoulder blade following a crash on Stage 11.

Rolf SÖRENSEN (DAN)
1991, Stage 5 Reims–Valenciennes : broken collarbone.

Stéphane HEULOT (FRA)
1996, Stage 7 Chambéry–Les Arcs : knee pains.

Chris BOARDMAN (GBR)
1998, Stage 2 Enniscorthy–Cork : crash.

Michael RASMUSSEN (DAN)
2007, Stage 16 Orthez-Gourette–Col d'Aubisque : dismissed by his team.

Tony MARTIN (GER)
2015, Stage 6 Abbeville – Le Havre : crash injury, open fracture of collarbone.

Tony Martin crosses the line with the help of team mates Michal Kwiatkowski (left) and Julien Vermote. Martin's Tour is now over.

1927

FRANCIS PÉLISSIER

PÉLISSIER, FIRST TO GO

Eugène Christophe had been one of the first ever to wear the yellow jersey in its inaugural year of 1919, but was forced to quit the race through bad luck when his forks broke. A few years later, however, Francis Pélissier would have the dubious honour of being the first rider to drop out of the Tour with the yellow jersey on his back. It happened on Stage 6 of the 1927 Tour, from Dinan to Brest, as the Tour crossed Brittany. 'I'm sorry,' said Pélissier, nicknamed 'The Big Guy'. 'I just don't have anything left to do this. After about 50km I could tell I was having trouble keeping up with the team. I tried to dig in and push on, but I can't do this anymore. My team mates waited for me, but I told them to just keep going. To win back the yellow jersey that I've just lost.' By the time he reached Morlaix, Francis Pélissier was cramping up, and finally got into a support car in front of derisive whistles from the spectators. Later that day in Brest, Ferdinand Le Drogo, on his home turf, would become the first Breton to wear the yellow jersey.

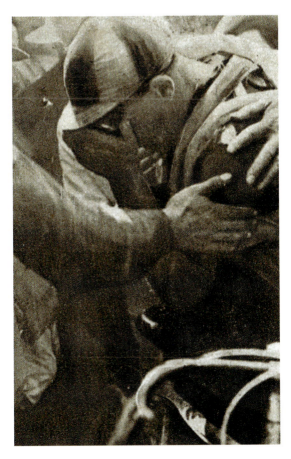

1929

VICTOR FONTAN

BROKEN FORKS, BROKEN DREAMS

The story came out in an early-morning bulletin from Jean Antoine and Alex Virot, French pioneers of radio news: the Tour favourite, Victor Fontan had dropped out of the race on 11 July. It was unexpected. Fontan was 37, but looked a likely winner after he took the yellow in the Pyrenees with a lead of more than ten minutes. The next stage down into Perpignan would allow him to strengthen his lead, and perhaps even extend it. The Tour made a night-time start from Luchon, and Tour director Henri Desgrange followed on behind at the wheel of his Hotchkiss. After 9km the car's headlights picked out the figure of a man in a yellow jersey – Fontan – walking down the road in front of him. Just like Eugène Christophe, Fontan's forks had broken. A passing cyclist offered to lend him his old bike, but Fontan declined and walked to a garage a few kilometres further on to find a better machine. But at the Portet d'Aspet he was already 36 minutes behind the leader, and by dawn, 151km from the start, he got off his bike and gave up.

WHY THEY QUIT

The most common reason for a yellow jersey to quit the Tour is a crash (Van Est, Ocaña, Boardman) or the results of a crash emerging later (Bartali, Sörensen, Simon, Martin), with seven such instances in the record books. The other main cause is sickness or physical injury (Pélissier, Van De Kerckhove, Hinault, Heulot) with four instances on record. Beyond these, there are also riders who quit deliberately (Maes, Magni), were disqualified (Pollentier) or suffered mechanical problems (Fontan).

LOST LEADERS

The 1937 Tour was notable for losing not one, but two of its top riders.

SYLVÈRE MAES

It is hard to imagine a more dramatic crash. Italian racing superstar Gino 'The Pious' Bartali was well into the Alpine stages of the 1937 Tour, when a short distance beyond Embrun he crashed over the side of a stone bridge and ended up in the torrent of icy water below.

'Fate clearly decreed that I should fall just so that my victory would be even more brilliant!' declared a gung-ho (and unscathed) Bartali the morning after his dramatic fall on Stage 8, from Grenoble to Briançon. But it was not to be. Four difficult stages later, Bartali would find himself in Marseille with a high fever, unable to continue racing. 'I already had pneumonia in the spring, and falling into that icy water made me very ill,' he said later. Bartali quit the Tour and took a train home to Florence, explaining that he could not tolerate being 'the worst rider on the Tour, the guy who is always first to be dropped'. With Bartali out, race leadership passed to Belgian rider Sylvère Maes.

A HOSTILE ENVIRONMENT

Maes, too, was also about to depart the race. The Belgian team had been facing an extraordinary level of hostility from the fiercely partisan French crowds, and felt that the race organizers were discriminating against them too. Maes and his Belgian team were crying foul over a 15 second penalty that had been imposed on the yellow jersey, relating to help he allegedly received from spectators when fixing a puncture during Stage 16 from Pau to Bordeaux.

Meanwhile his Belgian team mate Éloi Meulenberg claimed someone had thrown pepper into his face, while another, Hubert Deltour, said he had been threatened by a man wielding a club. Tour director Jacques Goddet, editor of *L'Auto* newspaper, was dismissive: 'I was with the Belgian team the whole time,' he wrote, 'and as the only official on the route I can report that no such incidents occurred.' Goddet also dismissed claims of an alleged incident at a level crossing, where the Belgians believed the peloton deliberately stopped to allow the French breakaway group to get ahead, even though no train was passing. 'I too was blocked at this level crossing,' wrote Goddet, 'and I saw the train pass three minutes later.'

The atmosphere on the race was becoming toxic. Goddet described the scene as French favourite Roger Lapébie arrived in his home city of Bordeaux: 'The Belgians were being booed, people shook their fists, it was sickening,' he wrote. 'But there were still nine out of ten who were applauding, as we have always cheered on the foreign riders on our routes for the last 40 years.'

The Belgian press treated the whole thing almost as a diplomatic incident. As for Sylvère Maes, his mind was made up. 'I will not be leaving Bordeaux with the yellow jersey. I have a wife and family at home and I don't want to be attacked. There is just too much hostility around me right now.' With Maes out, the way was now clear for Roger Lapébie to take the yellow jersey – for France – at Royan later that same day. ∎

Six riders wore the yellow jersey during the 1937 Tour, but it was the first time ever that two race leaders quit the race in succession.

Gino Bartali will take the yellow jersey after an electrifying ride to Grenoble on 7 July 1937. The next day, a crash into an icy stream will force him to abandon the Tour a few days later.

Wim Van Est is joined by Louison Bobet (left) at the stage start in Dax. A few hours later, Van Est will finish up in a ravine.

1950-1951

MAGNI / VAN EST

MADE IN SWITZERLAND

The 'Two Ks' of Swiss cycling, Ferdi Kübler and Hugo Koblet, both won the Tour in consecutive years (in 1950 and 1951 respectively) but they had something else in common: they both took over from a yellow jersey who had dropped out of the race. Kübler picked up from Fiorenzo Magni after the mass walk-out by the Italian team at Saint-Gaudens (on the morning of Stage 12). A year later, Koblet won the Tour after Wim Van Est crashed and fell into a ravine on the Aubisque during Stage 13 from Dax to Tarbes. Gilbert Bauvin first took the leader's jersey for a brief interlude, before Koblet powered into the lead. It is likely he would have won even without Van Est's dramatic exit.

1950
FIORENZO MAGNI

JERSEY IN THE BAG AS ITALIAN TEAM QUITS

If you have to make a difficult decision, sleep on it. Not that this helped change the minds of the Italian team in 1950, or that of its star rider and team captain Gino Bartali in particular. Just one hour before the scheduled departure of Stage 12 from Saint-Gaudens to Perpignan, the choice had been made: the Italians would be leaving the race. All of them.

So how come? Throughout the race, the French public had become increasingly wound up by the attitude of the Italians, who had fielded two national teams – the 'Nazionale' of Gino Bartali and the 'Cadetti' of Fiorenzo Magni – which seemed openly to be supporting each other (forbidden under Tour rules). What's more, the Italian team boss Alfredo Binda made no secret of it: 'The Italians,' he declared, 'will be marching to orders.'

On the Col d'Aspin in the first Pyrenees stage, the French crowds hurled insults at the Italian riders. There was no actual physical violence, but there were threats, which escalated when French favourite Jean Robic came off his bike after contact with another rider during Stage 11. 'The idiots thought it was me who deliberately brought down Robic,' said Bartali, who went on to win the stage. 'They hit me, they threatened to grab my bike.'

The animosity was raw and palpable, as was the expression of nationalist sentiment on both sides. It became politically charged, the French National Assembly got involved, and for a moment the entire Tour looked to be at risk. To diffuse potential flashpoints, the organizers re-routed one of the forthcoming stages to finish at Menton (in France) instead of further east in San Remo (in Italy). Whatever else happened, nobody would get Bartali to change his mind to quit the race, not even team manager Binda. 'I talked to Gino the whole evening, and talked with the team until three in the morning. They are all of one mind. I don't know what else to do.' he said as he announced the decision to quit.

One idea had been to get Magni, the yellow jersey, to continue the race accompanied by various volunteers from Bartali's team, an idea the organizers strongly favoured. This created a difficult decision for Fiorenzo Magni. He was riding at the top of his form and looked capable of winning, but felt honour-bound to follow Bartali's decision. 'It grieves me,' he said, 'but I was hired to support Bartali, not hired to win the Tour. I can't go back on the promise I made at the start. What would they take me for?'

Magni fell in with the team decision. He had become, in a sense, a hostage to Bartali, who could perhaps see the threat posed by his younger rival. 'I think I had never been on such great form,' said Magni (who would go on to win the Giro the following year for the second time). 'And to think, I had to fold up the yellow jersey and put it into my suitcase.' ∎

Florenzo Magni's race leadership is over: he is about to put the jersey into his suitcase and quit the tour, part of a mass walk-out by the Italian teams.

EXCLUSIF : LE FILM DE LA CHUTE
SENSATIONNELLE DE VAN EST

A makeshift rope made from inner tubes is used to haul Wim Van Est up the final part of the ravine where he fell while descending the Aubisque. He escaped with a few cuts and bruises.

1951

WIM VAN EST

BETWEEN A ROCK AND ANOTHER ROCK

Wim Van Est's dramatic crash on the descent from the Aubisque could have been fatal. Luckily things turned out differently...

Wim Van Est was the first Dutchman in Tour history to wear the yellow jersey, winning it at the end of Stage 12 of the 1951 Tour from Agen to Dax. But he would not keep it for long. More accustomed to cycling on the flat, Van Est crashed off the road during his descent from the Aubisque and ended up in a ravine.

On the rocky wall at the edge of the road, a brass plaque commemorates the event: 'On this spot the cyclist Wim Van Est fell 70 metres during the Tour de France on 17 July 1951. He survived the fall, but lost the yellow jersey.'

Wim Van Est could easily have lost his life too. At that point, the road winds around the cliff edge, with spectacular views over the precipice towards the Cirque du Litor. The Dutch rider was extremely lucky, narrowly avoiding two huge rocks and then sliding down a patch of loose scree which slowed his descent. His team manager Kees Pellenaers and journalist Albert De Wetter managed to rig up a makeshift rope by interlinking dozens of inner tubes. They lowered them down to Van Est, who had escaped largely unscathed, and managed to haul him up, back to the road, where he immediately took time to thank all his rescuers. The image became a classic in Tour history, and even inspired a magazine advertisement for the Pontiac brand of watches: 'I just fell 70 metres into a ravine,' says the bruised and battered Van Est, grimacing into the camera. 'My heart missed a beat. But my Pontiac didn't!'

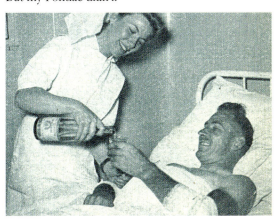

1965

BERNARD VAN DE KERKHOVE

FEELING THE HEAT

Belgian rider Bernard Van De Kerckhove showed early promise on the 1965 Tour with a Stage 2 win into Roubaix, getting ahead of Felice Gimondi (who would go on to win the Tour that year). A few days later Van De Kerckhove picked up the yellow jersey in La Rochelle at the end of Stage 7, but after just 48 hours he was forced to drop out of the race in the Pyrenees. The Solo-Supéria rider was not a great mountain climber, and was one of a number of riders to suffer heat exhaustion that day on the Aubisque.

– 1971 –
LUIS OCAÑA

GOING DOWN
A STORM

**The Spaniard had finally beaten Eddy Merckx.
But suddenly a storm broke over the Col de Menté.**

The dramatic departure of Luis Ocaña from the 1971 Tour shows how even the toughest competitors are made out of flesh and blood, just like the rest of us. And Luis Ocaña was certainly tough. He was a man who was single-mindedly pursuing an obsession that could be summed up in just six letters: M-E-R-C-K-X. He had even given this same name to his dog, just for the pure pleasure of being able to say 'Merckx, heel! Merckx, lie down!' Ocaña finally had it his way in 1971, crushing Merckx easily on Stage 9 from Grenoble to Orcières-Merlette.

It was a huge day, and Ocaña was unstoppable with a flying breakaway that is now seen as one of the most dramatic solo performances in the Tour's history (alongside Koblet from Brive to Agen in 1951, Charly Gaul on the Chartreuse in 1958, and Eddy Merckx himself at Mourenx in 1969).

Ocaña's team manager at Bic, Maurice de Muer, was incredulous as he saw the lead growing: 'It's six minutes! No way! It's gone up to seven!' He began to worry about his man burning out. 'You know, you could slow down a bit,' he suggested to Ocaña, who ignored the advice, finishing the stage with a lead of 8'42" over Merckx and Zoetemelk. ■ ■ ■

The Spaniard thought his dreams had come true in July 1971. He, rather than Eddy Merckx, was the yellow jersey.

Luis Ocaña's hopes were cruelly dashed in the violent storm on the Col de Menté.

1971. Luis Ocaña's crash scared everyone, not least the rider himself. Tour director Jacques Goddet (here, by his bedside) and the team staff had been fearing the worst.

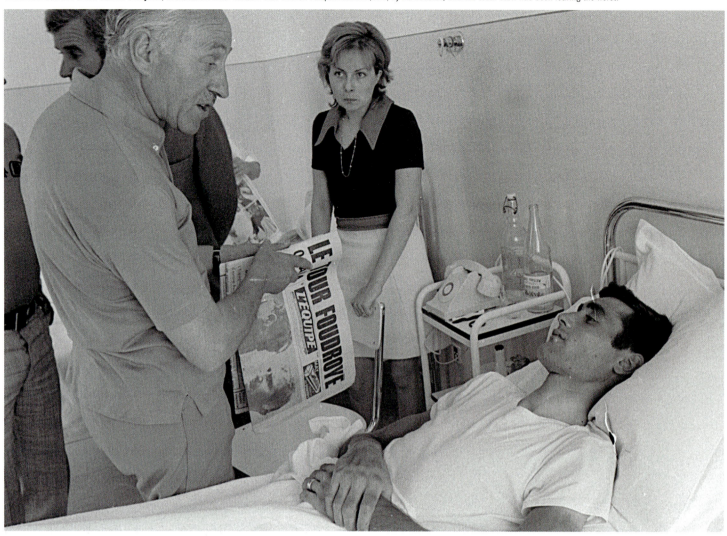

1971. For Eddy Merckx, the race was not the same without the presence of his great rival.

1973. Luis Ocaña takes his revenge at the Cipale velodrome in Paris.

■■■

But four days later on Stage 14 (from Revel to Luchon) this apparently unassailable lead was gone in a flash – during a massive thunderstorm over the Col de Menté in the Pyrenees – the same mountains Ocaña's father had crossed to escape the Franco regime in Spain. The sky darkened, and when the race crested the summit, the heavens opened and a deluge of rain turned the road into a torrent. Merckx piled on the pressure on the way down, and Ocaña – despite his already comfortable lead – set his mind to stay on Merkx's wheel at any cost. Suddenly, Merckx missed a left-hand bend. 'I can only remember one thing: I saw Merckx fall right in front of me, and I swerved to get round him. I was ready to get going. After that, it all goes black.'

" I'm in a lot of pain, especially in my shoulder. But this physical pain is nothing. What really hurts is losing the yellow jersey. To have lost the Tour. "

Luis Ocaña

At this point, brakes were useless. Joop Zoetemelk slammed straight into the Spaniard as he was getting up, and then Joaquim Agostinho was next into the pile-up. 'I thought immediately of Roger Rivière* and was fearing the worst,' wrote Tour director Jacques Goddet, who was alongside the injured Ocaña as they waited for a helicopter to get him to hospital. After extensive tests, there was better news: Ocaña had no fractures, but had suffered heavy bruising to his chest. 'I'm in a lot of pain, especially in my shoulder,' he said later that evening, speaking from his hospital bed. 'But all this physical pain is nothing. It's nothing. What really hurts is having lost the yellow jersey. To have lost the Tour.'

'I was going to win it – I was absolutely certain of it,' said the Spaniard. 'But no, it's not going to happen. It's unbelievable.'

In Luchon, Eddy Merckx asked the organizers for a favour – not to have to wear the yellow jersey the following day out of respect for the injured Ocaña. His heart was just not in it: 'In these kind of circumstances, there's no pleasure in winning the Tour,' he said, feeling acutely the sudden loss of his fiercest and most tenacious rival. 'After fighting against him every single day, I would rather have finished in second place,' Merckx added.

Luis Ocaña would be back, however, and his moment would come in 1973 with a stunning Tour victory. But with Merckx absent from the 1973 line-up, it was perhaps not quite the victory of Ocaña's dreams. ■

* The French rider whose career was ended after a crash on the Col du Perjuret in 1960.

–1980–
BERNARD HINAULT

HINAULT QUITS TOUR BY BACK DOOR

In 1980, Hinault's reign over the Tour was hit by a recurrent knee injury. In Pau, he quit the race via the hotel kitchen.

When **Bernard Hinault** was forced to drop out of the race, team boss **Cyrille Guimard** (top) did everything he could to hide the fact from the media. Race leader **Joop Zoetemelk** (above) rode the following day without the yellow jersey, out of respect for Hinault.

'Everything is OK.' Bernard Hinault passed on this briefest of messages, on the evening of Stage 12 (from Agen to Pau) while he took part in the weekly lottery draw on live TV, broadcast from the team hotel. At around the same time, Hubert Arbès had driven the 40km from his home in Lourdes to visit his Renault team mates at the Pau hotel. Arbès had been forced to quit the race at Bordeaux after injuries sustained in a crash earlier on. Amid the usual throng of journalists in the hotel lobby, Arbès ran into Cyrille Guimard (his Renault team manager) who was looking worried. 'Come eat with us, I'm going to need your help,' whispered Guimard. At the dinner table, Arbès was surprised to see Martine Hinault, Bernard's wife. Then Guimard leaned over to him and said urgently: 'Go and get your car. Bernard is going to have to drop out, and I don't want him mobbed by all those journalists. Wait for him out in the service yard, behind the kitchens.'

Bernard Hinault, the clear favourite to win the 1980 Tour de France, quit the race under cover of darkness, via the kitchen door of the team hotel. Hinault had been riding at the height of his powers, and the race was his to win. But his victory in the gruelling Liège–Bastogne–Liège one-day race the previous April had put his body through hell. And the weather conditions on the Tour were atrocious, with torrential rain on almost every stage. On the Stage 7 team time trial between Beauvais and Rouen, there were signs that all was not quite right. Hinault skipped his turns in the lead and was left to sit in behind, and the team had to slow down for him on some of the gentle climbs. Even so, Hinault was in yellow from the individual time trial in Gascony, between Damazan and Laplume, and he managed to drop Joop Zoetemelk (21 seconds off in the general classification) to get the best time. But the stabbing knee pain remained, and each turn of the crank seemed to make it worse. In Pau, the evening before the first Pyrenean stage, his mind was made up.

It was 10.30pm when team manager Cyrille Guimard gave the news to Félix Lévitan, the Tour director, during a dinner at the Hotel Continental with the leader of the French Communist Party Georges Marchais. Outside, Hubert Arbès was sitting in his car in the service yard, the engine idling, waiting for his friend to appear. Hinault made his escape with Arbès as planned, but as they were leaving Pau, a passer-by recognized Hinault as the car was waiting at a stop light. 'Get going Hubert! We can't have anyone following us!' shouted Hinault.

> **" Go and get your car. Bernard has to drop out, and I don't want him mobbed by all those journalists. Wait for him out in the service yard, behind the kitchens. "**
> Cyrille Guimard

Hinault's exit had been premeditated and meticulously planned. That evening he stayed at Arbès's house in Lourdes. Martine Hinault then drove their own car to Lourdes, and parked it out of sight in Arbès's garage.

'I think Hinault realized a few days earlier that the race was lost,' said Arbès. 'And he was trying to figure out how we would manage this with all the journalists.' At dawn the following day, Joop Zoetemelk received the news. He became the new leader of the Tour de France, and would go on to win it, at last, at the age of 34 – having already finished in second place an astonishing five times. Zoetemelk, respectful of Hinault's misfortune, did not wear yellow that day. ∎

DANGER: PYRENEES!
Of 16 riders who have dropped out wearing the yellow jersey, seven were forced to give up in the Pyrenees.

-1983-

THE AGONY OF NOT QUITTING

Leaving the Pyrenees, the 1983 Tour looked to be in the bag for Pascal Simon. But he scarcely had time to put on the yellow jersey before his shoulder was fractured, and with it, his dreams of winning the Tour.

It was game over. Pascal Simon would be going no further. His ordeal came to an end on the slopes of La Table, on Stage 17 from La Tour du Pin to the Alpe d'Huez. Simon loosened his toe-clips and dismounted. For one final time he thanked his Peugeot team mate Frédéric Brun, who had supported him for six tortuous days.

Simon had quit the race, but the real story was one of bravery: his fierce determination to fight on, even when it looked as if the race was lost. He had the yellow jersey, and he did not want to give it up to anyone.

Simon took the yellow after a storming performance in the Pyrenees and with a lead of more than four minutes (4'22") over second-placed Laurent Fignon. 'I was really flying!' he said, confident he had a serious chance of winning the Tour. But the race, just like life, can turn at any moment. On his first morning wearing yellow, 40km out from the start at Bagnères-de-Luchon, the peloton was coasting gently through the town of Montréjeau in Haute-Garonne. The day was set to be sunny and calm, and perhaps some of the riders were feeling just a little too relaxed. Two bikes came together and a pile-up ensued. Simon managed to swerve to the right and at least get himself a soft landing in a field of wheat. He got back on immediately, thinking he was unhurt. But he wasn't. 'I was suffering so much, I was thinking: how am I going to manage to finish the Tour?' he said later. At the stage finish that evening, he went to hospital in Auch where he discovered he had fractured his shoulder blade.

Each morning, it was the same ritual. The team medic bandaged his shoulder to immobilize it completely. During the race, Simon could not reach back to the pocket in his jersey, so it became the job of Frédéric Brun to hand food and drink across to the injured rider. Despite the pain, Simon had to ride through the Causses, climb the sharp ascents of the Massif Central, and withstand any and all attacks without getting out of his saddle, and with traction from only one hand. He managed to keep the yellow jersey, but lost a lot of time in the Puy-de-Dôme time trial. 'If I quit,' he said, 'it will not be from my hotel room. It will be on the bike.'

With each day that passed Simon continued to hold onto the yellow jersey, though the organizers spared him the physical agony of having to put it on at the traditional evening ceremony, as he could barely get his arm through the sleeve. In the end, just as he had promised, he quit on the road. The yellow jersey was then up for grabs, and this seemed to galvanize Laurent Fignon, who was first to the line on the Alpe d'Huez that same day, and went on to win the Tour. Pascal Simon would never again wear yellow, but he remains convinced of one thing: 'I would definitely have won that Tour.' ■

A few kilometres after the start of Stage 17 (from La Tour du Pin to l'Alpe d'Huez), Pascal Simon got off his bike. His six days of agony were over.

1991
ROLF SÖRENSEN

FRACTURED HOPES

Rolf Sörensen, a Danish cyclist riding for the Italian Ariostea team, was a powerful, attacking rider who took the yellow jersey from Greg LeMond after Stage 2 of the 1991 Tour, a team time trial around Lyon. Sörensen went on to keep the yellow for a few more days, until his Tour ambitions came to an abrupt end. Just 4km from the end of Stage 5 he crashed on a roundabout coming into Valenciennes. With injuries to his face and a painful shoulder he made it to the finish line in 90th place, still within the peloton and still as race leader. However, a later X-ray showed that Sörensen had fractured his collarbone and would not be leaving Arras the following morning.

Greg LeMond, in overall second place, found himself race leader the following morning, but declined to wear the yellow jersey that day. In the tradition of Eddy Merckx (with respect for Luis Ocaña in 1971) and Joop Zoetemelk (after Hinault's withdrawal in 1980), he did not put on the jersey abandoned by the unlucky Sörensen. Thierry Marie, who made a long breakaway on the route through his native Normandy, would be in yellow that evening in Le Havre.

1996
STÉPHANE HEULOT

«IF YOU LOSE IT, YOU MUST HAVE HAD IT»

Stéphane Heulot took the yellow jersey on 3 July at the Lac de Madine in Lorraine, thanks to a dramatic breakaway that assured him a comfortable lead in the 1996 Tour. But his knee was already giving him trouble. Three days later he dropped out of the Tour at the top of the Cormet de Roselend in the Alps. He recalls what happened:

How much did your knee injury spoil the pleasure of wearing the yellow jersey?
I didn't get an ounce of pleasure from wearing the yellow jersey. Already, the night before the stage where I took yellow, I could feel the onset of knee pain. It was tendonitis, which I put down to the equipment – the new bikes that we had at the start of the Tour. And also the bad weather. Obviously, this was a real downer as I could see that my days on the Tour were numbered.

When you did take the yellow jersey, did you already know that you wouldn't be able to defend it for long?
I remember that on the evening of the stage to Aix-les-Bains (Stage 6) when it had been raining all day, my physio Jean-Louis Gauthier [himself a former yellow jersey in 1983] pointed out that [the tendon] had swollen to the size of his thumb. With the stage we had the following day [the Madeleine, Cormet de Roselend and La Plagne] it was going to get complicated. I tried to fight it, but on the cols I was suffering excruciating pain. It would have been stupid to carry on. I was finished.

So despite all this frustration, did you get anything out of having worn the yellow jersey?
I don't know how to answer that. If you lose it, you must have had it. But I admit, I had no time to enjoy the moment. It was tough, really tough. But look, it's not the end of the world. There are plenty of worse things in life. ∎

1998

IT'S ALL OVER IN IRELAND

'What just happened?' asked Chris Boardman, sprawled on the ground at the side of the road. The prologue specialist had already taken the Tour's first yellow jersey in both 1994 and 1997, and was able to do so once again in Dublin at the start of the 1998 Tour. This time, though, he would not be taking it to France. It was near the end of Stage 2 (from Enniscorthy to Cork) that Boardman clipped a rear wheel near the front of the densely packed peloton. Boardman ended up in a ditch at the side of the road, with cuts to his eyebrow and pain to his elbow and wrist. As a precaution, he was given a neck brace and taken to hospital in Cork, where he was shown to have sustained a cracked radius. That evening, Erik Zabel would be able to cross the Channel with the yellow jersey in his bag.

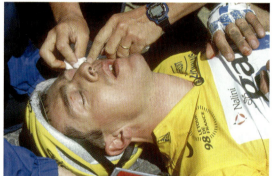

2015

OVER AND OUT FOR MARTIN'S TOUR

Since the previous evening, it was all too clear what was going to happen. Yellow jersey Tony Martin (pictured right) had a compound fracture of the collarbone and would not be leaving Livarot the next day for the Stage 7 route to Fougères. He was officially out of the race. The night before he had made it – just – into Le Havre after a collision in the peloton saw him crashing onto the road just 1km from the finish line. With the help of his Etixx-Quick Step team, he struggled painfully up the final hill to the finish line, where Zdenek Stybar, also from Quick Step had just won the stage. Martin's 2015 Tour, however, would end there.

124

Fausto Coppi (left) and Gino Bartali were complete
opposites, in physique, and in their background and
mindset. Even so, the pair came to be seen as Italian
cycling superstars, each leaving their own individual
mark on the Tour de France.

10

DOUBLE ACTS

The history of the Tour contains many legendary duels, marked by bitter rivalries as well as lifelong friendships.

COPPI-BARTALI
THE TWO FACES OF ITALY

Gino Bartali and Fausto Coppi were synonymous with Italian cycling on the Tour – even if the war got in the way of some of their best years.

There is a book about Italy during the post-war years by writer and journalist Curzio Malaparte called *Two Faces of Italy: Coppi and Bartali*. For a book dealing with the opposing forces of modernizing and traditional life, the title was a smart idea. Fausto Coppi, from Piedmont, was the poster boy for modernity. Gino Bartali, however, was depicted as being all about traditional, Catholic, rural Italy. While this was something of a caricature, the two riders divided public opinion, while also demonstrating what Italy at that time was all about.

Was the cycling world – and the Tour de France – big enough for these two huge champions to exist side by side? Sometimes the two riders (skilfully managed by national team boss Alfredo Binda) did exactly that: on the 1949 Tour on the Izoard, with the two riders out in front, Bartali suggested to Coppi that they finish together. 'It's my 35th birthday,' Bartali told Coppi, 'and tomorrow you will win the Tour.' Coppi agreed, and did indeed win the Tour the following day.

Gino Bartali would have only worn the yellow jersey for 20 days, and Fausto Coppi for just 19. But the legends they created have endured. Bartali was the older of the two by five years, and could have won his very first Tour in 1937 if he hadn't ended up in a ditch in the Alps (while wearing the yellow jersey). He did win the Tour the following year, so when he came back after the war in 1948, a full ten years had elapsed. Bartali had managed to carve out a lead of around 20 minutes over the young Frenchman Louison Bobet when he received an extraordinary phone call at his hotel that evening: It was the Italian prime minister, Alcide De Gasperi, on the line. De Gasperi was battling to hold together an Italy on the edge of insurrection, following an assassination attempt on the communist party leader Palmiro Togliatti.

'Bartali, we need your help,' announced De Gasperi.
'What can I do? I'm on the Tour de France,' replied Bartali.
'You could help us a lot by winning some stages,' De Gasperi shot back.

After that, Bartali seemed fired up, and won three Alpine stages in a row (Stage 13, Cannes to Briançon; Stage 14, Briançon to Aix-les-Bains and Stage 15, Aix-les-Bains to Lausanne), where the pre-war mountain ace seemed to regain his wings. He took the yellow jersey and kept it all the way to Paris, becoming the only racer to win the Tour both before (1938) and after (1948) the war.

As for Fausto Coppi, he raced in just three Tours de France, but of these three, he won two. Each time, it was a dazzling solo performance. On his debut Tour in 1949, he built a lead of 11 minutes on Bartali, and could have put more into him if he been totally ruthless over his countryman. He donned his first yellow jersey in the Italian town of Aoste on 19 July. In 1951 Coppi's brother Serse died tragically in a crash during the Tour of Piedmont in June, and the grieving Fausto finished tenth in the Tour de France that year, some 47 minutes behind winner Hugo Koblet. The following year Coppi was back with a vengeance, and nobody could touch him. He was scintillating on the Tour's first ascent up the Alpe d'Huez (Stage 10), on the road to Sestrières (Stage 11) and the Puy de Dôme (Stage 21). And he was so far ahead that the Tour organizers raised the prize money for second place (by 500,000 Francs) and third place (by 250,000 Francs). The Belgian Stan Ockers cashed in for second place, but was trailing nearly half an hour behind.∎

Fausto and Gino. The two Italian champions at the start of Stage 11 (Pau to Luchon) on the 1949 Tour de France.

Fausto Coppi had made meticulous preparations for the 1952 Tour, and it paid off, with his incredible pace and control of the race throughout. He was in a class of his own.

Antonin Magne was under pressure on the 1931 Tour, but his mental discipline and physical stamina won him the Tour.

LEDUCQ-MAGNE
DEFINING AN ERA

Winners of two Tours each at the start of the 1930s, Leducq and Magne came to symbolize the golden era of the French national team.

They were an odd couple. André 'Dédé' Leducq grew up near the flea-markets in the Paris suburb of Saint-Ouen and was full of cheeky Parisian banter. Antonin 'Tonin' Magne was from a farming family, the strong and silent type, and thoughtful with it. The Tour put the two men together at the start of the 1930s at a time when the creation of national teams gave a huge boost to the Tour's popularity.

The riders may have had a whole nation behind them, but at the cost of pain and hard graft with every kilometre. On Stage 16 from Grenoble to Évian, André Leducq had been leading since Stage 9, but broke a pedal on the Col du Galibier and crashed coming down from Télégraphe. His knee was covered in blood, and he was sitting at the side of the road, ready to give up. The French team stopped and gathered around him. 'That's enough of your snivelling, let's see your knee, there's nothing broken. It'll ease up once you start riding,' were the encouraging words of the France team manager Marcel Bidot. 'Dédé, you don't give up when you're wearing the yellow jersey,' insisted Charles Pélissier.

Antonin Magne and his brother Pierre were also at the scene. When Leducq finally got back on his bike, he had lost a quarter of an hour to his Italian rival Learco Guerra, supported by the Belgian rider Joseph Demuysere. In the Maurienne valley, a long pursuit got underway, and then, while crossing Albertville, the French riders spotted Guerra and Demuysere up ahead after an all-out chase covering 75km. Leducq, despite his sore knee, proved his mettle beyond doubt by winning back the stage at Évian, saving the yellow jersey, and going on to win the Tour. And he would be back again to do the same thing in two years' time. In the meantime, it would be the turn of Antonin Magne to take the Tour in 1931.

The two Frenchmen shared a room during the Tour, and would always spend time going through the bundles of fan mail they received at each evening stop. On the night before the penultimate stage of the 1931 Tour, Magne opened a letter from an anonymous writer: 'Monsieur Antonin Magne, I am writing to warn you that Rebry wrote to his mother that he will try a major attack with Demuysère in the stage from Charleville to Malo-les-Bains.'

Magne had been wearing the yellow jersey for the last two weeks since the Pyrenees, and so thanks to the tip-off, the French team were now on its guard for this last-ditch attack from the Belgians. As predicted, Rebry and Demuysère did mount an attack, but the French team were ready for it, and Magne took the yellow to Paris and won the Tour.

Three years later he would enjoy a second Tour victory in 1934, though not without an element of bad luck. Magne took the yellow on the Stage 2 (from Lille to Charleville), and went through the Alps without incident, 'just riding the race in my own way,' as he put it in *L'Auto*. But on Stage 15 in the Pyrenees (from Perpignan to Ax-les-Thermes), in a fast descent from Puymorens, Magne missed a turn and smashed his bike. René Vietto, the young mountain specialist from the Cote d'Azur, gave Magne his wheel. It was the same story the following day, only this time Vietto, who became a French national hero overnight, handed over his entire bike to Magne. Thanks to Leducq and Magne, as well as to Georges Speicher who won the 1933 Tour, France claimed victory in the first five Tours of the 1930s. And for the 1938 Tour, (won by Gino Bartali) Leducq and Magne would cross the line in Paris in a dead heat, arms across each other's shoulders: proof enough that in racing, and in cycling history, they would be inseparable. ∎

A dejected André Leducq with a bloody knee, the result of a crash while descending the Télégraphe in 1930.

Antonin 'Tonin' Magne was a popular Tour rider with the public, as indeed were the entire France national team which found enormous success in the 1930s.

FROOME-THOMAS
MAY THE
BEST MAN WIN

**Despite looking all set for a fifth Tour victory,
Chris Froome gave way for his Welsh partner Geraint Thomas in 2018.**

Right from the start of the 2018 pro cycling season, Geraint Thomas was beginning to look every inch a credible candidate for a Tour victory. In the previous year's Tour he had crashed out, but not before picking up the yellow jersey during the Dusseldorf time trial. But while Thomas had his eye on the prize, so too did Sky team mate Chris Froome. He had a chance to join the likes of Anquetil, Merckx, Hinault and Indurain in the exclusive club of five-times winners of the Tour. Froome had also just won the Giro in this critical year, raising the possibility of achieving a Giro-Tour double for 2018.

The Sky team had to move carefully in the run-up to the Tour, keeping all options open. There was still doubt over whether Froome would be allowed to compete following an 'adverse analytical finding' for elevated levels of the asthma drug salbutamol during the Spanish Vuelta. The process dragged on, with the Tour organizers asking Sky to take Froome off the team. After a long and complex investigation by lawyers and medical experts, the Tour wrote to Froome less than a week before the start of the race to formally block his participation. But the following day, on 2 July, the UCI (the International Cycling Union) overturned this ruling, announcing that there had been no breach and that Froome had no case to answer. Froome was back.

Just one question remained over his fitness, and specifically, whether he had recovered sufficiently from his Giro win, which marked his third Grand Tour win out of the last three he had entered (the Tour de France and the Vuelta in 2017, and the Giro in 2018). But soon after the start of the 2018 Tour in Vendée (from Noirmoutier-en-l'Île to Fontenay-Le-Comte), Froome crashed, losing almost a minute, while his team mate Geraint Thomas put in a faultless ride to end up close to the top of the general classification.

WHO'S THE LEADER?

From that point, Chris Froome could see that Sky could keep its options open. He was still being protected and supported, as was his due, and perhaps he would still take preference. But the proof of all this would only be seen out on the road. It would be in the Alps that Thomas emerged as the more powerful rider, showing that the Welshman known for his power on the flat could also perform on the climbs. He took two Alpine stages in a row (Stage 11 from Albertville to La Rosière, and Stage 12 from Bourg-Saint-Maurice to Alpe d'Huez) and from then, the yellow jersey would be his all the way to Paris. Froome struggled on the long Pyrenean Stage 17 (from Bagnères de Luchon to Col de Portet) but clung on to take third place on the podium. The question on everyone's mind was what would happen the following year: who would take precedence: the four-times Tour winner seeking a fifth, or the new yellow jersey victor of 2018? ∎

Geraint Thomas and Chris Froome indulge in the traditional glass of champagne on the final stage into Paris. The chance of fifth Tour de France victory would have to come later for 'Froomy'.

2018. The Tour de France was expecting Chris Froome. What it got was Geraint Thomas.

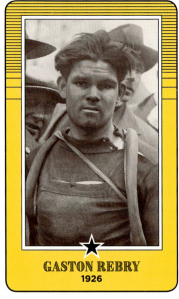

GASTON REBRY
1926

WILLI OBERBECK
1938

ARSÈNE MERSCH
1938

AMÉDÉE FOURNIER
1939

ANDREA CARREA
1952

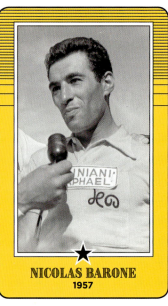

NICOLAS BARONE
1957

TOMMASSO DE PRÀ
1966
(Left) with Rudi Altig

JOSEPH SPRUYT
1970

SEAN KELLY
1983

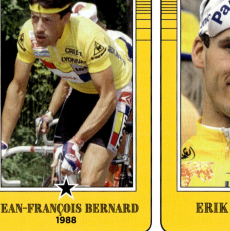

JEAN-FRANÇOIS BERNARD
1988

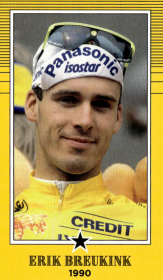

ERIK BREUKINK
1990

11

ONE DAY IN A LIFETIME

The yellow jersey is an all too brief experience for many riders, but it can still leave its mark on a cycling career – or even an entire lifetime.

Many of the riders who have taken the yellow jersey have not worn it for long. For them, the experience is a bit like a lightning strike: dramatic, bright, and then absent, gone. No less than a quarter* of yellow jerseys have been held for just 24 hours, and sometimes for even less time during the years when part-stages were a regular feature on the Tour.

Many of these have gone to relatively unknown riders who would have remained that way, were they not thrown into the spotlight unexpectedly: people like Arsène Mersch, Amédée Fournier, Willi Oberbeck, Nicolas Barone and plenty of others. Then there are the team riders who picked up the yellow almost by chance, and who subsequently felt pangs of guilt for denying their team leader the chance to take it: riders like Andrea Carrea, Tomasso De Pra or Joseph Spruyt. There are also many top racers for whom this day in yellow, had it not existed, would have been a gap in their illustrious careers: names such as Gaston Rebry, Rik Van Looy or Sean Kelly. And then there are the racers who mounted the winner's podium at the end of the Tour, having won the yellow just once throughout the race: Jean-François Bernard (third in 1988) or Erik Breukink (third in 1990) know what that is all about.

Finally, plenty of lesser-known riders within the peloton are not really cut out for the limelight. Jean-Louis Gauthier and Dominique Gaigne are just two examples among many, and were certainly not going to be dazzled by what they knew would be their one day of fame. On Richard Virenque's first Tour in 1992 he won the yellow but lost it the following evening in Bordeaux. 'A single day, it's just too short,' he lamented. 'I would have at least liked to keep it for a couple of days. And maybe I will never have another chance to wear it – even if it really is a fantastic thing to have happened.' Little did he know, he would in fact regain the yellow once again, 11 years later, in the 2003 Centennial Edition of the Tour. Between times, he found himself an alternative jersey – the red and white polka dots of the King of the Mountains. But even back in 1992, the young Virenque was totally into the spirit of the yellow jersey. That evening in Bordeaux, the prospect of having to give back the iconic jersey was bothering him, as he realized it would become little more than a cherished memory. 'I am afraid that people won't look at me in the same way, once it's gone,' he confessed. ∎

* Statistics up to the end of the 2011 Tour. 255 riders have held the Yellow jersey, of which 59 for a single day, and sometimes less (for a half-stage or third-stage).

> **" I would have at least liked to keep it for a couple of days. Maybe I will never have another chance.**
>
> **Richard Virenque** "

MARINUS WAGTMANS
1971

RINI WAGTMANS, SHORT AND SWEET

The Dutchman kept his yellow jersey for just two hours, twenty-nine minutes and thirty-one seconds.

Of all the riders who ever wore it, Marinus (nicknamed 'Rini') Wagtman's stewardship of the yellow jersey was over in a flash. For him, it lasted for less than three hours, and it came about almost by accident. On day one of the 1971 Tour, the Molteni team won the prologue, which that year was a team time trial in Mulhouse. Eddy Merckx took the first yellow, as expected. The next day's stage was divided into three sections. Éric Leman won the morning session, which was just 59.5km long, running from Mulhouse to Bâle, with Rini Wagtmans the highest placed of the Molteni riders in the sprint final (Wagtmans was in 20th position, while Huysmans was 38th and Merckx 49th). As the Molteni team had won the previous day, Wagtmans was therefore in line to take the yellow. 'I passed the finish line without realizing that I would take the Yellow jersey,' recalls Rini. 'I mean, me, I work for the team, for Eddy. And of course, Eddy didn't want me picking up another one.' Anyway, Merckx took back 'his' yellow that

same afternoon, at Fribourg-en-Brisgau where Joop Zoetemelk shook up the peloton and Wagtmans finished around a minute back. Then, at the end of the third segment of this very full day, Merckx was able to go to sleep with the yellow jersey in its usual place, on the chair at the foot of his bed.

Forty years later, Wagtmans still gets emotional when he remembers that day. 'Even just one hour with the yellow jersey is something that you will never forget. Never.' In fact, he would have worn it for precisely two hours, twenty-nine minutes and thirty-one seconds, the time it took for him to cover the second leg of the stage from Bâle to Fribourg (90km). And even though Rini Wagtmans would have well liked a little more time in yellow, he describes it as 'a gift' that he was given for life, like a Hollywood actor who wins an Oscar. 'I am part of the family of the Tour de France and that will be with me for the rest of my life, until the day I die,' he said. ■

A yellow jersey lasts a lifetime, whether it gets worn for just a few hours (like that of Wagtmans) or for close to three months, which was the case for Eddy Merckx.

Jean-Louis Gauthier only kept his yellow jersey for a single day, but it was a life-changing moment.

– 1983 –

JEAN-LOUIS GAUTHIER: 'IT FELL INTO MY LAP'

Jean-Louis Gauthier was not expecting to find himself wearing the yellow jersey in 1983. And while the moment was all too brief, his sense of pride lasted a lifetime.

Jean-Louis Gauthier picked up his yellow jersey as a result of the unexpected success of his Coop-Mercier team during a team time trial on Stage 2 of the 1983 Tour, from Soissons to Fontaine-au-Pire. Thinking back over those events years later (he died in 2014) he still harboured a few regrets over how it all happened: 'I didn't have the feeling that it was me, personally, who had won it. It was a yellow jersey that was to be shared,' he said. 'And what's more, the moment was over far too quickly.' Gauthier, from the Charentes region, said he had little time to fully appreciate it, though he did get the unique sensation of seeing it on the chair in his hotel room. 'When you see it, you say to yourself:

JEAN-LOUIS GAUTHIER
1983

I'd better raise my game!' Unfortunately for Gauthier, luck was against him. The Coop-Mercier team were at the top of the general classification the next day, and riding on cobbles it was Kim Andersen who was first to make his escape, along with the Belgian Rudy Matthijs. 'I was trapped,' Gauthier recalled. 'By sheer bad luck, the car belonging to Jean-Pierre Danguillaume [the team manager] had been held back when it ran into a ditch, and Joop [Zoetemelk, his team leader] had a puncture on one of the last sections of cobbles. The yellow jersey was out of the question for me. So I said to myself: "Never mind. I'll give him my wheel."' He eventually arrived, somewhat later, at the Roubaix velodrome at the end of the ■ ■ ■

Jean-Louis Gauthier in yellow, between Valenciennes and Roubaix on the 1983 Tour.

makes me feel pretty awkward to be described as "the former yellow jersey". But as I have remained in professional cycling [Gauthier worked with various French cycling teams right up to the time of his death] I can see the respect that it brings me in the eyes of the younger riders when they're told that yes, I did wear the yellow jersey. They must say to themselves that to have won a yellow jersey, back then, I must have really been quite something.'

At the time, Gauthier said he felt surprise, more than anything else. 'It's impossible!' he had exclaimed at the finish line, when reporters told him the result on that day, 3 July 1983. 'It just dropped into my lap,' he said later. 'I was really racing this team time trial, with no thought that I could take the jersey.'

With the passage of time, Gauthier realized he had achieved the dream of every competitive racer. 'At the time, it didn't strike me, but it's something that has become etched into my memory, and nobody can take that away from me. I'm happy to see myself in photographs, in books.' Gauthier is visibly moved by the memories. 'You know,' he added, 'inside of me, I can tell you, I'm very proud to have it'. ∎

■ ■ ■

stage, having kept the yellow jersey for just one day: 'I'm sure that if I'd held on to it for two or three days, it would have made more of an impression on me. But what can you do?'

Gauthier's single yellow jersey was mounted in a frame in the sitting room of the family home. It brought him neither wealth nor fame. The financial gains for this all-round team cyclist (a very strong road racer, a great sprinter, and Tour stage winner at Compiègne in 1980) were almost non-existent. Nonetheless, Gauthier's yellow jersey did change something in his own mindset. 'Outside of my cycling career, people don't really know me,' he said 'There is only Daniel Mangeas [the Tour's own commentator] to remind people who I am, and as I am quite shy, it always

> **"It's something that has become etched into my memory, and nobody can take that away.**
>
> Jean-Louis Gauthier

-2014-
TONY GALLOPIN, FOR FRANCE AND FAMILY

TONY GALLOPIN
2014

Writing as we approach the 2019 Tour de France and the centenary of the yellow jersey, Tony Gallopin's name is significant as the last French rider to wear the yellow jersey. He is the 84th name on a list that began a century earlier with Eugène Christophe. But Tony Gallopin, a stocky racer from the Beauce region (the 'corn belt' south of Paris) is a tough racer on the flat, decent in the mountains, and sharp on the attack – in short, a good all-rounder – who also comes from a distinguished cycling family, from fathers and brothers to sons. Joël, his father, competed in four Tours de France from the late 1970s into the early 1980s. His uncles, Guy and Alain, were also pro cyclists, with Alain becoming team manager at a number of international cycling teams. And another Gallopin, André, was also on his way to a solid career as an amateur cyclist. However, it was to be Tony Gallopin, on 13 July 2014 (Stage 9 from Gérardmer to Mulhouse), who was to create what his uncle Alain would describe as 'the greatest moment ever for the Gallopin family'. Alain had been driving a team car for the rival Trek team, and had been following the race (and his nephew Tony's progress) closely. The night before Stage 9, the two Gallopins talked tactics. Tony had an excellent start to the Tour with a series of strong placings in the first few stages, and was sixth in the general classification. Alain reasoned that during the long stage in the Vosges the next day, the race leaders were unlikely to chase after every rider, which gave Tony an excellent opportunity. The advice proved to be spot-on, and it was in a group of 28 riders, pursuing the breakaway Tony Martin (who would win the stage), that Tony Gallopin was able to move through and take the yellow jersey that evening.

Gallopin's attack had been premeditated, but the emotion of taking the yellow was raw and spontaneous, and affected the whole family. 'These things do not happen often in a lifetime, and only for champions. They are to be savoured. It's incredible,' Gallopin exclaimed. 'I am actually going to be wearing the yellow on 14 July. Mind you, I could have hoped for a rather easier stage!' Gallopin's slim lead over Vincenzo Nibali, along with tired legs, combined on the slopes of La Planche des Belles Filles to scupper the chances of keeping the yellow jersey longer than 24 hours, even though he managed to get a stage win a few days later at Oyonnax. Of course, the whole episode did little to change the outcome of the Tour, which would be won by Nibali, nor indeed to upset the life of Tony Gallopin himself, a man who had his feet very much on the ground. Even so, it remained one of the best days of Gallopin's life. ∎

Tony Gallopin fought hard to defend his yellow jersey on the stage from Mulhouse to La Planche des Belles Filles, but without success.

12

TALES OF THE UNEXPECTED

You often see the Tour favourites start to emerge right from the opening few stages. But some of the most dramatic Tours are those where all bets are off.

Roger Walkowiak on the individual time trial between Saint-Étienne and Lyon. He had taken the yellow jersey two days earlier, and would keep it right to the end.

-1956-

ROGER WALKOWIAK

THE OUTSIDER

**Winner of the Tour in 1956, Roger Walkowiak's victory
was not what the public were expecting**

The year before, it was Louison Bobet's final win. The year after, it would be Jacques Anquetil's first win. Between the two, in 1956, it would be the moment of glory for Roger Walkowiak. He was seen as the ultimate surprise winner. His victory in the 1956 Tour de France even created a new expression in the cycling lexicon: 'Doing a Walko', where a relative unknown wins a race ahead of all the big name riders.

To the public at large, there was something surprising, and perhaps even disappointing, about seeing the man from Montlucon take the yellow jersey in Paris. The previous year the hugely popular Louison Bobet had triumphed. 'I could sense that the public felt duped,' recalls Walkowiak, 'a feeling that the Tour was too important for a racer like me to win it.'

For Walkowiak himself though, his victory was not such a surprise. Already a great climber, he began to accumulate wins on the professional circuit which reinforced his self-belief.

> **" The press did not see me as someone who could win. And that stung.**
>
> Roger Walkowiak "

'I always told myself that if I did not lose too much time over the first stages on the flat, then I could be in with a chance for the '56 Tour.'

When he arrived at Reims for the start of the Tour, it looked do-able. Bobet was absent. Jacques Anquetil would only arrive on the scene the following year (as winner). 'Walko' stuck with four breakaways in the first week of the course, and then on Stage 7 the peloton split between Lorient and Angers. Walkowiak stayed with the massive leading group, giving him an 18-minute lead over most of the climbers. 'There were 31 in the breakaway, though it was basically me who was doing most of the work at the front,' he recalls. 'I was very focused on taking the yellow jersey, thinking that if I could wear it for just one day, it would really boost my chances.' Even so, it would take more than the yellow jersey (which he kept for the next three days) to get Walkowiak seen as a serious contender. Even his team manager on the Nord-Est-Centre regional team, Sauveur Ducazeaux, advised him to let the yellow go the next day, for fear of his small regional team burning out. 'People weren't talking much about me,' recalls Walkowiak. 'The press didn't see me as someone who could win the Tour. And that stung me a bit.'

Walkowiak had to give up the yellow jersey before the Pyrenees stages three days later. In the Soulor, Charly Gaul attacked. Walkowiak remembers thinking at the time: 'I'll test myself, see if I can go get him and stay with him.' He caught him easily. And in the Alps, Walkowiak was always near the front, ready to mount an ambush. 'Nobody out there looked unbeatable, I followed them without having to push myself to the limit. It just seemed to be OK.' On Stage 18 at Grenoble, he was still with Charly Gaul and Federico Bahamontès. This time he took the yellow jersey – for good.

Even so, Roger Walkowiak got little pleasure from a final victory which was tinged with bitterness. 'I wasn't exactly criticized,' he said many years later, 'it was more a case of being misunderstood.' Despite his evident prowess, he was seen as an interloper, an outsider, which today seems grossly unfair. He was clearly no showman, but he'd had to fight for a great Tour victory.

Tour director Jacques Goddet later honoured Walkowiak with a dedication in his book *L'Équipée Belle* (The Beautiful Team): 'To Roger Walkowiak,' Goddet wrote, 'an exemplary racer with the heart and mind of a champion, who won my favourite of all the Tours de France.' Walkowiak found solace in these few short lines: 'I could see how he would have enjoyed this Tour because there were breakaways and attacks all the time. In that dedication, Jacques Goddet helped put the record straight.' ■

YELLOW WHO? NOT JUST FOR THE BIG NAMES

It is not just the big name riders who get to put on the yellow jersey, and this is perhaps part of its mystique. A talented rider, on a good day, can find himself race leader by the end of the stage and wear the famous yellow the next morning. They are too numerous to mention, but here is just a selection. **Max Bulla**, for example, was the surprise winner of Stage 2 (from Caen to Dinan) in the 1931 Tour, giving the first and only yellow jersey to an Austrian rider. Bulla was a solid competitor who was part of the category of 'tourist racers' who rode as independents with no team support. Even more low key was the German **Willi Oberbeck** who became the first yellow jersey in the 1938 Tour from Paris to Caen. His prior form was fairly modest, winning just one stage of the Tour of Germany and one Bavarian Grand Prix. Then there was **Roger Levêque**, whose trophy cabinet remained empty over eight years of pro cycling from 1946 to 1953. His only win during this time was Stage 4 of the 1951 Tour, between Le Tréport and Paris, and this win, combined with a strong breakaway on Stage 6 between Caen and Rennes was enough to set him up for yellow some 48 hours later. He held onto the lead for a further five days, all the way down to Agen. ■

Wolkowiak defends the yellow jersey from Grenoble to Saint-Étienne, with Jean Forestier (right) in support.

The Austrian Max Bulla has something to smile about. The 'tourist-racer' rider without a team has just snatched the yellow jersey away from the Tour's big guns.

FROM HOPE TO DESPAIR

For some, the yellow jersey raises hopes of victory. And later in the Tour, the crushing reality of defeat.

In 1934, aged 20, René Vietto got the whole of France behind him with a selfless act of sacrifice for his team leader.

– 1934 • 1939 • 1947 –

VIETTO: IT JUST NEVER HAPPENED

**EVERYONE THOUGHT HE WOULD WIN THE TOUR,
NOT LEAST RENÉ VIETTO HIMSELF.
BUT EACH TIME, FORTUNE WAS AGAINST HIM.**

1934, BIG SACRIFICE

It has become a classic image in Tour history: a distraught René Vietto, sitting on a rough stone wall, alongside his bicycle which is missing a wheel. It was 20 July 1934, on Stage 15 from Perpignan to Ax-les-Thermes, and the former hotel bell-boy turned professional cyclist had become one of the stars of the Tour. Small in stature but a formidable climber, he had already won three Tour stages (Stage 7 from Aix-les-Bains to Grenoble; Stage 9 from Gap to Digne; and Stage 11 from Nice to Cannes) and had just been the first to the top of the Col de Puymorens. On the way down, yellow jersey Antonin Magne (the leader of Vietto's France national team) broke a wheel. Vietto stopped and handed over his own wheel, and when Magne set off, Vietto had to wait several long minutes for the support truck to arrive. He was beside himself with frustration, stamping and crying, 'like a kid that lost his parents in a store,' according to one

In 1939, Vietto discovers the joys of crossing France in the yellow jersey (here, on the Stage 10 time trial from Narbonne to Béziers).

of the support team. Amazingly, it was almost the same story the following day. On the descent from Portet d'Aspet, Magne's rear wheel locked up and his chain got snagged on the pedal. 'I thought my race was all over, but then I saw Vietto come round a corner further down the hill and start climbing back up the mountain at a crazy speed to give me his bicycle,' Magne told reporters later that day. Once again, Vietto would lose time before being able to set off again. 'I can't go on being the slave every day,' he was heard complaining later. Winning Stage 18 (from Tarbes to Pau) was not much consolation, but what he did win were the hearts of the French cycling fans. In Paris, Magne won the Tour, and Vietto was a creditable fifth place, and winner of the mountains classification. 'He was the hero of the Tour,' wrote Jacques Goddet in his editorial that day. Vietto was just 20 years old. Everyone knew that he would win it one day, surely?

1939, FIRST YELLOW

Tour boss Henri Desgrange delivered the good news to René Vietto: he had just won the first yellow jersey of his career. 'He winked at me with his left eye and smiled like had just won the national lottery,' wrote Desgrange in his daily column in *L'Auto*. For Vietto, that yellow jersey moment on 13 July became a whole 11 days as race leader, though not without struggle. Riding for the South-East France regional team, Vietto did not have his usual scintillating power on the climbs. He had caught a cold on Stage 6 (from La Rochelle to Royan) and it had worsened to bronchitis. He managed to protect his lead in the Pyrenees, but in the Alps it all proved too much. On Stage 15 (from Digne to Briançon) he had nothing left to give against an attack from Sylvère Maes on the Izoard, and conceded 17 minutes as well as the yellow jersey. During the following day's time trial from Bonneval-sur-Arc to Bourg-Saint-Maurice, Maes did it again on the climb up l'Iseran, and Vietto lost a further ten minutes to his rival. Vietto accepted some of the blame for making a poor choice of gear ratios: 'Of course, you're learning all the time. But look, I'm only 25, and not going to quit. Right now I am thinking of the 1940 Tour. I know I can win it.' But a month later, France was at war. There would be no 1940 Tour.

1947, CHANCE MISSED

Vietto was back with a vengeance on the first post-war Tour in 1947. On Stage 2 from Lille to Brussels he made an epic breakaway of an astonishing 180km, of which he completed 130km riding solo under the leaden sky. After a feat of such brilliance, the question on everyone's mind was: could he keep this up? Tour boss Jacques Goddet's daily column was sceptical: 'René my friend,' he wrote, 'we think you have just pulled off the most brilliant performance in your entire career. And it could also be your biggest ever mistake. We're afraid that by winning this battle today, you could have ended up losing the Tour.'

Vietto took the yellow, which he was able to defend for five days with the help of the French national team, before giving it up for two days in the Alps to newcomer Jean Robic who won in Grenoble. That evening, Vietto complained that he could feel the age in his legs. Even so, he was back in the yellow jersey in Digne and fought on to the Pyrenees, where he appeared to recover his energy and was able to apply 'his perfect knowledge of the race, the route, and also of himself,' as Goddet wrote. On the slopes of Tourmalet Vietto faltered, and asked Léo Veron, the team manager to send Edouard Fachleitner on the attack. But Vietto appeared to recover as he climbed the Aubisque, and kept the yellow jersey too. Everyone started to believe that this time, he really would win it. The arrival in Parc des Princes was scheduled two days after a final time trial between Vannes and Saint-Brieuc, but this proved to be too much for Vietto. He lost more than five minutes to Pierre Brambilla, which effectively lost him the Tour de France. That evening he could barely control his rage, talking of quitting the race and looking up the time of the next train out of town. But he didn't quit, and stayed on the Tour to help support the surprise victory of Jean Robic in Paris. ∎

René Vietto rides Stage 2 from Lille to Brussels, on the way to winning the stage and taking the yellow jersey. Despite leading for much of the 1947 Tour, he finishes in fifth place in Paris.

THE BETRAYAL OF GÉMINIANI

Raphaël Géminiani's relationship with the Tour de France was complicated. The yellow jersey that the Frenchman had coveted for so long arrived late in his career, and during a Tour that left a rather bitter taste. Géminiani took part in no fewer than 11 Tours between 1947 and 1959, but wore the yellow jersey just four times, all during the 1958 Tour. In 1951 he had a podium position at the finish, taking second place, some 22 minutes behind the unstoppable Hugo Koblet. In 1953 he had to park his personal Tour ambitions and help Louison Bobet achieve his first Tour victory. And then there was the 1958 Tour. Even before the start, he became the 'victim' of Jacques Anquetil, the previous year's winner and the new star of French cycling. Anquetil decided he didn't want both Louison Bobet and Géminiani on the France team, and persuaded manager Marcel Bidot to drop one of them. The axe fell on Géminiani, who was promptly snapped up by Centre-Midi, one of the regional teams competing in the Tour that year. Full of outrage at his demotion from the France national team, Géminiani rode like a demon and took the yellow jersey on Stage 13 from Dax to Pau, the first yellow of the 33-year-old's entire career. 'Far from getting anxious or worried, I feel fired up by the situation,' he said at the time. 'I am feeling pretty relaxed, not obsessing about winning. But I'm in for a major battle with Charly Gaul on Ventoux.' He was right. Gaul was Géminiani's biggest headache on

this Tour. Even if Géminiani still kept the yellow after the time trial on Ventoux (which was won by Gaul) and Gaul then gave up 15 minutes the next day on the road to Gap, Géminiani's Tour win was not a done deal. On Stage 21 from Briançon to Aix-les-Bains Gaul made an epic attack under torrential rain in the Chartreuse, an iconic moment in his career. But during his long and desperate pursuit of Gaul, Géminiani got zero support from any of his compatriots (and former team mates) on the France national team. When he crossed the finish line, his face deformed with pain and exhaustion, he summed it up in one word: 'Judas! All of them! Judas!' He finished the Tour in 13th place in Paris, nearly four minutes behind Gaul.

Betrayed: Géminiani felt let down by his compatriots on the French national team who forced him to take on Charly Gaul with no support.

Henri Pélissier on Stage 6 (from Bayonne to Luchon) of the 1923 Tour, which he went on to win two weeks later in Paris. Robert Jacquinot (right) crashed later that day climbing the Peyresourde.

14

BROTHERS IN ARMS

From the Pélissiers to the Schlecks (via the Buysses, Groussards and Simons) there are five sets of brothers who have been honoured with the yellow jersey.

– 1923 · 1931 –

HENRI, FRANCIS & CHARLES PÉLISSIER

THOSE PÉLISSIER LADS

Never was there a more illustrious cycling family than this one. Jean and Elisa-Augustine Pélissier moved to Paris from the Auvergne to set up a small dairy farm, one of the last to exist within the metropolis. They had four sons and a daughter. Jean, the youngest son, was killed in the Great War, and all three of his brothers became professional cyclists – and champions. The Pélissiers have remained the biggest and longest family saga on the Tour.

Henri, the eldest, picked up the richest collection of trophies. But Tour boss Henri Desgrange disliked him, finding him a shade neurotic and too fragile-looking to be a winner. (When it came to participants in his Tour, Desgranges preferred cart horses to thoroughbreds.) Henri Pélissier proved him wrong, winning the Tour in 1923, ten years after his Tour debut, and 12 years after the previous French winner, Gustave Garrigou.

As for Francis – 'the big guy' on account of his generally lanky appearance – he came on the scene in 1919. He had to wait until 1927 to put on the yellow jersey, but he kept it for five days in a row after winning Stage 1 from Paris to Dieppe.

Finally, there was Charles, 14 years younger than Henri, and adored by female fans of the Tour who would throw him flowers during his victory circuits. Charles was nicknamed 'Valentino', and set some style trends too, with his trademark white gloves and an assortment of different socks. He was also one of the first racers to be categorized as a sprint specialist, winning a total of 16 Tour stages, eight in 1930 alone including Stage 1 and four consecutive wins. Charles would have the yellow jersey again the following year. ∎

It took eight years of riding the Tour before Francis Pélissier managed to get a yellow jersey, at the end of the initial stage from Paris to Dieppe in 1927.

Yellow jersey or no yellow jersey, Charles Pélissier (right, alongside Learco Guerra) had a huge female following.

– 1926 –

JULES & LUCIEN BUYSSE

JERSEY BOYS

Belgian brothers Jules and Lucien Buysse were both members of the Automoto team. And to this day, they remain the only brothers to have both worn the yellow jersey during the same year's Tour. Jules, 24 years old, was the first Tour leader in 1926, and ended the Tour in 9th place. And Lucien, 33 years old, was the winner...

Jules Buysse can't quite believe it: he has the yellow jersey. His brother Lucien (right) will have his turn later, as victor of the 1923 Tour.

Joseph (left) and Georges Groussard had very different riding styles and abilities, but shared the same passion for the yellow jersey.

– 1960 • 1964 –

JOSEPH & GEORGES GROUSSARD

GROUSSARDS, A SPRINTER AND A CLIMBER

Joseph, the older brother was without doubt the better racer of the two brothers. His haul of trophies included a Milan–San Remo in 1963, and several prestigious national one-day races. He also won the final stage of the Tour in 1959 at the Parc des Princes. But it was the following year, in 1960 (aged 26), that the Breton, well known for his speed on the attack, managed to secure his day with the yellow jersey, during Stage 3 at Dieppe.

His brother Georges, three years younger, was a good deal smaller and a useful climber. He took the yellow jersey on Stage 8 of the 1964 Tour at Briançon. 'Little' Georges hung on to yellow for a further eight stages before having to give it up to Jacques Anquetil after a time trial between Peyrehorade and Bayonne (where bad luck once again struck Raymond Poulidor). Georges Groussard finished the Tour in fifth place. The newspaper shop that he later ran for many years in his home town of Fougères was called, not too surprisingly, 'The Yellow Jersey'.

The day had started well for Pascal Simon, who had picked up the yellow jersey the previous evening in Luchon. But a crash on the road to Fleurance put paid to his hopes for Tour glory in 1983.

– 1983 · 2001 –

PASCAL & FRANÇOIS SIMON

THE SIMON FAMILY

If three racing Pélissier brothers is already plenty, the Simon family managed to get four brothers onto the Tour. Pascal Simon seemed well on the way to winning the Tour in 1983 when a bad crash and a fractured shoulder put paid to all that (and he was forced to drop out after Stage 17, from La Tour-du-Pin to l'Alpe d'Huez). But his youngest brother François, 12 years his junior, had more luck during his Tour career some 18 years later. On Stage 8 of the 2001 Tour (from Colmar to Pontarlier) François was part of a large breakaway group of 13 riders who opened up a record-breaking gap of 36 minutes on the peloton. At the time, the yellow jersey was still with the celebrated Australian Stuart O'Grady, but it was on the Alpe d'Huez, the next day, that François Simon could cash in on the previous day's breakaway. He had to concede a dozen or so minutes to Lance Armstrong, but O'Grady was blocked, and Simon, who had been Champion of France in 1999, found himself with the yellow jersey.

The fightback came relatively quickly from Armstrong, and Simon's yellow would not make it beyond the Pyrenees stages. He did however, keep it for three days, before it inevitably went back to Armstrong on Stage 13 at Pla d'Adet. For Simon, though, the hardest work had been done, and he hung on to a very respectable sixth place in Paris.

Two other Simon brothers have also left their stamp on the Tour. Régis would win a half-stage in the Pyrenees (from Laruns to Pau) in 1985, and Jérôme would triumph in 1988 (on Stage 9, from Nancy to Strasbourg). ■

Léon Le Calvez (centre) poses for the cameras to celebrate his yellow jersey, joined by Charles Pélissier and Antonin Magne (right).

– 1953 –

FRANÇOIS MAHÉ

François Mahé (left) with Raphaël Géminiani, yellow jersey in Dax in 1958. Mahé himself had worn the yellow jersey five years earlier.

IMPRESSING THE IN-LAWS

Another unique case of family values: François Mahé, a member of the France West regional team, took the yellow in the 1953 Tour (Stage 12 from Luchon to Albi). His wife Yolande was the daughter of Léon Le Calvez, a Breton racer on the France national team who himself took the yellow jersey on the 1931 Tour (Stage 3 from Dinan to Brest).

Tour de France 2001: François Simon is led by his team mate Jean-Cyril Robin, with Spanish rider Javier Rodríguez on his flank during his third and final day in yellow between Foix and Saint-Lary-Soulan.

Andy Schleck (left) congratulates his brother Fränk who has just won the stage to Le Grand-Bornand in 2009. That year neither brother would be wearing the yellow jersey, but in 2010 Andy took race leadership in Stage 9 and would eventually be awarded a Tour victory.

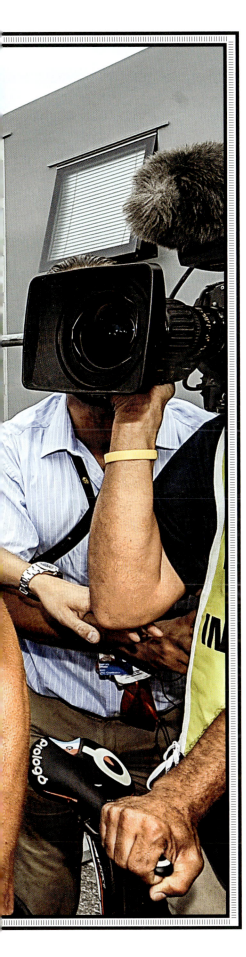

– 2008 • 2010 • 2011 –

FRÄNK & ANDY SCHLECK

TWO BROTHERS HONOURED ON PARIS PODIUM

Johny Schleck, born in Luxembourg, was a successful professional cyclist during the 1960s and 1970s, and later worked for Luis Ocaña on the Bic team. Johny had two sons, Fränk and Andy, who were the only brothers ever to have set foot together on the winners' podium on the Champs-Élysées. It was the end of the 2011 Tour, and Andy finished in second place with Fränk in third, while Cadel Evans stood between them on the top step. Both brothers had worn the yellow jersey too. Andy's came in 2010 when Alberto Contador was disqualified for doping offences. The following year, he took the yellow at the Alpe d'Huez (Stage 19), the same stage where Fränk had lost it in 2008. ■

– 1954 • 1956 –

WOUT WAGTMANS

– 1971 –

MARINUS «RINI» WAGTMANS

COUSINS IN ARMS

Dutchman Wout Wagtmans was one of the most bitter adversaries of Louison Bobet on the Tours in the mid-1950s. He took the yellow jersey three years in a row, from 1954 to 1956. His cousin, Marinus 'Rini' Wagtmans, was a team mate of Eddy Merckx on the Molteni team, and would also take the yellow, albeit for the shortest time on record – having won one-third of a stage at the start of the 1971 Tour.

Rini Wagtmans (left) made his mark as the man who wore the yellow jersey for the shortest time ever. His cousin **Wout Wagtmans (below)** meets Yvette Horner, official accordionist of the Tour de France.

Serafino Biagioni (right) keeps smiling as he gives up the yellow jersey to Roger Levêque at the arrival in Rennes in 1951. For 30-year-old Levêque, this is a huge moment. His only wins throughout his professional career to date had been a stage win in the Tour de France two days earlier.

15

JERSEY TRIVIA

Who would have thought it? Here are some fun facts with a yellow tinge.

YOU KNOW WHO I AM?

When he took the train home after his first Tour win in 1924, Ottavio Bottecchia did not pack the yellow jersey into his suitcase, but wore it proudly underneath his jacket.

A (VERY) RARE VICTORY

In 1951, Roger Levêque won Stage 4, from Le Tréport to Paris, the only win of his entire professional career. It set him up nicely to take the yellow jersey a couple of days later in Rennes.

LAST YEAR'S MODEL

Louison Bobet found himself without a yellow jersey at the start of Stage 6 of the 1954 Tour, from Saint-Brieuc to Brest. He had given his jersey to his sister, who had dropped in to visit him the previous evening. His trainer Raymond Le Bert just happened to live in Saint-Brieuc, and ran back to his house to fetch another jersey that the champion had given him the previous year.

TAKING A RAIN CHECK

In 1978 Jan Raas won the prologue in Leiden, the Netherlands. But chaos caused by rain meant the organizers did not count the prologue times in the general classification, so there would be no yellow jersey for Raas. His frustration was brief: he picked one up the following lunchtime at Sint Willebrord.

Impressing the neighbours: Marc Wauters rides through his village in the yellow jersey.

AN ON-OFF RELATIONSHIP

Ferdi Van Den Haute was about to experience the best day of his cycling career. It was the 1984 Tour, and the Belgian had just won Stage 4, and was being awarded the yellow jersey. He stood proudly on the podium at Béthune, relishing the kisses, the handshakes, and of course the jersey, which he put on, smoothing it down and smiling for the cameras. A few minutes later there were some urgent discussions nearby. A mistake had been made, and bonus seconds mid-stage had been omitted, so that it was actually the Dutchman Adri Van der Poel who was race leader. The unlucky Van den Haute had to get back into his own jersey again.

A CHRONO TO NOWHERE

The usual prologue was replaced by a rather convoluted 'preface' at the start of the 1988 Tour. There was a team time trial between Pornichet and La Baule, with each team designating a 'finisher' for the final kilometre. The Carrera team's Guido Bontempi was the winner, but the results did not form part of the general classification.

CYCLING'S COMING HOME

What were the chances of this? The one and only time that the Tour went through Lummen, a village in the Limbourg region of northern Belgium, it was local man Marc Wauters who was wearing the yellow jersey, part of his brief leadership of the 2001 Tour. A nice coincidence.

WORTH WAITING FOR

Oscar Pereiro, the Spanish winner of the 2006 Tour was the architect of an epic Stage 13 breakaway that gave him a stonking half-hour lead from Béziers to Montélimar. But he is also remembered as one of just two Tour champions not to have been awarded the yellow jersey on the Champs-Élysées podium in Paris. Following Floyd Landis's disqualifcation for doping offences, Pereiro (second in Paris) eventually picked up his champion's jersey in a ceremony in Madrid, in October the following year.

Guido Bontempi enjoys the moment, but this particular yellow jersey will not count.

CHRIS FROOME'S SPRINT FINISH!

During its long history, the Tour de France is full of moments where riders have had to get off their bike and walk, whether due to mechanical failure or slopes that were simply too steep for the gears to cope with. But how about the yellow jersey leaving his mangled bike on the road and sprinting – on foot – up a mountain? On 13 July 2016 there were gale-force winds at the top of Mont Ventoux, so the finish line was moved 6km further down the mountain, close to Chalet Reynard. A massive crowd closed in alongside the final kilometre of the race, which led to a motorbike having to stop suddenly. Richie Porte, at the front of the leading group of riders, rode straight into it, and Bauke Mollema and Chris Froome (the yellow jersey) were brought down in the escalating chaos. Mollema set off quickly, but Froome's bike was not rideable, and his support car was stuck somewhere in the massive traffic jam behind him. So Froome began running, 300 or 400m up the hill, at a good pace, tracked by a phalanx of motorbikes like a marathon runner. Finally he was able to pick up a bike from the

neutral service car, but his cleats were not compatible, and he struggled to make progress. Around 400m from the finish, the Sky car made its way through and gave him a replacement bike. He arrived in 25th place, 1'40" from Bauke Mollema, and would in theory have lost the yellow to fellow British rider Adam Yates who had somehow managed to weave through the crash scene unscathed. The organizers were at a loss as to how to handle this totally unprecedented situation, and decided to award Froome the same time as Mollema, allowing him to keep the yellow jersey. This was completely out of line with Tour regulations but seemed to be fairest – or the least unfair – way of dealing with it, and Adam Yates accepted the decision with more or less good grace. Completely overshadowed by all this drama was Thomas De Gendt, the Belgian who won the stage after a long and brave breakaway. ∎

After an earlier crash with a motorcycle on Stage 15 of the
1968 Tour (from Font-Romeu to Albi), Poulidor once again sees
his chances of a Tour victory slipping away.

16

POULIDOR: THE MAN WITH NO JERSEY

In all of Raymond Poulidor's 14 Tours de France, he never – not once, not even for a half-day stage – wore the yellow jersey. He was though, in his own unique way, an exceptional champion.

How could it NOT happen? Raymond 'Poupou' Poulidor took part in no fewer than 14 Tours de France between 1962 and 1976. He had eight podium finishes in Paris, including second place three times, and third place on a further five Tours. But during the whole of his illustrious Tour career he never, ever, found himself in the yellow jersey.

At the launch event of the 2019 Tour, marking 100 years of the yellow jersey, Poulidor was invited onto the platform alongside the three surviving five-times champions of the Tour (Eddy Merckx, Bernard Hinault and Miguel Indurain). Poulidor quipped: 'You know, on this podium we can count 15 Tour victories between the four of us!' The crowd loved it.

Poulidor often got close, very close to becoming a great Tour champion. But he was also like a magnet for bad luck. Perhaps it was a bad omen right from the start, but on his first Tour in 1962 he already had a hand in plaster, having crashed during training a few days before the start. But as his hand healed up, he showed what he could do later in the race, winning Stage 19 in the Chartreuse from Briançon to Aix-les-Bains. It's worth noting that at the end of the Tour he was 9'24" behind the winner Jacques Anquetil, not much more than the eight minutes he lost on Stage 1 with his painful hand injury. Team manager Antonin Magne subjected all his new riders to the famous 'pendulum test' (a bit of rural folklore to predict their future) and in Poulidor's case the results were a little troubling: 'The verdict of the pendulum got me worried,' Magne confided in an interview many years later. 'It revealed that Raymond was prone to bad luck during June and July.' For Poulidor, it would become the Tour of Lost Chances, and perhaps none more dramatic than in 1964. At the summit of Puy de Dôme on Stage 20, Poulidor was held off, just, by Anquetil and missed out on the yellow jersey ■■■

A bad moment for a puncture (here in 1964). Once again, the Tour gets away from him.

▪▪▪

by 14 seconds. But even more than this elbow-to-elbow battle, there had been a time trial three days earlier from Peyrehorade to Bayonne, where luck was against him again. Poulidor was in the lead on the split times, but had a puncture. What followed was almost slapstick. In the general rush, team mechanic Louis Billard (who was carrying the replacement bike on his shoulder) was thrown off balance by the team car and fell to the ground, with the bike pitching into a ditch. 'I went to get it myself,' recalled Poulidor, 'but my cleats were making it hard to walk. When I got back on the road, the handlebar was twisted so I had to straighten it. And the chain was off, so I had to fix that, and then I couldn't get into the clips. It was nothing but lost time!'

SECOND TO ANQUETIL. AND TO MERCKX!

During his exceptionally long career, Poulidor would have the privilege of coming second to Anqetil (in 1964) and also to Merckx (a full decade later). But perhaps Poulidor's real bad luck came by having his least successful years at a time when there was a power vacuum at the top, between the end of Anquetil's reign and the start of Merckx's. Poulidor was caught out by Felice Gimondi in 1965, attacked by Anquetil to the benefit of Lucien Aimar in 1966, and held up in 1967 on the Ballon d'Alsace waiting for a replacement bike when the France team car broke down. In the 1968 Tour he was knocked down by a motorcyclist on Stage 15 and forced to abandon the race. After that, Eddy Merckx came on the scene, and when 'the Cannibal' was absent from the 1973 Tour, it was Joop Zoetemelk (another seasoned runner up) who would deprive Poulidor of the yellow jersey by less than a second in the prologue at Scheveningen in the Netherlands. Could things have got any worse?

Raymond Poulidor's autobiography is, unsurprisingly, called *Glory Without The Yellow Jersey* and the Frenchman eventually got used to it. He was not a man particularly consumed with ambition. 'My popularity actually got in the way of things,' he admits. 'I would not have earned more money if I had actually won the Tour,' he believes. At times he almost seemed like a caricature of himself. In the 1970s, a famous Paris department store called La Samaritaine captured the spirit nicely: 'You can find everything you want at Samaritaine' went the slogan. And in the picture, a smiling Raymond Poulidor – with the yellow jersey. ▪

BY A WHISKER...

Raymond Poulidor often missed out on the yellow jersey by a hair's breadth. Here are some of the ones that got away.

0.8 SECONDS
The margin by which Joop Zoetemelk beat Poulidor into second place during the prologue of the 1973 Tour in Scheveningen.

6 SECONDS
Poulidor was holding the best time during the 5.8km prologue at Angers in 1967, when the Spaniard José Maria Errandonea snatched a surprise victory by just six seconds.

14 SECONDS
The gap that remained between Poulidor and the leader, Jacques Anquetil in 1964 after the Puy de Dôme stage. Poulidor had narrowed the gap by 42 seconds.

34 SECONDS
The narrowest margin between Felice Gimondi and Poulidor during the 1965 Tour after his Stage 14 victory on Ventoux.

17

THE PRIZE FOR BEST SUPPORTING ACTOR

Nobody wins a yellow jersey without the backing of a team. But sometimes, even team riders can find themselves finishing the day wearing the iconic jersey.

On the slopes of Mont Ventoux, Antonin Rolland (here alongside Ferdi Kubler) battled on to keep the yellow jersey for his France national team for more than a week. Ultimately, he knew that he would have to hand it over to Louison Bobet before Paris.

Joseph Bruyère stays ahead of Gerben Karstens on Stage 3 of the 1974, between Morlaix and Saint-Malo. Bruyère was in yellow, temporarily, with the jersey 'on loan' from his leader, Eddy Merckx.

KNOW YOUR PLACE

It can be a thankless task. There's no glory and no recognition. You push yourself to your physical limits, and then have to give up a wheel or hand out water bottles. But team riders play a key part in both team and individual wins, and above all, in helping defend the yellow jersey. They have played an integral part in the history of the Tour, and sometimes, completely out of the blue, they will find themselves wearing the yellow jersey. Historically, you can go all the way back to Maurice Archambaud, a cornerstone of the France team during the 1930s. He was a talented racer, with a number of yellow jerseys to his name (in 1933 and 1936) and the potential, some thought, to win the Tour. But the Alpine stages all too often brought him back to earth, where he would typically revert to his team role and leave the history-making to others. Fast-forward to the 1955 tour, and the story of Antonin Rolland. France team manager Marcel Bidot had issued him with clear orders: 'Control the breakaways, and don't work with anyone, whoever it might be.' Rolland obeyed, and took the yellow on Stage 4 from Namur to Metz. He continued into the mountains, still race leader, and left the Alps on Stage 8 still holding an eight-minute lead over his own team leader Louison Bobet. Was it just a lack of ambition that kept Rolland from capitalizing on the 12 days he spent in the yellow jersey? More likely, he knew that his job was simply to prepare the ground for Bobet (the future three-times Tour champion), and that is what he did. There are other examples too: the likes of Raymond Riotte (team mate of Pingeon, Poulidor and Aimar) who led the Tour on 5 July 1967 in Strasbourg; or Jean-Pierre Genêt (again, riding with Pingeon and Poulidor) who was leader at Rouen on 1 July 1968; and José Catieau, whose big day was 3 July 1973 and the huge attack by the Bic team in Stage 3 from Roubaix to Reims. He would get to keep the yellow jersey for four days, before handing it on to Luis Ocaña for the remainder of the Tour.

'THE YELLOW JERSEY HAS NOT LEFT EDDY'S ROOM. HE'LL GET IT BACK WHEN HE WANTS IT.'

By contrast, Pascal Lino seemed to have it easy when he started his campaign for the yellow jersey in a large breakaway group on Stage 3 of the 1992 Tour, from Pau to Bordeaux, and he went on to keep it for a full ten days. 'It was very simple, we just needed to get into every attack going,' he said later. 'After that, we could just stay in the pack, neither in front nor behind, because we had the jersey. It was the ideal situation.'

Team racing has its advantages, even for team mates of Eddy Merckx, who was not one to share too much of the glory. Julien Stevens (1969), Italo Zilioli (1970), Marinus Wagtmans (1971) and Joseph Bruyère would all find a way to get the yellow, albeit briefly. 'Well done, Joseph, I'm happy for you,' Merckx reassured Bruyère, who felt awkward at having deposed Merckx at Saint-Pol-de-Léon on Stage 1 of the 1974 Tour. 'All I did was follow Van Springel and Gualazzini, with absolutely no relaying. Just waiting for the peloton to chase us down,' explained Bruyère. At the time he was rooming with Merckx on the Tour. 'So nothing's really changed,' Bruyère added wryly. 'The yellow jersey has therefore not left Eddy's room, and he'll get it back when he wants it.' Which he did, three days later. ∎

– 1952 –

ANDREA CARREA

'A POOR KID LIKE ME!'

The Italian was devoted to his hero, Fausto Coppi.
So depriving the 'campionissimo' of a yellow jersey was just not in the script.

ndrea Carrea was a typical 'gregario', a team man through and through, completely devoted to his leader. He did his job as if every single moment was an honour, there to serve the 'campionissimo', the great champion Fausto Coppi. But fate was about to turn the old order upside down

On Stage 9 of the 1952 Tour (from Mulhouse to Lausanne), Carrea was doing the job he was paid to do, maintaining the Italian team's presence within a breakaway group of 12 riders. At the finish, they had a seven-minute gap on the peloton. The Swiss rider Walter Diggelmann won the stage on home ground, but it was the Italian, Carrea, in seventh place, who had no idea he was about to become race leader. 'I went straight to my hotel after the finish,' he recalls. 'And the police came to get me. I said to them: "What have I done?" And they replied: "We have orders to take you back to the finish line. You won the yellow jersey". I was actually scared, really scared,' he says. 'I said to myself, "How is Fausto going to take this?" I put on the yellow jersey, I was in tears. So I went over to Fausto. "What's up?" he says, so I said: "Fausto, look at this! I got no right to wear this jersey! A poor kid like me!"'

Coppi, however, congratulated his faithful team mate with his usual generosity. The next day the Tour made its first ever climb of Alpe d'Huez. Coppi smashed it, and Carrea reached the top in sixth place (which shows how good he actually was). Coppi had pushed Carrea back into second place with a lead of just five seconds. So with a sense of relief, the two riders were back in their habitual roles.■

Between Bagnères-de-Bigorre and Pau, Andrea Carrea (ahead of Stan Ockers and Fausto Coppi) does what he does best: protecting his leader Coppi, like a truly devoted 'gregario'.

18

HANDING ON THE TORCH

The exert total domination on the Tour for years, and then, suddenly, it's all over. Someone is quicker.

The deed is done: the moment when Bernard Thévenet passes Eddy Merckx on the ascent of Pra-Loup in the Pyrenees. Merckx's reign comes to a close.

– 1975 –

MERCKX / THÉVENET

THÉVENET, GIANT KILLER

Bernard Thévenet was a two-times champion of the Tour (in 1975 and 1977) but is perhaps best remembered as the man who beat Eddy Merckx.

At the start of the 1975 Tour, Joop Zoetemelk was asked who was his favourite to win. 'Merckx. Because he's Merckx,' he replied. Eddy Merckx was still World Champion, and his campaign through the spring-time Classics (the one-day races) had been one of his best, winning Milan–San Remo for the sixth time, the Tour of Flanders, the Amstel Gold Race and a fifth victory in the Liège–Bastogne–Liège. Only Roger De Vlaeminck was ahead of him on the road to Roubaix. Obviously, Merckx was not getting any younger, but after so many years as undisputed champion, who could believe that his reign was coming to a close. In the Dauphiné, though, Merckx had already been largely dominated by Bernard Thévenet in the Chartreuse. And as the Tour got underway, the Pyrenees climb up to Pla-d'Adet began to show the limits of Merckx's powers. He was going to have to fight hard for this Tour.

As usual, Merckx was in yellow before the end of the first week, taking it from Francesco Moser, and winning the time trials on Stage 6 (at Merlin Plage in the Vendée) and Stage 9 (from Fleurance to Auch). But the Stage 14 ascent of Puy de Dôme showed once again Merckx's ongoing struggle on the climbs. Joop Zoetemelk, Lucien Van Impe and above all Bernard Thévenet were proving the better climbers. And on the approaches of the Géant d'Auvergne, Merckx was inexplicably punched in the side by a spectator. In a later investigation, the spectator claimed it was an accident, as he had been shoved forward by the excited crowd. He was named as Nello Breton, and was represented in court by one Daniel Thévenet, no relation, in fact, to Merckx's Tour rival. At the summit of the Puy de Dôme on that 11 July evening, Merckx was still race leader. But after a tumultous day, he looked vulnerable. ■ ■ ■

'I TRIED EVERYTHING, AND I LOST'

Merckx's reign was coming to an end. His attack on the Col d'Allos on Stage 15 (from Nice to Pra-Loup) gave the false impression that 'the Cannibal' was back, ready to take his sixth Tour win. But it was not to be. The final climb on Stage 15 up to Pra-Loup, a new feature on the Tour, was to be the scene of a dramatic reversal. To his great surprise, Bernard Thévenet came up behind Merckx, moved alongside, and then dropped him. The Belgian had nothing more to give. 'I tried everything, and I lost. I don't think I can win this Tour. It's over,' he said at the finish that day.

From that day on, Bernard Thévenet would be known as the man who brought down Merckx. He was 27 years old, from the Burgundy region, and he exuded a quiet sense of power. He had begun Stage 15 some 58 seconds behind Merckx in the general classification. And he finished that day 58 seconds ahead. The same evening he got a visit from Louison Bobet, who suggested that the next day it should be Thévenet who leads the team across the Izoard on Stage 16 from Barcelonnette to Serre-Chevalier, an honour befitting the Tour's star riders. So it was, with Thévenet riding alone as he approached the Col, thinking of Bobet, who was following in the car, and of Bartali, Coppi, and Merckx. This would be his second stage victory in a row, and Merckx was now trailing by two and a half minutes. Victory, with the Tour's first ever arrival in Paris on the Champs-Élysées, was assured.

Thévenet won a second Tour in 1977. With Merckx, he had gained a reputation as being something of a giant killer. But another giant of cycling was waiting in the wings. Team boss Cyrille Guimard had persuaded a young Bernard Hinault to sit out the 1977 Tour and make his debut the following year when he would have a better chance of winning. So in 1977 Hinault was watching the Tour from the sidelines, and sharing his impressions with the sports writer Daniel Pautrat. To provide a bit of material for his column, Hinault had a dry run on the time trial route in Dijon in advance of the Tour stage. Thévenet takes up the story: 'I had worked out roughly how much time it would take for us to complete this time trial,' he recalls. 'When someone told me the time that Hinault had managed, I was not that surprised, because my first thought was that it was a joke: they were having me on.' That afternoon, he won the time trial, and a Tour win looked almost certain. But Thévenet's time was roughly the same as that recorded by Hinault on his solo training ride. 'So I'm thinking, "What the hell! It took me ages to get Merckx under control. And now here comes another one!"' ∎

Bernard Thévenet seems hardly able to believe that he has just taken the yellow jersey from Merckx, as he is mobbed by reporters on the podium after Stage 15, from Nice to Pra-Loup. It had looked like an impossible task.

– 1966 –

ANQUETIL BACKS AIMAR

By 1965, five-times Tour champion Jacques Anquetil could already sense that his era was coming to an end, and opted not to compete that year. 'My earning power won't go up any more if I win a sixth Tour, but if I lose a sixth Tour, it will probably do down,' he reasoned. Instead, he took on a new challenge, winning both the Dauphiné and the Bordeaux–Paris races back to back, seen as an insane challenge that just added to the Anquetil legend. He did return to the Tour in 1966, but with the twin and interlinked missions of first, trying to ensure that his French rival Poulidor did not win, and secondly, riding in support of his former 'domestique' on the Ford team, Lucien Aimar, whom he would help to set up to become champion of the 1966 Tour in Paris. Anquetil, his job done, retired from the race during Stage 19 from Chamonix to Saint-Étienne, which was his final appearance on the Tour.

– 1956 –

BOBET / WALKOWIAK

BOBET'S EXIT OPENS DOOR FOR WALKO

Louison Bobet is the first man ever to win three consecutive Tours (in 1953, 1954 and 1955) but it took time for him to recover from surgery and he sat out the 1956 Tour. His absence left the field wide open, and Roger Walkowiak capitalised to take his first and only Tour victory. The Bobet era was finished. But the Anquetil reign was about to start.

– 1983 –

HINAULT / FIGNON

FIGNON FILLS THE GAP

Racing in the 1983 Vuelta in Spain was a costly decision for Bernard Hinault, already four-times winner of the Tour from 1978 to 1982. Hinault had to undergo a knee operation and so withdrew from the 1983 Tour. Laurent Fignon saw the gap left by Hinault and was quick to fill it. Hinault was back the following year, but not riding at his best, and Fignon, at peak fitness, was able to pull off a second Tour win. Hinault, though, got the last word in 1985, for then it was Fignon who had to go and seek surgery.

– 1986 –

HINAULT / LEMOND

LEMOND, THE HEIR APPARENT

The superior power and strength of the American cyclist Greg LeMond was already showing through in the 1985 Tour, when he was still supporting Bernard Hinault in the La Vie Claire team. Something had to give. So Hinault, five-times winner of the Tour, gave LeMond the impression that he was ready to hand over the torch: 'Next year,' he told LeMond, 'the Tour will be yours. I'll be there to support you.' Despite the promises, however, when it came to the Pyrenees stages of the 1986 Tour, Hinault looked very strong, and more determined than ever to take a sixth Tour victory. But the American was even stronger. With Hinault's victory hopes fading, he then went all out to support his team mate, with the two finishing hand in hand on the Alpe d'Huez. LeMond went on to win his first Tour, while Hinault made his exit as a veritable Tour champion.

On the final climb to the Alpe d'Huez, Bernard Hinault stays ahead of Greg LeMond and shows, for one final time, the quality that made him a world-class cycling legend. His Tour hopes are over, but he aims to finish in style.

INDURAIN / RIIS

DANE STEALS THE SHOW

Tour champion five times in a row from 1991 to 1995, Miguel Indurain looked set for a sixth victory in 1996. But he was not quite at his peak form, and the cold and wet weather conditions had not helped him to shed a little excess weight. Indurain became victim of a defeat as brutal as it was unexpected at the end of the final climb up to Les Arcs on Stage 7. He would finish in 11th place in Paris, with the victor Bjarne Riis looking untouchable. He dropped everyone at Sestrières with a concerted attack at the end of Stage 9 which had been cut short because of a snow storm. And he did the same again on Stage 16 from Agen to Hautacam. Just over a decade later the Dane admitted he had used several banned drugs in the course of his Tour. There were some dark times ahead.

- 1991 -

LEMOND / INDURAIN

DAWN OF A NEW ERA

Greg LeMond had already won the Tour in 1986, 1989 and 1990, and seemed set to take a fourth victory in 1991. He took the yellow jersey at the end of the time trial from Argentan to Alençon, and (apart from Luc Leblanc's brief tenure of the jersey after Stage 12 from Pau to Jaca) the American looked every inch the Tour favourite. But the following day, from Jaca to Val Louron, LeMond cracked on the final kilometre of the climb to Tourmalet. On the other side of the summit, Claudio Chiappucci and Miguel Indurain partnered up, with the Italian winning the stage and the Spaniard taking the first of what would become 60 yellow jerseys. The era of Indurain had arrived.

– 2006 –

ARMSTRONG AFTERMATH

THE REIGN OF SPAIN

While Tour history sometimes resembles a succession of dominant riders, each giving way to the next, the immediate aftermath of the disgraced Armstrong era in 2005 was less easy to define. Armstrong had won seven times between 1999 and 2005, but was stripped of his titles for systematic doping offences. His former team mate Floyd Landis thought he had won the 2006 Tour, but then he was disqualified for doping. The tour victory was finally held by Oscar Pereiro. Spanish cycling then came into its own – not without controversy – with the little-known Carlos Sastre winning in 2008, amid victories by the brilliant Alberto Contador in 2007 and 2009. Contador rode into Paris in 2010 as race leader, but failed a doping test, leading to an

18-month enquiry and an eventual sanction in February 2012. Contador was suspended retroactively for two years, and so stripped of his 2010 win, which passed on to second-placed Andy Schleck. Alberto Contador ended up with two Tour victories to his credit.

– 2011 –

THE NEW ERA: AUSSIES AND BRITS

ENGLISH SPOKEN HERE!

With Armstrong stripped of his victories, Greg LeMond remains as the only US winner of the Tour. And in 2011, the Tour saw the appearance of its first ever Australian winner, Cadel Evans, who unknowingly heralded in a new era of English-speaking champions. The following year, Sir Bradley Wiggins became the first British winner of the Tour. His compatriot Chris Froome would become a four-times winner from 2013 to 2017, while in 2018 it was the turn of Welshman Geraint Thomas. Seven of the last eight Tours de France have been won by English-speaking winners, of whom six of the seven were riding for Sky.

Georges Groussard had no illusions about his chances on the 1964 Tour, knowing full well that Jacques Anquetil would almost certainly win in Paris. Even so, the climbing specialist took the yellow jersey for a full ten days.

19 THE ENCYCLOPEDIA OF THE YELLOW JERSEY

WHEN YOU JUST CAN'T LET IT GO

The Tour has had its share of unexpected leaders who have managed to hang on to the yellow jersey for as long as possible. Here are just a few of them.

– 1964 –

GEORGES GROUSSARD

'LITTLE GEORGE' BIG CLIMBER

There is little doubt that Georges Groussard was a less talented all-round racer than his brother Joseph, who was yellow jersey (briefly) in 1960, and winner of the Milan–San Remo in 1963. But with his slight build (just 1m 59cm), 'Little Georges' as he was known was a pretty useful climber. He proved this on the 1964 Tour, taking the yellow at Briançon (Stage 8) where he finished sixth. 'I was thinking, OK then, I just need to stick with the big guys. And at the summit, I knew I had won the jersey,' he recalls. Having won it, he did not want to let it go. In Andorra, after the first Pyrenean stage, he was still race leader. 'Now I think I can go on a bit further,' he thought. Two days later on the famous stage from Andorra to Toulouse, he saw Jacques Anquetil struggling at the Port d'Envalira and again secured yellow for another day, despite Anquetil's recovery and a blistering race with his Pelforth team on the flat plain. 'Each day people were saying to me I was going to lose the jersey, and each day I managed to keep it,' he recalls. Eventually, reality caught up with him. On the Stage 17 time trial between Peyrehorade and Bayonne,

Groussard and the yellow jersey parted company. 'Don't get me wrong: I knew I was not going to be keeping the jersey all the way to Paris,' he said later. Groussard finished in a very respectable fifth place, and after retiring from competitive cycling he opened a paper shop in Fougères. The shop, of course, was called 'Le Maillot Jaune'.

– 1980 –

RUDY PEVENAGE

LEADER FOR HALF A TOUR

It was pouring with rain when a sizeable breakaway group took off on Stage 2 of the 1980 Tour on the road from Frankfurt to Metz. Behind Jacques Bossis, Pierre Bazzo, Yvon Bertin and the Belgian Rudy Pévenage, the TI-Raleigh team (who had won the team time trial the previous evening) were not interested in defending Knetemann's yellow jersey in the atrocious riding conditions, and let them go. Their lead at the finish was just under ten minutes, with Rudy Pévenage winning the stage and Bertin taking the yellow jersey. Pévenage then took the yellow the next day at Liège, and thanks to his substantial lead he kept it for almost half the Tour as it travelled

down Western France. Eight days later the old order was re-established on the time trial to La-plume, where Pévenage finished back in 74th place, more than seven minutes down on Zoetemelk (who won the Tour). Pévenage himself finished the 1980 Tour in 42nd place.

Rudy Pévenage raced an entire half of the 1980 Tour in yellow.

Jacques Marinelli crosses the line on the penultimate stage of the 1949 Tour (from Colmar to Nancy). The public were still celebrating his six days in yellow during the earlier part of the Tour.

– 1949 –

'THE BUDGIE' FLIES FREE

With his small stature, endless banter, and of course the yellow jersey which he wore for six days in a row, his nickname 'the Budgie' seemed apt. Marinelli found fame in the 1949 Tour, wearing yellow all the way from Rouen to Pau, and finishing in third place behind the giants of the Tour – Coppi and Bartali. But the adventures of Jacques Marinelli kept France on tenterhooks well beyond his six days as race leader, as the pocket-sized rider on the France national team fought to maintain his third place all through the second half of the Tour: a struggle of David-and-Goliath proportions. The whole of France seemed to be backing Marinelli who was leading the race with a 30-minute gap over Fausto Coppi, the 'campionissimo' who had been held back by a crash at Saint-Malo. He also had a 15-minute lead over the other favourites, including Ferdi Kübler. Marinelli was young, just 24, starting out in pro cycling, and didn't look like a

potential champion. But he touched a chord with the French public, and the press adored him. The previous year, *L'Equipe* had seen huge popular interest in Frenchman Marcel Cerdan who won the World Championships. But for the 1949 Tour, the paper upped its print run to a record high of 600,000 copies per day, thanks to a hugely popular daily column where Marinelli shared his hopes and fears with the nation. 'I know what I have to do. Get on the wheel of Bartali and don't let go,' he wrote in his column as the Tour hit the Pyrenees. And how about the threat from Coppi? 'When I can't go any further, when I am dead, that's when Coppi will have won. But not before,' he wrote. 'And now goodnight. I'm going to bed, and I want to dream that the Tour de France is over.' Even so, Marinelli kept his biggest anxieties to himself: 'I had to hide those moments when I was feeling weaker. If the others spotted that, they would have beaten me. I felt really alone, really quite vulnerable in the middle of all this,' he revealed in later interviews.

Reality caught up with Marinelli on Stage 10 (from Saint-Sébastien to Pau) where he lost the yellow jersey to Fiorenzo Magni. But he kept his promise, finishing in the group with Bartali and Coppi. The next day in Luchon he lost 15 minutes to Coppi who had now closed more than half the earlier gap. The dream was over, but it did not turn into a complete nightmare. Marinelli clung on to finish third on the podium, to a tumultuous reception from his fans in the Parc des Princes.

The summer of 1949 made Marinelli one of the most popular French riders on the circuit, and he knew how to make the most of it. 'With the yellow jersey, everything just sort of blossomed,' he recalled decades later. 'Suddenly I was hugely popular, and this jersey became the foundation for everything else.' Marinelli later opened his own cycle shop, and was elected mayor of Melun from 1989 to 2002.

– 1984 –

VINCENT BARTEAU

BARTEAU IS READY TO GO

The early bird, as they say, catches the worm. When Maurice Le Guilloux and Vincent Barteau joined Portuguese rider Paulo Ferreira on a breakaway just 20km into Stage 5 of the 1984 Tour, they had some great days ahead of them. Nobody was chasing them on the road from Béthune to Cergy-Pontoise, the wind was in their favour, and they managed to put a lead of 25 minutes into the trailing peloton. When the peloton finally responded, it was already too late, and the trio crossed the finish with a substantial margin of 17 minutes. The little-known Paulo Ferreira won the stage, while Vincent Barteau took the yellow jersey. The hard-working Maurice Le Guilloux had, quite literally, been taken for a ride, and came away with nothing to show for his efforts. Vincent Barteau was from Normandy, and at 22 years old was a level-headed rider with great potential. He had already taken the yellow in the Pyrenees, where his team leader Lauren Fignon began wondering if Barteau might even win the Tour. Barteau now found himself with a ten-minute lead over Fignon, and could hardly believe his luck. 'I never thought I had it in me,' he said. He held onto the jersey as far as the Alpe d'Huez where his 12-day stint came to an end and the jersey passed, as widely predicted, to Fignon. Barteau showed flashes of brilliance throughout his career, and a sense of occasion too: five years later he won a stage at Marseille on 14 July 1989 – the 200th anniversary of the French Revolution.

He could scarcely believe it at the time, but Vincent Barteau had indeed just taken the yellow jersey. An unforgettable moment in any cycling career.

Claudio Chiappucci with the yellow jersey, not defending but attacking on the slopes of the Col du Tourmalet.

– 1990 –

CLAUDIO CHIAPPUCCI

CHIAPPUCCI'S EPIC DEFENCE FROM STAGE 1

The peloton appeared to have thrown in the towel at the start of the 1990 Tour when it gave up 10'35" to the breakaway of Frans Maassen, Steve Bauer, Ronan Pensec and Claudio Chiappucci on Stage 1 at Futuroscope. From then on, Tour favourite Greg LeMond was forced into a long chase that would finish a full three weeks later on the penultimate stage, a time trial at the Lac de Vassivière. Claudio Chiappucci, who had taken over the yellow jersey from Bauer and Pensec after a Stage 12 time trial from Fontaine to Villard-de-Lans, was still wearing yellow as the Lac de Vassivière trial began. But with a lead of just five seconds over the American, it looked like a lost cause, and it was. LeMond, the time trial specialist, took the jersey that evening and went on to win the Tour, with Chiappucci second on the podium in Paris.

– 1992 –

PASCAL LINO

LINO, THE 'INTERIM' LEADER

Pascal Lino seemed to have little trouble getting hold of the yellow jersey in the 1992 Tour. He was virtually coasting in the middle of a breakaway group that made its way along the flat roads in the Landes on Stage 3 from Pau to Bordeaux. His team mate Richard Virenque (who had the yellow jersey the previous day) was stuck further back in the peloton, and Lino picked up the jersey that evening. After that, recalls Lino, 'It was simple. We just needed to get into every attack going. And we could just stay in the middle of the pack because whatever else happened, we had the jersey.' Lino's team was RMO, sponsored by a temporary staffing agency, and Lino himself seemed to take on the role of 'temp' leader for the next ten days. His seven-minute lead allowed him to survive the time trial in Luxembourg (Stage 9) where Miguel Indurain's campaign took off, and even for three more stages. Lino only relinquished the yellow jersey at Stage 13 from Saint-Gervais to Sestrières, where Claudio Chiappucci won the stage and Indurain took back the yellow and kept it all the way to Paris. Lino finished in a highly creditable fifth place.

No confusion here between Pascal Lino (above, yellow jersey) and Richard Virenque (green jersey). The two RMO men were leading each classification for a couple of days during the 1992 Tour. Right, Lino's time trial in Luxembourg.

– 2004 • 2011 –

THOMAS VOECKLER

VOECKLER AND THE SEVEN-YEAR ITCH

The French rider competed in 15 Tours, but over the course of just two of them, he came away with a haul of 20 yellow jerseys.

Not exactly a household name outside of his native France, Thomas Voeckler nonetheless built up a creditable stack of some 20 yellow jerseys during his professional cycling career. The amazing thing is, however, that all these came from just two Tours. He won ten yellow jerseys in 2004, a year after his Tour debut, at the age of 25. He then participated annually in the Tour, and in 2011 he suddenly excelled again, winning another ten jerseys and narrowly missing a podium place in Paris (he was fourth).

With 20 yellow jerseys, he is in good company. Gino Bartali managed no more than 20 days as race leader, and over the last century only 17 riders have done better than Voeckler and Bartali.* (And of riders who never won the Tour, only René Vietto, with 26 days, and the Swiss rider Fabian Cancellara with 29 days have done better.)

Voeckler used to joke that he would 'sometimes work the occasional shift' in the yellow jersey. Like someone nursing a cold beer on a café terrace for the best part of a long hot afternoon, Voeckler knew how to make a good thing last a long time. When he started the 2011 Tour he says he could sense that the French supporters got solidly behind him, inspired by his hunger to win and the promise of a re-run of his 2004 performance. Voeckler is down to earth, grounded and pragmatic, and at heart he is a realist. On both Tours, Voeckler's yellow jersey run ended at the top of the Alpe d'Huez. 'I had been nurturing this vague dream of getting onto the podium,' he said of his performance in 2011. 'But that would have to remain a dream.'

For Voeckler, those moments as race leader meant a great deal. 'It is not being the race leader that matters,' he said. 'It is having that yellow jersey.' Success, in the grand scheme of things, can be gone in a flash. But for Voeckler, with his 20 days as race leader, he had time to enjoy it.

'NO EMOTION. JUST SUFFERING.

Some of the time, Voeckler seemed to have luck on his side, especially in his 2004 Tour. On Stage 5, he was part of a five-man breakaway (with Sandy Casar, Magnus Backstedt, Brabantse Pijl and Stuart O'Grady) between Amiens and Chartres, and the gap opened dramatically when Lance Armstrong slowed down the peloton after several of his team mates crashed. Armstrong was probably not too bothered at handing over the task of defending the yellow jersey to an obscure Frenchman for a few days. Voeckler and the young Brioches La Boulangère team could do the heavy lifting instead.

But Voeckler also knew that the best luck was generally found at the front of the race. 'When you're not the best rider in the world,' he reasoned, 'you have to attack. And attack to win.' When he took his first yellow jersey in 2011, there was a sense of history repeating itself. He made his breakaway on Stage 9 in the Massif Central, again with Sandy Cesar and several others including Luis Leon Sanchez (who would cross the finish line first at Saint-Flour). Two others in the group had worse luck: Juan Antonio Flecha and Johnny Hoogerland were both knocked off their bikes by a support car.

Voeckler was a tenacious competitor. In 2004 he had to dig deep on the Beille plateau, where he still had 22 seconds on Lance Armstrong – enough to see him through to the Alps in yellow. Seven years later, at the same spot, he was once again taking on the big names of the peloton. He was still in yellow when he crossed the line at the summit of Galibier. 'No, there was no emotion,' he told the waiting journalists. 'Just suffering.' He was 72 hours from Paris, and again lost the race on the Alpe d'Huez. Voeckler eventually retired from professional cycling in 2017, having completed his 15th Tour de France. ∎

* Figures to the end of the 2018 Tour

Arriving on the Plateau de Beille in 2004 (left) and at the Col du Galibier in 2011 (above), Thomas Voeckler was never a Tour winner but he knew how to push himself to the limit, winning huge support from fans for his fighting spirit and determination.

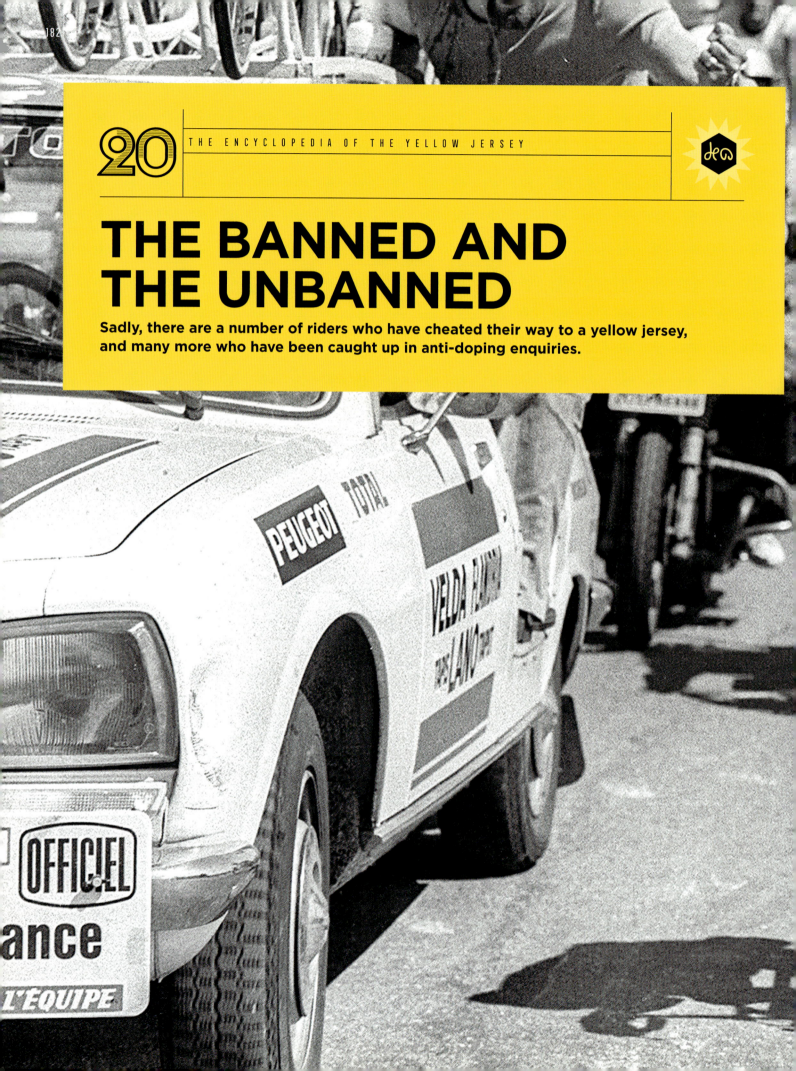

THE BANNED AND THE UNBANNED

Sadly, there are a number of riders who have cheated their way to a yellow jersey, and many more who have been caught up in anti-doping enquiries.

Michel Pollentier drives on towards the yellow jersey at the Alpe d'Huez… and disqualification

– 1978 –

MICHEL POLLENTIER

POLLENTIER'S RUSE GOES PEAR-SHAPED

Michel Pollentier has the dubious honour of being the first yellow jersey to be excluded from the Tour for cheating. The inauspicious date was 16 July 1978.

The press could not stop talking about Michel Pollentier's success that day, winning the stage at the Alpe d'Huez. But the Belgian rider's performance in front of the anti-doping controls would put paid to all that.

It was Stage 16 of the 1978 Tour, and Michel Pollentier was pushing hard in a bid to secure his lead in the mountain stages. When he crossed the line on the Alpe d'Huez, he could swap his red and white polka dot jersey for the yellow, taking it over from a struggling Joseph Bruyère. Joop Zoetemelk and Bernard Hinault (on his Tour debut) finished the day second and third in the general classification. The race was set to be a nail-biter, and the last week would be interesting. Everyone was looking forward to it.

Just after crossing the finish line at 4.10pm Pollentier duly attended the ceremony and received his jersey, before heading back to the Castillan hotel where he and his Flandria team mates were staying. Around 5pm he entered the doping control centre (a small white caravan) for a urine test. Oddly, he did not leave the caravan for a full two hours. That evening, standing in the hotel bar with a glass of champagne in his hand, he said nothing about the inexplicably long doping test, and instead talked at length about the day's cycling. But one hour later, while dining with his team, an official statement was released from the Tour commissioners: Michel Pollentier would be immediately disqualified from the race for having been 'caught in the act of blatant cheating'. It was earth-shattering news: the yellow jersey kicked off the race for cheating. Later that night, the (former) Tour leader tried to explain what had happened. 'It took me a long time to urinate, but nobody said anything to me about that…I can't understand it…' The truth, however, was rather different. In reality, the doping controllers had discovered a 'pear-shaped' rubber bag hidden under his armpit, containing someone else's urine. The container was connected with a tube fixed to his back with sticking plaster, running all the way down to the front of his cycling shorts. Pollentier had been taking Alupen, an asthma drug that was banned on the race, and was hoping to get away with a clean urine test. He had apparently used this technique more than once, and it looks like he was not the only one to do so. This time, though, the drug testers had enforced the rule (usually ignored) that requires a cyclist to lift his jersey up to the chest, and drop his shorts to the knees. So for Pollentier, there was nowhere to hide. The following afternoon, while the Tour was on a rest day, he admitted what he had done and wrote to the organizers asking for clemency – but in vain. His Flandria team had mulled over the idea of quitting the Tour before the following stage, but decided to stay in the race without their leader. Pollentier was handed a two-month suspension, and took a train back to Belgium. He would never again wear a yellow jersey. Despite vowing never to return to the Tour, he did come back in 1979, 1980 and 1981. He failed to finish all three races. ∎

Michel Pollentier held the yellow jersey for just a few hours, on the evening before being disqualified during the 1978 Tour for cheating a doping control test. The jersey went back to Belgium with him in his bag. He never wore it on the road.

—1988—

PEDRO DELGADO

UCI LIST GETS DELGADO OFF THE HOOK

Spanish rider Pedro Delgado had reason to be cheerful. Even though a second set of lab results had just confirmed a positive test for probenecid (a diuretic suspected of having masking effects), he would not be required to quit the race. The leader of the Reynolds team (and yellow jersey since the Alpe d'Huez a week earlier), saw the case against him dismissed on a technicality on 21 July 1988. The drug was indeed on the list of substances banned by the International Olympic Committee, but it was not, however, on the anti-doping list of the UCI, the International Cycling Union. Delgado could therefore continue his race, and keep the yellow jersey, which he did, all the way to Paris. 'I want to forget everything about this business,' Delgado said. 'I am the only yellow jersey on this Tour.'

The controversy dragged on for several days, but by the end of the stage from Limoge to Puy de Dôme, Pedro Delgado was off the hook. Even if he had a positive result for probenecid, the drug was not yet banned by cycling's international governing body, and he would arrive in Paris as winner of the 1988 Tour.

Bjarn Riis seemed to have wings as he attacked on the slopes of Hautacam, ahead of Miguel Indurain. But it was all an illusion. Riis was fuelled up with EPO.

– 1996 –

BJARNE RIIS

RIIS COMES CLEAN AFTER 11 YEARS

My yellow jersey is in a cardboard box in my garage, and you can come and get it any time. It's just a jersey. It means nothing to me. I won't be wearing it again.

Bjarne Riis

'I probably don't deserve my Tour de France victory. My yellow jersey is in a cardboard box in my garage, and you can come over and take it away any time. It's just a jersey. It means nothing to me. I won't be wearing it again.' In May 2007, close to 11 years after his victory in 1996, Bjarne Riis, the first ever Dane to win the Tour, admitted at a press conference in Copenhagen that he was taking the banned drug EPO throughout the 1990s. 'At the time,' he said, 'it was just part of everyday life.' History now needs some rewriting. Remember Riis's effortless climb in Les Arcs on 6 July 1996, where he dropped Miguel Indurain? Forget about it. Strike from the records too his blistering attack two days later, where he took the yellow jersey at Sestrières. Not to mention his 'victory' ten days later at Hautacam, where Indurain noticed that Riis was the only rider to climb using the largest chain ring. The name Bjarne Riis then, is still part of Tour history. But for all the wrong reasons.

– 2002 –

IGOR GONZALEZ DE GALDEANO

THERAPEUTIC? A MATTER OF OPINION

In 2002, yellow jersey Igor Gonzalez de Galdeano found himself mired in controversy. During the evening on Stage 6 (from Forges-les-Eaux to Alençon) traces of the anti-asthma drug salbutamol were found in his urine, enough to affect performance. For the World Anti-Doping Agency, this was a positive test result. But the UCI (cycling's international governing body) accepted the racer's claim the use was therapeutic, so Gonzalez de Galdeano could continue the race. He had worn the yellow since Stage 4 (from Épernay to Château-Thierry) and held on to it for the next four days, eventually finishing in fifth place in Paris. He would subsequently be handed a six-month suspension from competitive racing in France by the French anti-doping agency.

Igor Gonzalez de Galdeano kept his yellow jersey, thanks to a favourable interpretation of the anti-doping regulations.

Floyd Landis did not have long to enjoy his victory in the 2006 Tour. Just two days later, news came out about his positive doping control.

– 2006 –

FLOYD LANDIS

DENIAL, THEN CONFESSION

Floyd Landis can claim to be the first winner of the Tour de France to have his victory overturned for doping offences. In the summer of 2006 the American was still celebrating his victory two days after arriving in Paris. Then the results came in from a urine test taken on 20 July in Morzine (where he had performed a heroic breakaway to gain seven minutes on race leader Oscar Pereiro over just 130km). The test showed abnormal levels of testosterone. Landis came up with plenty of explanations: his own naturally high level of testosterone, a thyroid disorder, alcohol abuse (he had downed two beers and four whiskeys the previous evening after a poor performance on the previous day's stage to La Toussuire). Then he questioned the credibility of the tests themselves, spending a fortune on lawyers, but convincing nobody. After a long legal battle, he was given a two-year suspension. Oscar Pereiro would regain the yellow jersey at a ceremony in Madrid some 15 months later. In 2010, Landis finally owned up to doping during a large part of his career, and this admission would lead to the enquiry that eventually brought down Lance Armstrong.

Michael Rasmussen prepares to start Stage 12 from Montpellier to Castres. Little does he know that his drugs cheating will cost him the 2007 Tour and a two-year suspension.

– 2007 –

MICHAEL RASMUSSEN

LEAVING UNDER COVER OF DARKNESS

Michael Rasmussen dominated the 2007 Tour, holding (and keeping) the yellow jersey from Stage 8 onwards, after a long breakaway between Le Grand-Bornand and Tignes. He put in an exceptionally fast time (for a climber) on the Stage 13 time trial at Albi where he took 11th position (just three minutes behind Alexandre Vinokourov who had a positive doping test result that evening). As the peloton struggled on the Plateau de Beille (Stage 14), Rasmussen pedalled effortlessly. The Dane had been warned several times before about evading random doping tests, and one of his pretexts (that he was on holiday in Mexico) turned out to be a blatant lie. The atmosphere on the Tour became poisonous, and Rasmussen was booed by the crowd as he won the stage at the Aubisque. Finally, under pressure from the Tour organizers, Rasmussen's team bosses at Rabobank had to act. On 25th July at 11.10pm and under cover of darkness, Rasmussen quietly left the Tour, leaving his yellow jersey to Alberto Contador. A few weeks later, traces of EPO would be found in further doping tests carried out retrospectively. Rasmussen was given a two-year suspension.

– 2008 –

STEFAN SCHUMACHER

SCHUMACHER TOO GOOD TO BE TRUE

Stefan Schumacher, winner of the Stage 4 time trial in Cholet, took the yellow jersey on 8 July 2008. But it was a controversial win. With no great track record as a time trialist, he had managed to dominate a field that included the likes of David Millar and Fabien Cancellara – the Olympic champion at the time. Schumacher lost the yellow jersey the following day on the ascent of Superbesse, but on the eve of the final day's ride into Paris, he again produced scintillating speed in the time trial between Cérilly and Saint-Amand-Montrond, once again, leaving world-class riders for dust. Such performances invite suspicion. Schumacher had sporadic dealings with the anti-doping authorities over his career. In 2005 he was cleared after a positive test (for a medicine prescribed for him by mistake). A random doping test just before the 2007 World Championships did however reveal abnormalities in the blood works. In the autumn following his 2008 Tour performance, he was found guilty of doping with a third generation EPO called Mircera, after a series of retrospective controls by the French anti-doping authorities. He was given a two-year suspension.

– 2010 –

ALBERTO CONTADOR

CONTADOR'S 'STEAKGATE' ODYSSEY

Alberto Contador stood on the podium on the Champs-Élysées, savouring the moment. It was 25 July, and he had just won the 2010 Tour de France, his third Tour victory. One month later, the results of a doping test taken on a rest day of the Tour were revealed, and showed a positive result for clenbuterol (a banned anabolic sterioid). The quantity found was miniscule, but was confirmed in a second set of tests. The Spanish cyclist blamed a contaminated steak that he ate the day before the tests were taken – leading to the affair being known as 'Steakgate' in the press. He was suspended for a year by the Spanish federation, and then cleared by them in February 2011. However, both the World Anti-Doping Agency and the UCI (cycling's international governing body) weighed in to appeal this decision, leading to a tribunal that ran on for just over ten months. On 7 February 2012, Alberto Contador was officially suspended for two years (enforced retroactively from 25 January 2011) and stripped of his 2010 Tour title – which was handed to the second-placed rider, Andy Schleck.

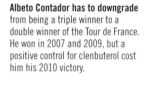

ALBERTO CONTADOR

Albeto Contador has to downgrade from being a triple winner to a double winner of the Tour de France. He won in 2007 and 2009, but a positive control for clenbuterol cost him his 2010 victory.

ARMSTRONG: THE BIG LIE

In October 2012, Armstrong's use of doping throughout his career was confirmed. His seven Tour victories were erased. Three months later, he admitted publicly that he had cheated.

I want to send a message to people who do not believe in cycling, the cynics and the sceptics. I am sorry they do not believe in miracles, in dreams. And that's too bad for them.' With these words, aimed squarely at his doubters and detractors, Lance Armstrong announced he was retiring from the Tour, having just taken his seventh Tour victory in 2005. He had comprehensively smashed the record for the most Tour de France victories, but his performance had provoked not jubilation but unease and suspicion.

Seven and a half years later, on 18 January 2013, and having returned to the Tour on two further occasions (in 2009, with a third place, and the following year, when he was in 23rd place), he found himself in a TV studio facing talk show host Oprah Winfrey. She asked him: 'Have you ever taken any performance-enhancing drugs?' To which Armstrong replied: 'Yes.'

Lance Armstrong had just admitted to what the whole world had suspected for a very long time, especially after the revelations in French newspaper *L'Équipe* in August 2005, which claimed that six of his urine samples taken during the 1999 Tour contained traces of the powerful performance-enhancing drug EPO. The story prompted a media storm at the time, but Armstrong himself was not being hounded by the anti-doping authorities. He had never been subject to a positive test, and his stock response to any claims to the contrary was unwavering: 'It's nothing but lies.' He appeared invincible, just as he had been during those seven Tour victories. 'I feel nothing special with the yellow jersey,' he even said on one occasion. 'If it were green, blue or white, it wouldn't change anything. The real satisfaction is to succeed at what you've been working hard at all year long.'

The US Anti-Doping Agency (USADA) had been investigating Armstrong following accusations from his former team mate Floyd Landis. In October 2010, the agency published a 1,000-page report which confirmed the use of performance-enhancing drugs by the Texan. There were emails, scientific data, lab tests and transfers of funds all proving his deep involvement in what looked like systematic cheating. So Armstrong's admission of guilt to Oprah Winfrey came at a point where he had little choice but to admit the truth.

A few months before the Winfrey interview, USADA had called for him to be banned for life, and to strike off all his competitive wins over the previous 14 years. The International Cycling Union (the UCI) followed these recommendations and chose to leave the Tour winner positions blank on all seven of the Tours that Armstrong had claimed as victor.

The house of cards had collapsed, taking others with it. ('Of course, I cheated, but everyone is cheating,' Armstrong had told Winfrey.) His sponsors are now long gone. And the myth of the man who made an incredible comeback after testicular cancer (metastizing in his brain and lungs) is no more. Gone too is the myth of the Armstrong 'method' for winning the Tour, such as limiting the number of race days, an intimate knowledge of the mountain topography, his particular pedalling cadence – all of this now looks like a huge confidence trick, just like his control of the peloton, installing his team up front to maintain the tempo, appearing to turn cycling into a form of precision science.

After his admission of guilt, there was a price to be paid for his deceit: some $5 million to be precise, which he paid on 20 April 2018 to settle a Federal lawsuit. The US government had been seeking $100million for misuse of public funds following the sponsorship of his team by the US Postal Service until 2004. That case is now closed. ∎

Lance Armstrong's habitual victory lap on the Champs-Élysées with the stars and stripes: seven years of deceit.

III
STATISTICS

All the key stats on the yellow jersey and the 266 race leaders who have worn it.

DAYS IN YELLOW: THE COMPLETE RANKING

Number of days in yellow

| 97 | 96 | 95 | 94 | 93 | 92 | 91 | 90 | 89 | 87 | 86 | 85 | 84 | 83 | 82 | 81 | 80 | 79 | 78 | 77 | 76 | 75 | 74 |

97
(111 TIMES)
EDDY MERCKX
(BEL)

From 1969 to 1975 Eddy Merckx spent the equivalent of more than three months wearing the yellow jersey!

76
(79 TIMES)
BERNARD HINAULT
(FRA)

71 70 69 68 67 66 65 64 63 62 61 60 59 58 57 56 55 54 53 52 51 50 49 ...

60 (60 TIMES)
MIGUEL INDURAIN
(ESP)

59 (59 TIMES)
CHRIS
FROOME
(GBR)

51 (52 TIMES)
JACQUES
ANQUETIL
(FRA)

METHODOLOGY

HOW WE CALCULATED
THE NUMBER OF DAYS IN YELLOW

Who were the kings of the yellow jersey? Eddy Merckx is the clear winner, ahead of Bernard Hinault and Miguel Indurain, followed in turn by Chris Froome (who may yet pick up more jerseys and move into third place). But what's the difference between 'days in yellow' and 'times in yellow'? Here is a guide to how it works:

A 'day in yellow' signifies the presenting of a yellow jersey each evening of a stage, which allows the recipient to wear the yellow jersey the following day. In the cases of both Jean Robic (1947) and Jan Janssen (1968) who won the Tour de France without having ever worn the yellow jersey in that year (except for the lap of honour in Paris) then the final 'day in yellow' is counted, just as it is for all the Tour winners, for whom the yellow jersey received in Paris counts as an additional day.

In some cases, there is a difference between the number of 'days in yellow' and the number of 'times' that the yellow jersey was received, because of the various part-stages with two or three legs in a day, popular in the 1930s and then from the mid-1950s to the early 1990s. This explains why 'the number of times' can be higher than 'the number of days', notably for the record holder Eddy Merckx (with 97 days and 111 'times')

It is also worth noting that when a rider, for whatever reason, does not wear the yellow jersey during a stage (for example Merckx the day after Ocaña's accident in 1971), the day is still counted in the overall tally of 'days in yellow'.

Rest days (in yellow) are not, of course, counted in the total.

AND A WORD ABOUT
DISQUALIFICATIONS

Cases of doping, or of later admissions of substance abuse have affected the calculations of 'days in yellow.' Lance Armstrong, in particular, wore the yellow jersey on 83 days between 1999 and 2005 (theoretically placing him second behind Merckx) and won seven Tour 'victories' during this time. He was later stripped of all his wins, but without any benefit to any other competitor, with the various wins being simply left blank in the Tour de France records.

The consequences of Floyd Landis's disqualification in 2006 and Alberto Contador's in 2010 were more complex. The Tour victory in these two editions went, respectively, to Oscar Pereiro and Andy Schleck. As they subsequently received the yellow jersey, it makes sense to credit them with the 'days in yellow' that Landis and Contador were forced to give up. (Pereiro and Andy Schleck had finished second in the general classification.) This is the method we have chosen here, even if they did not actually wear the yellow jersey in the race at that time. Oscar Pereiro and Andy Schleck are thus credited with, respectively, two and six additional days in yellow, a number deducted, of course, from the totals of Landis and Contador. However, for the disqualifications of David Zabriskie in 2005, George Hincapie in 2006 and Stefan Schumacher in 2008, no other riders have been credited in their place.

| 48 | 47 | 46 | 45 | 44 | 43 | 42 | 41 | 40 | 39 | 38 | 37 | 36 | 35 | 34 | 33 | 32 | 31 | 30 | 29 | 28 | 27 | 26 |

Antonin MAGNE (FRA). **38**

Nicolas FRANTZ (LUX). **37**

André LEDUCQ (FRA). **34.5**

Ottavio BOTTECCHIA (ITA) ; Louison BOBET (FRA). **34**

Fabian CANCELLARA (SUI). **29**

Sylvère MAES (BEL) ; René VIETTO (FRA). **26**

Joop ZOETEMELK (NED) ;

Romain MAES

Gino

38
ANTONIN MAGNE
(FRA)

22
LAURENT FIGNON
(FRA)

6
EUGÈNE CHRISTOPHE
(FRA)

2
CHARLY GAUL
(FRA)

13
GEORGES SPEICHER
(FRA)

3
STEPHEN ROCHE
(IRL)

6
HENRI PÉLISSIER
(FRA)

14
PHILIPPE THYS
(BEL)

19
FAUSTO COPPI
(FRA)

NOTES

Lance Armstrong was stripped of all his wins, having worn the yellow jersey 83 times from 1999 to 2005. The Americans **David Zabriskie** (2005), **George Hincapie** (2006), **Floyd Landis** (2006) and the German **Stefan Schumacher** (2008) all wore the yellow jersey, and were disqualified.
Oscar Pereiro wore the yellow jersey five days in the 2006 Tour which he won following the disqualification of Floyd Landis. The final yellow jersey was presented to him in October 2007. He can also be credited with an additional two days in yellow, given that he was in second place (behind Landis) in the general classification at the end of the 15th and 19th stages, giving him a total of eight days. **Andy Schleck** is also credited with six additional days where he would have worn the yellow jersey following the disqualification of **Alberto Contador** in 2010. In turn, Contador's total is reduced by the same number of days.

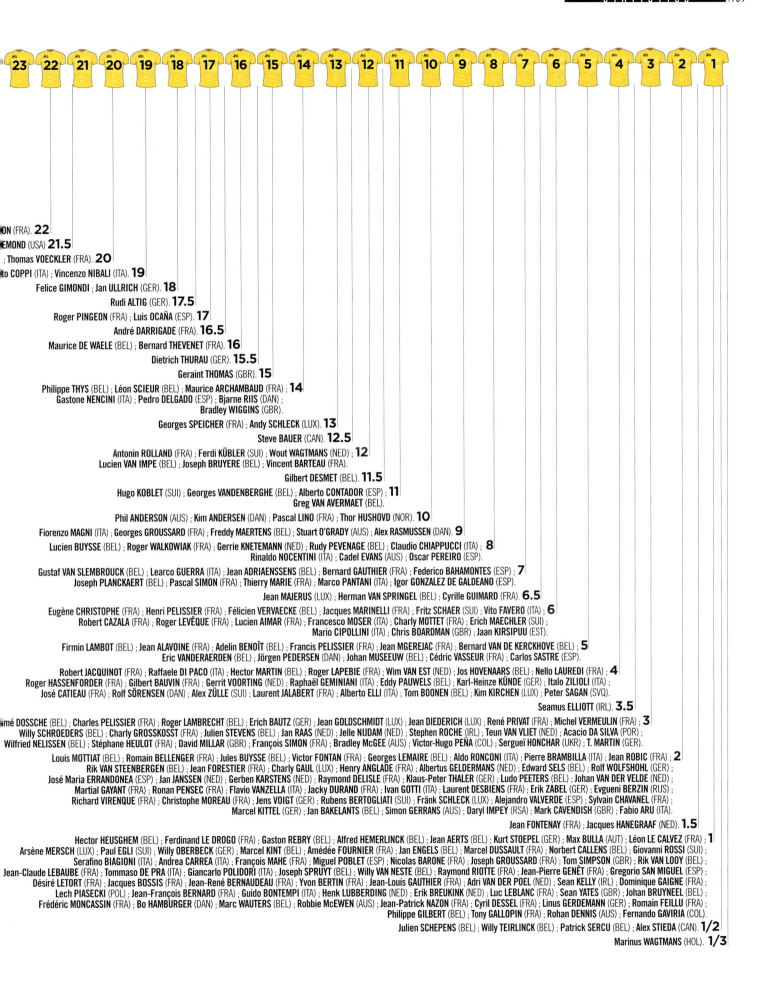

ON (FRA). **22**

EMOND (USA) **21.5**

; Thomas VOECKLER (FRA). **20**

to COPPI (ITA) ; Vincenzo NIBALI (ITA). **19**

Felice GIMONDI ; Jan ULLRICH (GER). **18**

Rudi ALTIG (GER). **17.5**

Roger PINGEON (FRA) ; Luis OCAÑA (ESP). **17**

André DARRIGADE (FRA). **16.5**

Maurice DE WAELE (BEL) ; Bernard THEVENET (FRA). **16**

Dietrich THURAU (GER). **15.5**

Geraint THOMAS (GBR). **15**

Philippe THYS (BEL) ; Léon SCIEUR (BEL) ; Maurice ARCHAMBAUD (FRA) ; **14**
Gastone NENCINI (ITA) ; Pedro DELGADO (ESP) ; Bjarne RIIS (DAN) ;
Bradley WIGGINS (GBR).

Georges SPEICHER (FRA) ; Andy SCHLECK (LUX). **13**

Steve BAUER (CAN). **12.5**

Antonin ROLLAND (FRA) ; Ferdi KÜBLER (SUI) ; Wout WAGTMANS (NED) ; **12**
Lucien VAN IMPE (BEL) ; Joseph BRUYERE (BEL) ; Vincent BARTEAU (FRA).

Gilbert DESMET (BEL). **11.5**

Hugo KOBLET (SUI) ; Georges VANDENBERGHE (BEL) ; Alberto CONTADOR (ESP) ; **11**
Greg VAN AVERMAET (BEL).

Phil ANDERSON (AUS) ; Kim ANDERSEN (DAN) ; Pascal LINO (FRA) ; Thor HUSHOVD (NOR). **10**

Fiorenzo MAGNI (ITA) ; Georges GROUSSARD (FRA) ; Freddy MAERTENS (BEL) ; Stuart O'GRADY (AUS) ; Alex RASMUSSEN (DAN). **9**

Lucien BUYSSE (BEL) ; Roger WALKOWIAK (FRA) ; Gerrie KNETEMANN (NED) ; Rudy PEVENAGE (BEL) ; Claudio CHIAPPUCCI (ITA) ; **8**
Rinaldo NOCENTINI (ITA) ; Cadel EVANS (AUS) ; Oscar PEREIRO (ESP).

Gustaf VAN SLEMBROUCK (BEL) ; Learco GUERRA (ITA) ; Jean ADRIAENSSENS (BEL) ; Bernard GAUTHIER (FRA) ; Federico BAHAMONTES (ESP) ; **7**
Joseph PLANCKAERT (BEL) ; Pascal SIMON (FRA) ; Thierry MARIE (FRA) ; Marco PANTANI (ITA) ; Igor GONZALEZ DE GALDEANO (ESP).

Jean MAJERUS (LUX) ; Herman VAN SPRINGEL (BEL) ; Cyrille GUIMARD (FRA). **6.5**

Eugène CHRISTOPHE (FRA) ; Henri PELISSIER (FRA) ; Félicien VERVAECKE (BEL) ; Jacques MARINELLI (FRA) ; Fritz SCHAER (SUI) ; Vito FAVERO (ITA) ; **6**
Robert CAZALA (FRA) ; Roger LEVÊQUE (FRA) ; Lucien AIMAR (FRA) ; Francesco MOSER (ITA) ; Charly MOTTET (FRA) ; Erich MAECHLER (SUI) ;
Mario CIPOLLINI (ITA) ; Chris BOARDMAN (GBR) ; Jaan KIRSIPUU (EST).

Firmin LAMBOT (BEL) ; Jean ALAVOINE (FRA) ; Adelin BENOÎT (BEL) ; Francis PELISSIER (FRA) ; Jean MGEREJAC (FRA) ; Bernard VAN DE KERCKHOVE (BEL) ; **5**
Eric VANDERAERDEN (BEL) ; Jörgen PEDERSEN (DAN) ; Johan MUSEEUW (BEL) ; Cédric VASSEUR (FRA) ; Carlos SASTRE (ESP).

Robert JACQUINOT (FRA) ; Raffaele DI PACO (ITA) ; Hector MARTIN (BEL) ; Roger LAPEBIE (FRA) ; Wim VAN EST (NED) ; Jos HOVENAARS (BEL) ; Nello LAUREDI (FRA) ; **4**
Roger HASSENFORDER (FRA) ; Gilbert BAUVIN (FRA) ; Gerrit VOORTING (NED) ; Raphaël GEMINIANI (FRA) ; Eddy PAUWELS (BEL) ; Karl-Heinze KÜNDE (GER) ; Italo ZILIOLI (ITA) ;
José CATIEAU (FRA) ; Rolf SÖRENSEN (DAN) ; Alex ZÜLLE (SUI) ; Laurent JALABERT (FRA) ; Alberto ELLI (ITA) ; Tom BOONEN (BEL) ; Kim KIRCHEN (GER) ; Peter SAGAN (SVQ).

Seamus ELLIOTT (IRL). **3.5**

mé DOSSCHE (BEL) ; Charles PELISSIER (FRA) ; Roger LAMBRECHT (BEL) ; Erich BAUTZ (GER) ; Jean GOLDSCHMIDT (LUX) ; Jean DIEDERICH (LUX) ; René PRIVAT (FRA) ; Michel VERMEULIN (FRA) ; **3**
Willy SCHROEDERS (BEL) ; Charly GROSSKOSST (FRA) ; Julien STEVENS (BEL) ; Jan RAAS (NED) ; Jelle NIJDAM (NED) ; Stephen ROCHE (IRL) ; Teun VAN VLIET (NED) ; Acacio DA SILVA (POR) ;
Wilfried NELISSEN (BEL) ; Stéphane HEULOT (FRA) ; David MILLAR (GBR) ; François SIMON (FRA) ; Bradley McGEE (AUS) ; Victor-Hugo PEÑA (COL) ; Sergueï HONCHAR (UKR) ; T. MARTIN (GER).

Louis MOTTIAT (BEL) ; Romain BELLENGER (FRA) ; Jules BUYSSE (BEL) ; Victor FONTAN (FRA) ; Georges LEMAIRE (BEL) ; Aldo RONCONI (ITA) ; Pierre BRAMBILLA (ITA) ; Jean ROBIC (FRA) ; **2**
Rik VAN STEENBERGEN (BEL) ; Jean FORESTIER (FRA) ; Charly GAUL (LUX) ; Henry ANGLADE (FRA) ; Albertus GELDERMANS (NED) ; Edward SELS (BEL) ; Rolf WOLFSHOHL (GER) ;
José Maria ERRANDONEA (ESP) ; Jan JANSSEN (NED) ; Gerben KARSTENS (NED) ; Raymond DELISLE (FRA) ; Klaus-Peter THALER (GER) ; Ludo PEETERS (BEL) ; Johan VAN DER VELDE (NED) ;
Martial GAYANT (FRA) ; Ronan PENSEC (FRA) ; Flavio VANZELLA (ITA) ; Jacky DURAND (FRA) ; Ivan GOTTI (ITA) ; Laurent DESBIENS (FRA) ; Erik ZABEL (GER) ; Evgueni BERZIN (RUS) ;
Richard VIRENQUE (FRA) ; Christophe MOREAU (FRA) ; Jens VOIGT (GER) ; Rubens BERTOGLIATI (SUI) ; Fränk SCHLECK (LUX) ; Alejandro VALVERDE (ESP) ; Sylvain CHAVANEL (FRA) ;
Marcel KITTEL (GER) ; Jan BAKELANTS (BEL) ; Simon GERRANS (AUS) ; Daryl IMPEY (RSA) ; Mark CAVENDISH (GBR) ; Fabio ARU (ITA).

Jean FONTENAY (FRA) ; Jacques HANEGRAAF (NED). **1.5**

Hector HEUSGHEM (BEL) ; Ferdinand LE DROGO (FRA) ; Gaston REBRY (BEL) ; Alfred HEMERLINCK (BEL) ; Jean AERTS (BEL) ; Kurt STOEPEL (GER) ; Max BULLA (AUT) ; Léon LE CALVEZ (FRA) ; **1**
Arsène MERSCH (LUX) ; Paul EGLI (SUI) ; Willy OBERBECK (GER) ; Marcel KINT (BEL) ; Amédée FOURNIER (FRA) ; Jan ENGELS (BEL) ; Marcel DUSSAULT (FRA) ; Norbert CALLENS (BEL) ; Giovanni ROSSI (SUI) ;
Serafino BIAGIONI (ITA) ; Andrea CARREA (ITA) ; François MAHE (FRA) ; Miguel POBLET (ESP) ; Nicolas BARONE (FRA) ; Joseph GROUSSARD (FRA) ; Tom SIMPSON (GBR) ; Rik VAN LOOY (BEL) ;
Jean-Claude LEBAUBE (FRA) ; Tommaso DE PRA (ITA) ; Giancarlo POLIDORI (ITA) ; Joseph SPRUYT (BEL) ; Willy VAN NESTE (BEL) ; Raymond RIOTTE (FRA) ; Jean-Pierre GENÊT (FRA) ; Gregorio SAN MIGUEL (ESP) ;
Désiré LETORT (FRA) ; Jacques BOSSIS (FRA) ; Jean-René BERNAUDEAU (FRA) ; Yvon BERTIN (FRA) ; Jean-Louis GAUTHIER (FRA) ; Adri VAN DER POEL (NED) ; Sean KELLY (IRL) ; Dominique GAIGNE (FRA) ;
Lech PIASECKI (POL) ; Jean-François BERNARD (FRA) ; Guido BONTEMPI (ITA) ; Henk LUBBERDING (NED) ; Erik BREUKINK (NED) ; Luc LEBLANC (FRA) ; Sean YATES (GBR) ; Johan BRUYNEEL (BEL) ;
Frédéric MONCASSIN (FRA) ; Bo HAMBURGER (DAN) ; Marc WAUTERS (BEL) ; Robbie McEWEN (AUS) ; Jean-Patrick NAZON (FRA) ; Cyril DESSEL (FRA) ; Linus GERDEMANN (GER) ; Romain FEILLU (FRA) ;
Philippe GILBERT (BEL) ; Tony GALLOPIN (FRA) ; Rohan DENNIS (AUS) ; Fernando GAVIRIA (COL).

Julien SCHEPENS (BEL) ; Willy TEIRLINCK (BEL) ; Patrick SERCU (BEL) ; Alex STIEDA (CAN). **1/2**

Marinus WAGTMANS (HOL). **1/3**

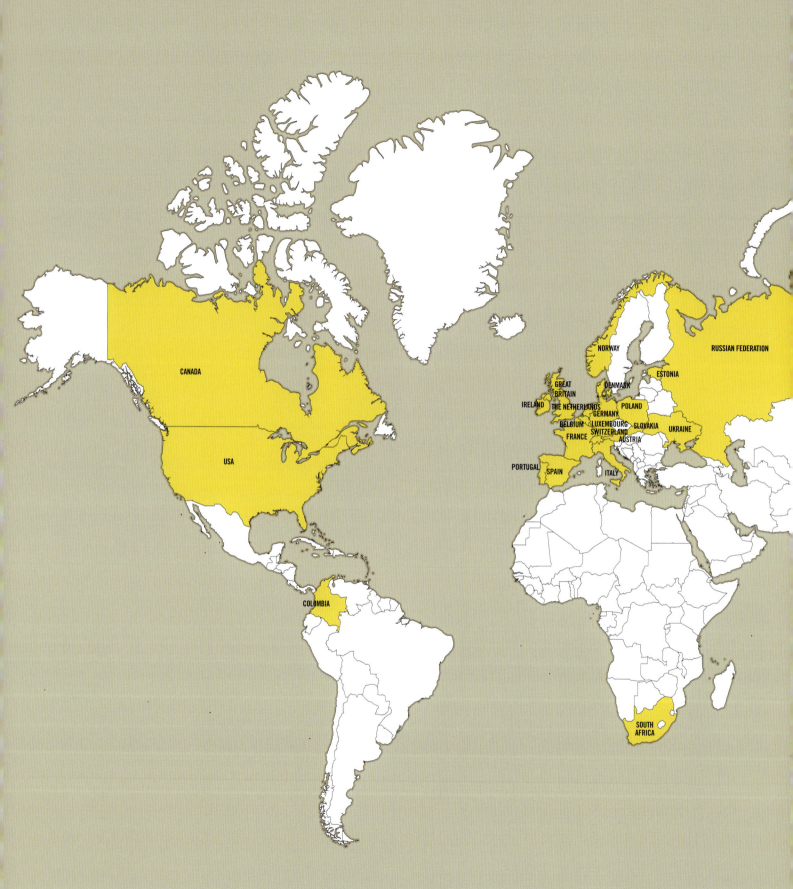

CANADA

USA

COLOMBIA

NORWAY

GREAT
BRITAIN
IRELAND
THE NETHERLANDS
BELGIUM
GERMANY
LUXEMBOURG
SWITZERLAND
FRANCE
AUSTRIA

DENMARK

ESTONIA

RUSSIAN FEDERATION

POLAND

SLOVAKIA
UKRAINE

PORTUGAL
SPAIN
ITALY

SOUTH
AFRICA

THE YELLOW JERSEY BY COUNTRY

The 266 wearers of the yellow jersey come from 24 different countries in an increasingly globalizing Tour

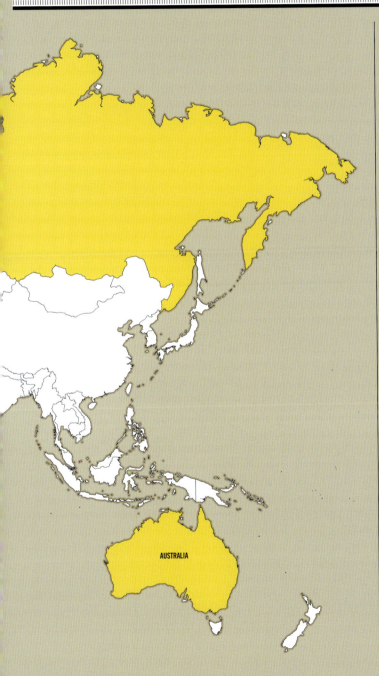

AUSTRALIA

84 🔵

FRANCE

1. **Eugène Christophe**, 1919, 3 days
2. **Robert Jacquinot**, 1922, 3 days
   Eugène Christophe, 1922, 3 days
3. **Jean Alavoine**, 1922, 5 days
   Robert Jacquinot, 1923, 1 day
4. **Romain Bellenger**, 1923, 2 days
5. **Henri Pélissier**, 1923, 6 days
6. **Francis Pélissier**, 1927, 5 days
7. **Ferdinand Le Drogo**, 1927, 1 day
8. **Victor Fontan**, 1929, 2 days
9. **André Leducq**, 1929, 1 day
10. **Charles Pélissier**, 1930, 1 day
    André Leducq, 1930, 13 days
11. **Léon Le Calvez**, 1931, 1 day
    Charles Pélissier 1931, 2 days
12. **Antonin Magne**, 1931, 16 days
    André Leducq, 1932, 19 days
13. **Maurice Archambaud**, 1933, 9 days
14. **Georges Speicher**, 1933, 12 days
    Georges Speicher, 1934, 1 day
    Antonin Magne, 1934, 22 days
    Maurice Archambaud, 1936, 5 days
15. **Roger Lapébie**, 1937, 4 days
    André Leducq, 1938, 1½ days
16. **Amédée Fournier**, 1939, 1 day
17. **Jean Fontenay**, 1939, 1½ days
18. **René Vietto**, 1939, 11 days
    René Vietto, 1947, 15 days
19. **Jean Robic**, 1947, 1 day
20. **Louison Bobet**, 1948, 9 days
21. **Marcel Dussault**, 1949, 1 day
22. **Jacques Marinelli**, 1949, 6 days
23. **Bernard Gauthier**, 1950, 7 days
24. **Roger Levêque**, 1951, 6 days
25. **Gilbert Bauvin**, 1951, 1 day
26. **Nello Lauredi**, 1952, 4 days
27. **Roger Hassenforder**, 1953, 4 days
    Jean Robic, 1953, 1 day
28. **François Mahé**, 1953, 1 day
29. **Jean Malléjac**, 1953, 5 days
    Louison Bobet, 1953, 5 days
    Gilbert Bauvin, 1954, 2 days
    Louison Bobet, 1954, 14 days
30. **Antonin Rolland**, 1955, 12 days
    Louison Bobet, 1955, 6 days
31. **André Darrigade**, 1956, 6 days
32. **Roger Walkowiak**, 1956, 8 days
    André Darrigade, 1957, 1 day
33. **René Privat**, 1957, 3 days
34. **Jacques Anquetil**, 1957, 16 days
35. **Nicolas Barone**, 1957, 1 day
36. **Jean Forestier**, 1957, 2 days
    André Darrigade, 1958, 5 days
    Gilbert Bauvin, 1958, 1 day
37. **Raphaël Géminiani**, 1958, 4 days
    André Darrigade, 1959, 2 days
38. **Robert Cazala**, 1959, 6 days
39. **Michel Vermeulin**, 1959, 3 days
40. **Joseph Groussard**, 1960, 1 day
41. **Henry Anglade**, 1960, 2 days
    André Darrigade, 1961, ½ day
    Jacques Anquetil, 1961, 21 days
    André Darrigade, 1962, 2 days
    Jacques Anquetil, 1962, 3 days
    Jacques Anquetil, 1963, 5 days
42. **Georges Groussard**, 1964, 9 days
    Jacques Anquetil, 6 days
43. **Jean-Claude Lebaube**, 1966, 1 day
44. **Lucien Aimar**, 1966, 6 days
45. **Roger Pingeon**, 1967, 17 days
46. **Raymond Riotte**, 1967, 1 day
47. **Charly Grosskost**, 1968, 3 days
48. **Jean-Pierre Genêt**, 1968, 1 day
49. **Désiré Letort**, 1969, 1 day
50. **Cyrille Guimard**, 1972, 6½ days
51. **José Catieau**, 1973, 4 days
52. **Bernard Thévenet**, 1975, 8 days
53. **Raymond Delisle**, 1976, 2 days
    Bernard Thévenet, 1977, 8 days
54. **Jacques Bossis**, 1978, 1 day
55. **Bernard Hinault**, 1978, 3 days
56. **Jean-René Bernaudeau**, 1979, 1 day
    Bernard Hinault, 1979, 17 days
    Bernard Hinault, 1980, 3½ days
57. **Yvon Bertin, 1980**, 1 day
    Bernard Hinault, 1981, 18½ days
    Bernard Hinault, 1982, 12 days
58. **Jean-Louis Gauthier**, 1983, 1 day
59. **Pascal Simon**, 1983, 7 days
60. **Laurent Fignon**, 1983, 6 days
    Bernard Hinault, 1984, 1 day

■■■

61. Vincent Barteau, 1984, 12 days
    Laurent Fignon, 1984, 7 days
    Bernard Hinault, 1985, 16 days
62. Thierry Marie, 1986, 3 days
63. Dominique Gaigne, 1986, 1 day
    Bernard Hinault, 1986, 5 days
64. Charly Mottet, 1987, 6 days
65. Martial Gayant, 1987, 2 days
66. Jean-François Bernard, 1987, 1 day
    Laurent Fignon, 1989, 9 days
    Thierry Marie, 1990, 1 day
67. Ronan Pensec, 1990, 2 days
    Thierry Marie, 1991, 3 days
68. Luc Leblanc, 1991, 1 day
69. Richard Virenque, 1992, 1 day
70. Pascal Lino, 1992, 10 days
71. Jacky Durand, 1995, 2 days
72. Laurent Jalabert, 1995, 2 days
73. Frédéric Moncassin, 1996, 1 day
74. Stéphane Heulot, 1996, 3 days
75. Cédric Vasseur, 1997, 5 days
76. Laurent Desbiens, 1998, 2 days
    Laurent Jalabert, 2000, 2 days
77. Christophe Moreau, 2001, 2 days
78. François Simon, 2001, 3 days
79. Jean-Patrick Nazon, 2003, 1 day
    Richard Virenque, 2003, 1 day
80. Thomas Voeckler, 2004, 10 days
81. Cyril Dessel, 2006, 1 day
82. Romain Feillu, 2008, 1 day
83. Sylvain Chavanel, 2010, 2 days
    Thomas Voeckler, 2011, 10 days
84. Tony Gallopin, 2014, 1 day

56

BELGIUM

1. Firmin Lambot, 1919, 2 days
2. Louis Mottiat, 1920, 1 day
3. Philippe Thys, 1920, 14 days
    Louis Mottiat, 1921, 1 day
4. Léon Scieur, 1921, 14 days
5. Hector Heusghem, 1922, 1 day
    Firmin Lambot, 1922, 3 days
6. Adelin Benoît, 1925, 5 days
7. Jules Buysse, 1926, 2 days
8. Gustaaf Van Slembrouck, 1926, 7 days
9. Lucien Buysse, 1926, 8 days
10. Hector Martin, 1927, 4 days
11. Aimé Dossche, 1929, 3 days
12. Maurice De Waele, 1929, 16 days
13. Gaston Rebry, 1929, 1 day
14. Alfred Hamerlinck, 1931, 1 day
15. Jean Aerts, 1932, 1 day
16. Georges Lemaire, 1933, 2 days
17. Romain Maes, 1935, 21 days
18. Sylvère Maes, 1936, 14 days
19. Marcel Kint, 1937, 1 day
    Sylvère Maes, 1937, 8 days
20. Félicien Vervaecke, 1938, 6 days

Romain Maes, 1939, ½ day
Sylvère Maes, 1939, 4 days
21. Jan Engels, 1948, 1 day
22. Roger Lambrecht, 1948, 2 days
    Roger Lambrecht, 1949, 1 day
23. Norbert Callens, 1949, 1 day
24. Rik Van Steenbergen, 1952, 2 days
25. Gilbert Desmet, 1956, 1½ days
26. Jean Adriaenssens, 1956, 3 days
27. Jos Hoevenaars, 1958, 1 day
28. Eddy Pauwels, 1959, 2 days
    Jos Hoevenaars, 1959, 3 days
29. Julien Schepens, 1960, ½ day
    Jean Adriaenssens, 1960, 4 days
30. Willy Schroeders, 1962, 3 days
31. Josef Planckaert, 1962, 7 days
    Eddy Pauwels, 1963, 2 days
    Gilbert Desmet, 1963, 10 days
32. Edward Sels, 1964, 2 days
33. Bernard Van De Kerckhove, 1964, 2 days
34. Rik Van Looy, 1965, 1 day
    Bernard Van De Kerckhove, 1965, 3 days
35. Willy Van Neste, 1967, 1 day
36. Joseph Spruyt, 1967, 1 day
37. Herman Van Springel, 1968, 4 ½ days
38. Georges Vandenberghe, 1968, 11 days
39. Eddy Merckx, 1969, 18 days
40. Julien Stevens, 1969, 3 days
    Eddy Merckx, 1970, 20 days
    Eddy Merckx, 1971, 17 days
    Eddy Merckx, 1972, 15 days
41. Willy Teirlinck, 1973, ½ day
    Herman Van Springel, 1973, 2 days
42. Joseph Bruyère, 1974, 3 days
43. Patrick Sercu, 1974, ½ day
    Eddy Merckx, 1974, 18 days
    Eddy Merckx, 1975, 9 days
44. Freddy Maertens, 1976, 9 days
45. Lucien Van Impe, 1976, 12 days
    Joseph Bruyère, 1978, 8 days
46. Rudy Pevenage, 1980, 8 days
47. Ludo Peeters, 1982, 1 day
48. Eric Vanderaerden, 1983, 2 days
    Ludo Peeters, 1984, 1 day
    Eric Vanderaerden, 1985, 3 days
49. Wilfried Nelissen, 1993, 3 days
50. Johan Museeuw, 1993, 2 days
    Johan Museeuw, 1994, 3 days
51. Johan Bruyneel, 1995, 1 day
52. Marc Wauters, 2001, 1 day
53. Tom Boonen, 2006, 4 days
54. Philippe Gilbert, 2011, 1 day
55. Jan Bakelants, 2013, 2 days
56. Greg Van Avermaet, 2016, 3 days
    Greg Van Avermaet, 2018, 8 days

27

ITALY

1. Ottavio Bottecchia, 1923, 6 days
    Ottavio Bottecchia, 1924, 15 days

Ottavio Bottecchia, 1925, 13 days
2. Learco Guerra, 1930, 7 days
3. Raffaele Di Paco, 1931, 4 days
4. Gino Bartali, 1937, 2 days
    Gino Bartali, 1938, 8 days
5. Aldo Ronconi, 1947, 2 days
6. Pierre Brambilla, 1947, 2 days
    Gino Bartali, 1948, 9 days
7. Fiorenzo Magni, 1949, 6 days
    Gino Bartali, 1949, 1 day
8. Fausto Coppi, 1949, 5 days
    Fiorenzo Magni, 1950, 1 day
9. Serafino Biagioni, 1951, 1 day
    Fiorenzo Magni, 1952, 2 days
10. Andrea Carrea, 1952, 1 day
    Fausto Coppi, 1952, 14 days
11. Vito Favero, 1958, 6 days
12. Gastone Nencini, 1960, 14 days
13. Felice Gimondi, 1965, 18 days
14. Tommaso De Pra, 1966, 1 day
15. Giancarlo Polidori, 1967, 1 day
16. Italo Zilioli, 1970, 4 days
17. Francesco Moser, 1975, 6 days
18. Guido Bontempi, 1988, 1 day
19. Claudio Chiappucci, 1990, 8 days
20. Mario Cipollini, 1993, 2 days
21. Flavio Vanzella, 1994, 2 days
22. Ivan Gotti, 1995, 2 days
    Mario Cipollini, 1997, 4 days
23. Marco Pantani, 1998, 7 days
24. Alberto Elli, 2000, 4 days
25. Rinaldo Nocentini, 2009, 8 days
26. Vincenzo Nibali, 2014, 19 days
27. Fabio Aru, 2017, 2 days

9

LUXEMBOURG

1. Nicolas Frantz, 1927, 14 days
    Nicolas Frantz, 1928, 22 days
    Nicolas Frantz, 1929, 1 day
2. Arsène Mersch, 1936, 1 day
3. Jean Majérus, 1937, 2 days
    Jean Majérus, 1938, 4½ days
4. Jean Goldschmidt, 1950, 3 days
5. Jean Diederich, 1951, 3 days
6. Charly Gaul, 1958, 2 days
7. Kim Kirchen, 2008, 4 days
8. Fränk Schleck, 2008, 2 days
9. Andy Schleck, 2010, 6 days
    Andy Schleck, 2011, 1 day

1

AUSTRIA

1. Max Bulla, 1931, 1 day

14

GERMANY

1. Kurt Stoepel, 1932, 1 day
2. Erich Bautz, 1937, 3 days
3. Willi Oberbeck, 1938, 1 day
4. Rudi Altig, 1962, 4 days
    Rudi Altig, 1964, 3 days
    Rudi Altig, 1966, 9 days
5. Karl-Heinze Kunde, 1966, 4 days
6. Rolf Wolfshohl, 1968, 2 days
    Rudi Altig, 1969, 1½ days
7. Dietrich Thurau, 1977, 15½ days
8. Klaus-Peter Thaler, 1978, 2 days
9. Jan Ullrich, 1997, 12 days
10. Erik Zabel, 1998, 1 day
    Jan Ullrich, 1998, 6 days
11. Jens Voigt, 2001, 1 day
    Erik Zabel, 2002, 1 day
    Jens Voigt, 2005, 1 day
12. Linus Gerdemann, 2007, 1 day
13. Marcel Kittel, 2013, 1 day
    Marcel Kittel, 2014, 1 day
14. Tony Martin, 2015, 3 days

9

SWITZERLAND

1. Paul Egli, 1936, 1 day
2. Ferdi Kubler, 1947, 1 day
    Ferdi Kubler, 1950, 11 days
3. Giovanni Rossi, 1951, 1 day
4. Hugo Koblet, 1951, 11 days
5. Fritz Schaer, 1953, 6 days
6. Erich Maechler, 1987, 6 days
7. Alex Zülle, 1992, 1 day
    Alex Zülle, 1996, 3 days
8. Rubens Bertogliati, 2002, 2 days
9. Fabian Cancellara, 2004, 2 days
    Fabian Cancellara, 2007, 7 days
    Fabian Cancellara, 2009, 6 days
    Fabian Cancellara, 2010, 6 days
    Fabian Cancellara, 2012, 7 days
    Fabian Cancellara, 2015, 1 day

17

THE NETHERLANDS

1. Wim Van Est, 1951, 1 day
2. Wout Wagtmans, 1954, 7 days
    Wout Wagtmans, 1955, 2 days
    Wim Van Est, 1955, 1 day
3. Gerrit Voorting, 1956, 1 day
    Wout Wagtmans, 1956, 3 days
    Wim Van Est, 1958, 2 days
    Gerrit Voorting, 1958, 3 days
4. Albertus Geldermans, 1962, 2 days

5. Jan Janssen, 1966, 1 day
   Jan Janssen, 1968, 1 day
6. Marinus Wagtmans, 1971, 1/3 day
7. Joop Zoetemelk, 1971, 1 day
   Joop Zoetemelk, 1973, 1 day
8. Gerben Karstens, 1974, 1 day
9. Jan Raas, 1978, 3 days
10. Gerrie Knetemann, 1978, 2 days
    Joop Zoetemelk, 1978, 4 days
    Gerrie Knetemann, 1979, 1 day
    Joop Zoetemelk, 1979, 6 days
    Gerrie Knetemann, 1980, 1 day
    Joop Zoetemelk, 1980, 10 days
    Gerrie Knetemann, 1981, 4 days
11. Jacques Hanegraaf, 1984, 1½ days
12. Adri Van der Poel, 1984, 1 day
13. Johan Van der Velde, 1986, 2 days
14. Jelle Nijdam, 1987, 1 day
15. Teun Van Vliet, 1988, 3 days
16. Henk Lubberding, 1988, 1 day
    Jelle Nijdam, 1988, 2 days
17. Erik Breukink, 1989, 1 day

12

SPAIN

1. Miguel Poblet, 1955, 1 day
2. Federico Bahamontes, 1959, 6 days
   Federico Bahamontes, 1963, 1 day
3. José Maria Errandonea, 1967, 2 days
4. Gregorio San Miguel, 1968, 1 day
5. Luis Ocaña, 1971, 3 days
   Luis Ocaña, 1973, 14 days
6. Pedro Delgado, 1987, 4 days
   Pedro Delgado, 1988, 10 days
7. Miguel Indurain, 1991, 10 days
   Miguel Indurain, 1992, 10 days
   Miguel Indurain, 1993, 14 days
   Miguel Indurain, 1994, 13 days
   Miguel Indurain, 1995, 13 days
8. Igor Gonzalez de Galdeano, 2002, 7 days
9. Oscar Pereiro, 2006, 5 days
   (+3 days after disqualification of Landis)
10. Alberto Contador, 2007, 4 days
11. Alejandro Valverde, 2008, 2 days
12. Carlos Sastre, 2008, 5 days
    Alberto Contador, 2009, 7 days

8

GREAT BRITAIN

1. Tom Simpson, 1962, 1 day
2. Chris Boardman, 1994, 3 days
3. Sean Yates, 1994, 1 day
   Chris Boardman, 1997, 1 day
   Chris Boardman, 1998, 2 days
4. David Millar, 2000, 3 days

5. Bradley Wiggins, 2012, 14 days
6. Christopher Froome, 2013, 14 days
   Christopher Froome, 2015, 16 days
7. Mark Cavendish, 2016, 1 day
   Christopher Froome, 2016, 14 days
8. Geraint Thomas, 2017, 4 days
   Christopher Froome, 2017, 15 days
   Geraint Thomas, 2018, 11 days

3

IRELAND

1. Seamus Elliott, 1963, 3½ days
2. Sean Kelly, 1983, 1 day
3. Stephen Roche, 1987, 3 days

7

AUSTRALIA

1. Phil Anderson, 1981, 1 day
   Phil Anderson, 1982, 9 days
2. Stuart O'Grady, 1998, 3 days
   Stuart O'Grady, 2001, 6 days
3. Bradley McGee, 2003, 3 days
4. Robbie McEwen, 2004, 1 day
5. Cadel Evans, 2008, 5 days
   Cadel Evans, 2010, 1 day
   Cadel Evans, 2011, 2 days
6. Simon Gerrans, 2013, 2 days
7. Rohan Dennis, 2015, 1 day

6

DENMARK

1. Kim Andersen, 1983, 6 days
   Kim Andersen, 1985, 4 days
2. Jörgen-Vagn Pedersen, 1986, 5 days
3. Rolf Sörensen, 1991, 4 days
4. Bjarne Riis, 1995, 1 day
   Bjarne Riis, 1996, 13 days
5. Bo Hamburger, 1998, 1 day
6. Michael Rasmussen, 2007, 9 days
   (excluded for lack of ethics)

2

CANADA

1. Alex Stieda, 1986, ½ day
2. Steve Bauer, 1988, 4½ days
   Steve Bauer, 1990, 8 days

1

USA

Greg LeMond, 1986, 7 days
Greg LeMond, 1989, 8 days
Greg LeMond, 1990, 2 days
Greg LeMond, 1991, 4½ days

1

POLAND

Lech Piasecki, 1987, 1 day

1

PORTUGAL

Acacio Da Silva, 1989, 3 days

1

RUSSIA

Evgueni Berzin, 1996, 2 days

1

ESTONIA

Jaan Kirsipuu, 1999, 6 days

2

COLOMBIA

1. Victor-Hugo Peña, 2003, 3 days
2. Fernando Gaviria, 2018, 1 day

1

NORWAY

Thor Hushovd, 2004, 1 day
Thor Hushovd, 2006, 2 days
Thor Hushovd, 2011, 7 days

1

UKRAINE

Serguei Honchar, 2006, 3 days

1

SOUTH AFRICA

Daryl Impey, 2013, 2 days

1

SLOVAKIA

Peter Sagan, 2016, 3 days
Peter Sagan, 2018, 1 day

MOST RECENT JERSEYS BY NATIONALITY

2018
Great Britain (Geraint Thomas)
Belgium (Greg Van Avermaet)
Slovakia (Peter Sagan)
Colombia (Fernando Gaviria)

2017
Italy (Fabio Aru)

2015
Australia (Rohan Dennis)
Switzerland (Fabian Cancellara)
Germany (Tony Martin)

2014
France (Tony Gallopin)

2013
South Africa (Daryl Impey)

2011
Norway (Thor Hushovd)

2010
Luxembourg (Andy Schleck)

2009
Spain (Alberto Contador)

2007
Denmark (Michael Rasmussen)

2006
Ukraine (Serguei Honchar)

1999
Estonia (Jaan Kirsipuu)

1996
Russia (Evgueni Berzin)

1991
USA (Greg LeMond)

1990
Canada (Steve Bauer)

1989
The Netherlands (Erik Breukink)
Portugal (Acacio Da Silva)

1987
Poland (Lech Piasecki)
Ireland (Stephen Roche)

1931
Austria (Max Bulla)

1919

NATIONAL FIRSTS

The first cyclist ever to wear the yellow jersey was a Frenchman, Eugène Christophe. Since then, riders from 23 other country have followed suit. Here are the first from each nation.

1919
FIRMIN LAMBOT
BELGIUM

1923
OTTAVIO BOTTECCHIA
ITALY

1927
NICOLAS FRANTZ
LUXEMBOURG

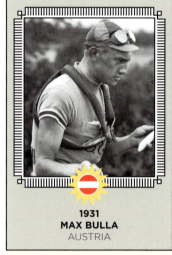

1931
MAX BULLA
AUSTRIA

It was cold and wet as the Tour de France crossed North-Eastern France, in a landscape decimated by the Great War. Eugène Christophe looked set to win this first Tour since the signing of the Armistice, but on the penultimate stage from Metz to Dunkirk he was hit by an all too familiar setback: his forks broke. It was deeply unlucky. Christophe took more than an hour to try to fix his bike, and then had to try to salvage his race leadership, which proved an impossible task. Instead it was Firmin Lambot who became, at 33 years old, the first yellow jersey on the podium in Paris, as well as the first Belgian to wear the jersey. Back in 1913 (another year when Christophe's forks broke) and in 1914, the Tour was won by the Belgian Philippe Thys, but that was before the yellow jersey had been introduced. Thys won the Tour again in 1920, and Lambot repeated his victory in 1922, becoming the oldest ever winner of the Tour at 36 years, 4 months and 9 days.

The 1923 Tour was just underway when former stonemason Ottavio Bottechia took the lead on Stage 2 from Le Havre to Cherbourg, winning the first yellow jersey for any Italian rider. Bottechia, 29 at the time, had joined the race as an unassuming team rider making his Tour debut, and his inexperience showed. He kept the jersey for two days, then lost it, before regaining it in the Pyrenees and then losing it four days later. Despite his evident climbing skills he had yet to learn how to conserve his energy and stay properly hydrated and fed during the race. But he still managed to finish in second place on the podium in Paris. In 1924 he took the yellow jersey from start to finish, and in 1925 he won again, showing that he had not only the talent, but also the technique and tactics to go with it. He died in mysterious circumstances in June 1927, while on a training ride.

The first ever Tour winner from Luxembourg was the brilliant François Faber in 1909. However, that was a full ten years before the yellow jersey got started. So it was only in 1927, 18 years later, that Nicolas Frantz took the first yellow jersey for Luxembourg. He seized his chance on 30 June 1927 at the end of Stage 11 (from Bayonne to Luchon), and from then he managed to keep the yellow all the way to Paris. The following year he was in yellow again, this time from the start of the race right through to the finish. The talented Frantz was a natural climber, but had many other strengths that made him a winner. Tour director Henri Desgrange put it down to Frantz's meticulous attention to detail, even down to bringing 22 sets of underwear with him on the Tour to avoid the risk of badly washed clothing provoking a saddle sore. And he hardly ever got a puncture. 'He spots the sharp stones and avoids them,' said Desgrange. 'He is always looking at the road in front.'

When Max Bulla became the first Austrian yellow jersey on the Tour de France, it was the result of a unique solo achievement: Bulla had entered the race in 1931 as an independent competitor, without the support of any team. Riding as a 'tourist racer' (as the independents were known) meant he had to set off ten minutes after the mass of team riders, and the 25-year-old Viennese rider launched into a sustained attack over almost half the entire 212km stage from Caen to Dinan. While Charles Pélissier was the first of a group of 30 team riders to cross the finishing line, Max Bulla arrived just seven minutes later. He had effectively taken a three-minute lead over Pélissier to earn him both the stage win and the yellow jersey. Sitting on the terrace of his hotel that evening, he said he was delighted to get his picture into the newspaper. 'Finally,' he said, 'cycling will get the recognition it deserves in my country.' He finished in 15th place, the best ranking of his career.

1932
KURT STOEPEL
GERMANY

For the 1932 Tour, Henri Desgranges introduced a new system of 'bonus seconds' for the first to arrive at the end of Stage 2. The stage winner would get four seconds deducted from their total time, the second placed rider would shed two seconds, and the third placed, one second. Three Belgian riders (Aerts, Demuysere and Sieronski) were first to finish and scooped up all the time bonuses, but squandered them the next day on the 300km route to Nantes. The race came alive in the final kilometre with 13 riders sprinting for the finish. The winner was the 24-year-old German Kurt Stoepel, who as well as winning the stage found himself leading the race and became the first German to wear the yellow jersey. He lost it the very next day to André Leducq in Bordeaux, who kept it right through to Paris. Stoepel dug in, however, and finished the Tour in second place. Leducq's lead, thanks to yet more time bonuses, was a formidable 24 minutes.

1936
PAUL EGLI
SWITZERLAND

'I can't quite believe I've actually got the yellow jersey,' the Swiss rider Paul Egli told *L'Auto* newspaper the day after his unexpected victory in the first stage of the 1936 Tour. 'If someone had told me in Paris that I was going to be taking first place in Lille, I would have punched them on the nose for making fun of me,' he added. Egli had worked hard for the jersey on that first stage, battling through torrential rain and taking on the French star rider Maurice Archambaud (who took back the jersey the next day). For most of the day, Egli had not even been in the lead, as he was unfamiliar with the route and was unsure of the distance remaining. 'I only began to think I could win when I got to Lille,' he said.

The atrocious weather also played its part: 'When the Lord opened those celestial floodgates, he answered my prayers. Rain and mud? Bring it on!' Egli vowed to defend the jersey, the first for any Swiss rider, but he was eventually forced to drop out of the race at the end of Stage 10 in Nice.

1951
WIM VAN EST
THE NETHERLANDS

Wim Van Est was a solid rider who won the Bordeaux–Paris in 1950, and came second in 1951. On Stage 12 of the Tour de France the same year, Van Est dug deep to take a comfortable race lead after a long ten-man breakaway near the start of the stage from Agen to Dax. The next day, proudly sporting the first yellow jersey worn by any Dutch rider, he tackled the Aubisque, digging in again on the ascent, and then tearing down the other side as a thunderstorm raged above. The result was three crashes, with the final one pitching Van Est into the bottom of a ravine. He was hauled out via a makeshift rope that his team manager put together using interlinked inner tubes. 'Miraculously, he saved his life,' wrote Tour director Jacques Goddet in his newspaper column the following day. 'And he left the shredded remains of his yellow jersey down by the rocks.'

1955
MIGUEL POBLET
SPAIN

A summer's evening in Dieppe: the sky was deep blue, the sea was calm, and popular Belgian singer Annie Cordy was warming up for the Tour's evening parade in the town centre. And then, for the first time in Tour history, a Spanish rider took the yellow jersey. During Stage 1 from Le Havre to Dieppe, Miguel Poblet had been part of a dozen riders in a breakaway group (that included Jean Robic and Wout Wagtmans) and then managed to win the final sprint finish in Dieppe. There was no need for a photo-finish (although the new camera equipment had just been installed) and the Catalan rider, 27 years old, was a popular winner. He was already a star of the six-day events, and *L'Equipe* journalist Pierre Chany described Poblet's win as 'pure class'. The next day Poblet kept his jersey when the Dutch won the team time trial, and three weeks later he won the final stage from Tours to Paris, again with a sprint. Between times, he even managed to take first place to the summit of the Tourmalet. Pure class indeed!

1963
SEAMUS ELLIOTT
IRELAND

It was cold and wet as Seamus Elliot approached the Roubaix velodrome, but he was oblivious to all that. As he pounded on, he was picturing his 16-month son Pascal, whose godfather, Jean Stablinski, had been World Champion the previous year. Stablinski was now a little distance behind Elliot on the road, having led him on the 150km breakaway that began in Jambes in Belgium and would shortly end in Roubaix. Six kilometres from the Roubaix velodrome, Stablinski had told Elliot to get going – and make his final solo attack to win the stage. So Elliot gave it everything over those final slippery kilometres, getting ever nearer to becoming the first Irishman to wear the yellow jersey. 'I had always dreamed of the yellow jersey,' said Elliot, a mechanic in Ireland who had moved to France in 1955. He felt he owed his jersey in part to Jacques Anquetil, his team leader on Saint-Raphaël-Gitanes, who was on his way to a fourth Tour victory. 'He chose me early in the season for the team, and yesterday, seeing that I was going well, he told me to get to the front of the peloton to go with the breakaway.' Nice work.

■ ■ ■

■■■

1962
TOM SIMPSON
GREAT BRITAIN

Nobody will forget his tragic death on the slopes of Mont Ventoux on 13 July 1967, nor the footage of him zigzagging his final few metres under the relentless sun, losing consciousness. But Simpson had made his mark on the Tour in a different way five years earlier, becoming the first British rider to wear the yellow jersey. It took place on Stage 12 of the 1962 Tour from Pau to Saint-Gaudens on 5 July. That evening, he celebrated his yellow jersey with tea and biscuits, posing for the cameras with a bowler hat and umbrella. A popular rider in the peloton, Simpson gained little recognition in Britain for his achievement. 'If it's raining in Wimbledon, I'll no doubt have the chance of seeing a few articles a bit longer than normal in the press,' he said. 'Otherwise, there's a risk this will go unnoticed.' In France, where he lived since the late 1950s, he got a good deal more attention.

Valenciennes to Roubaix. It was a hard day. Just after the start, he went to work to support his Coop-Mercier team leader Joop Zoetemelk as well as Jean-Louis Gauthier (yellow jersey since the previous evening). Andersen had been battling the whole day, moving up to the leading group to stay with the Belgian Rudy Matthys's breakaway, and taking second place in the stage and first place in the general classification. Andersen felt a little sorry to have deposed Gauthier – a good friend – but nobody was complaining. He kept the yellow jersey as far as Pau, and would be wearing it again two years later.

1986
GREG LEMOND
USA

Greg LeMond took the first yellow jersey for the USA on 20 July 1986 at the summit of Granon in the Alps. It was no big surprise. Ever since the previous year, with Bernard Hinault's pledge to help LeMond to win, the entire Tour was just waiting to see an American at the top of the general classification for the first time. Not that things were quite so simple. Hinault was in great shape, and in the Pyrenees showed that he was not yet ready to give way to LeMond. A few days later in the Alps the tension within the team was palpable, and LeMond moved up a gear, showing his unquestionable superiority over the five-times Tour winner on the ascent of Superbagnères. 'We've talked it through, and everything's settled,' said LeMond that evening. 'He's going to work for me.' The next day saw the iconic display of friendship between the two men at the Alpe d'Huez, arriving hand in hand, with LeMond knowing that his first Tour victory was assured.

1981
PHIL ANDERSON
AUSTRALIA

Lucien Van Impe was out in front, on the way to winning Stage 5 with the final climb up to Saint-Lary-Soulan. Meanwhile, Bernard Hinault, reigning World Champion, was aiming for the yellow jersey, except that he could not shake off Phil Anderson, the big, fun-loving Australian from Melbourne, who was following Hinault closely in the final 4km to Saint-Lary. Anderson, just 23 years old, took third place in the stage, and snapped up the race leadership with a margin of just 17 seconds, thus becoming the first Australian to wear the yellow jersey. Brimming with confidence, Anderson was convinced he could win the yellow, just as much as he was sure he could speak some broken French to express

delight at his achievement. The day's racing had been a hard struggle for Anderson, and the following day he gave up the yellow to Hinault, but nonetheless managed to stay in touch in subsequent stages to take a worthy tenth place in Paris. He would wear the yellow jersey for nine more days the following year.

1983
KIM ANDERSEN
DENMARK

'Not bad, huh?' gasped an exhausted Kim Anderson as he struggled to get his breath back, his face covered in dust from the rough tracks on the road to Roubaix. The Dane had just taken the yellow jersey, the first ever for a Danish rider, at the end of Stage 3 from

1986
ALEX STIEDA
CANADA

Alex Stieda was racing with the number 210 on his back – the very last number attributed for the 1986 Tour de France. But the last, as they say, shall be first, and at midday on 5 July, Stieda found himself as race leader. This was the first ever yellow jersey for a Canadian, and Stieda was incredulous. 'I wanted to do the sprint at Levallois, and that was it. And as nobody was following, I just carried on hard, without thinking about the rest.' Stieda went solo for 52km before being joined by a chasing group. Pol Verschuere, the Belgian who would win the stage later, shouted at Stieda 'Get going! You've got the yellow jersey!' and Stieda took off, consolidating his lead with time bonuses. In the afternoon, the former Vancouver medical student ran out of juice, dropping off the back of his 7-Eleven team 10km from the end of the time trial. He lost the yellow jersey and was close to elimination, but that morning of 5 July would stay with him forever.

**1987
LECH PIASECKI**
POLAND

Just as Bernard Hinault retired, the Tour began to spread further beyond the borders of France. The 1987 Tour departed from Berlin on 1 July, even while the Berlin Wall was still intact. Polish rider Lech Piasecki got off to a lightning start to finish in second place behind Jelle Jijdam, and the following morning he took his chance with an eight-man breakaway, giving him the yellow jersey by lunchtime, the first ever for a Polish rider. Short and stocky and sporting a dark moustache, Piasecki looked back on form after being badly injured the previous year in the Coors Classic. That afternoon he had to defend the jersey in the team time trial, and happily for him, his Del Tongo team made the grade, allowing the Pole to keep the jersey for the night. A devout Catholic, Piasecki had an audience with the Pope earlier that year, but no amount of divine intervention would help him keep the jersey for a further day, and he gave it up in Stuttgart the following evening.

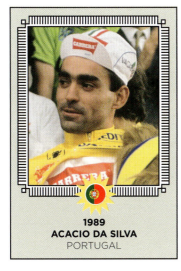

**1989
ACACIO DA SILVA**
PORTUGAL

Acacio Da Silva had it all figured out. The 1989 Tour would be starting from Luxembourg, a country that he knew well, even though he currently lived in Switzerland and was cycling for Carrera, an Italian team. Da Silva had lived in Luxembourg since he was six, and that was where he began learning to ride competitively, along with his two older brothers. By lucky coincidence, the first half-stage of the 1989 Tour (on 2 July) would take the peloton to Dudelange, where his family still lived. Surely this would be the ideal place to take the yellow jersey? Da Silva had form: he had already worn the pink jersey in the Giro the previous month, and had been a stage winner in the Tour de France in 1987 and 1988. So on the 2 July, he made his breakaway, opening up enough of a gap to stop and greet his family, and then to push on to win both the stage and the yellow jersey, the first for a Portuguese rider. He managed to keep it for three days.

**1996
EVGUENI BERZIN**
RUSSIA

One of the most skilful 'followers' of his generation, Evgeni Berzin took the Giro in 1994 and was thus the only rider to have beaten the great Miguel Indurain in a Grand Tour. Berzin did not finish the 1995 Tour, but looked promising for 1996. In the prologue, and wearing number 51, he was just three seconds away from the yellow jersey, narrowly beaten by Alex Zülle and Chris Boardman. A week later as the Tour climbed to Les Arcs and Indurain's campaign fell apart, Berzin finally took the yellow jersey, winning by just 0.16 seconds. He kept it the next day, winning the Val d'Isère time trial ahead of the likes of Riis and Olano, but would not get much further, mainly because the Gewiss team could not provide the solid support that he needed. The next day, on the shortened (because of snow) stage to Sestrières, Bjarne Riis took over. Berzin finished in 20th place in Paris, and would not impress again on the Tour de France.

**1999
JAAN KIRSIPUU**
ESTONIA

The Tour had only just begun, and the first week was shaping up to be a battle of the sprinters. Jaan Kirsipuu, a 30-year-old Estonian based in France for the last decade, had just won his first ever Tour stage and was just 16 seconds behind race leader Lance Armstrong. Kirsipuu began to run through possible scenarios for the next day. How about becoming the first Estonian to take the yellow jersey? So on 5 July 1999, a determined Kirsipuu proved to be untouchable on the road to Saint-Nazaire. When a large part of the peloton crashed on the slimy stones of the tidal Passage du Gois, Kirsipuu stayed at the front and picked up a string of bonuses in the intermediate sprints. The yellow jersey was his, and the timing was welcome: his team needed a new sponsor, and was about to get six full days of yellow jersey glory.

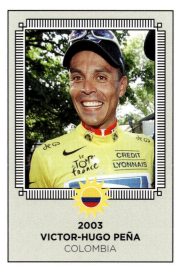

**2003
VICTOR-HUGO PEÑA**
COLOMBIA

As they crossed the finish line, Lance Armstrong and his team were punching the air. For the first time, the USPS team had just won a team time trial, tasting victory at the end of the hot and sun-drenched route from Joinville to Saint-Dizier. What's more, USPS rider Victor-Hugo Peña had just won the yellow jersey, the first for a Colombian. Peña was the son of a talented track cyclist, and was a successful competitive swimmer before switching to cycling, training at the velodrome situated alongside the public swimming pool in Santander, north of Bogota. Winning the yellow jersey was something that his childhood heroes (the Colombian riders Lucho Herrera and Fabio Parra) had never managed to achieve, and he dedicated his jersey to Herrera and kept it for three days. In the Alps, however he lost the yellow to Virenque, and Peña resumed his role in support of Armstrong.

■ ■ ■

...

2004
THOR HUSHOVD
NORWAY

2006
SERGUEÏ HONCHAR
UKRAINE

Serhiy Honchar remains the first Ukrainian to wear the yellow jersey, but his achievement is tarnished by doping offences that came to light the following year. He took the yellow on 8 July 2006 at the end of the time trial from Saint-Grégoire to Rennes, and his T-Mobile team perhaps breathed a sigh of relief: here, at last, was some good news after the devastation of losing their leader, Jan Ullrich, excluded from the race following a blood doping scandal. 'I had been waiting for this moment for a long time,' said Honchar. 'Despite being 36, I still feel young.' Honchar also won the Stage 19 individual time trial from Le Creusot to Montceau-les-Mines on the penultimate day. Floyd Landis won in Paris, but was caught up in the doping scandal a few days later. Honchar himself had to wait a few months more before T-Mobile

When Thor Hushovd first saw the route for the 2004 Tour during the preceding winter, he realized exactly what he had to do: a good prologue performance, plenty of bonus seconds from the intermediate sprints, and the yellow jersey could be his, the first one ever for a Norwegian rider. And that is exactly what he did, arriving on 5 July in second place on Stage 2 from Charleroi to Namur behind Robbie McEwen. Second place was enough to take the jersey, though, and Hushovd's family were there to congratulate him. 'Today, I have become a great cyclist,' said Hushovd, a man who discovered cycle racing relatively late in life. 'This jersey is going to change my life.' He wasn't so wrong, and he would wear the yellow again in 2006 and in 2011.

suspended him for irregularities in his blood samples, and subsequently terminated his contract.

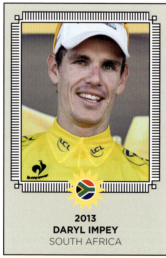

2013
DARYL IMPEY
SOUTH AFRICA

How's this for a tale of generosity? Australian rider Simon Gerrans won the yellow jersey with Orica-GreenEDGE in the team time trial around Nice, narrowly ahead of his team mate Daryl Impey. The next day, on the road to Marseille, Gerrans decided to let Impey have his turn in yellow too. So two days later, on 4 July, as Matthew Goss launched into his sprint to the finish line in Montpellier, Gerrans made sure that Impey was a few places in front, and thus assured of becoming the first African rider to wear the yellow jersey. 'I had so much enjoyed having the jersey, and Daryl had

worked so hard for me during the Tour that I wanted him to experience that too,' Gerrans explained later. 'I had my stage victory, my yellow jersey, my moment of glory. It was his turn. One or two more days in yellow would change nothing for me. But it could change everything for him.' Impey kept the yellow for two further days, and finished the race in Paris in 74th place.

2016
PETER SAGAN
SLOVAKIA

Sagan was already a big name on the Tour with a number of stage wins under his belt. When he won his fifth Tour stage (in Cherbourg in the early part of the 2016 Tour) there was an added twist: he had just become the first Slovakian to take the yellow jersey. Despite the sense of occasion, he admitted to being a bit 'bored' by the day's racing. 'For the people watching, it is only in the last 20 or 30km that things become interesting. Before, it's just a journey from A to B.' The final part of the race at least allowed him to fine-tune his sprint, though he thought there were still some of the breakaway riders ahead of him: 'I didn't realize I was going to win the stage.' Let alone the yellow jersey, which the World Champion clearly enjoyed getting. 'If I lose it tomorrow, or the day after, I'll still have the green jersey, which is the prize I want in Paris. And then, if not, I'll get the rainbow jersey. So I've got a choice, which is not too bad, is it?' That year, he kept the yellow for three days, won the green jersey in Paris, and maintained his World Champion title. Sagan was on a roll.

THE FIRST FOR ALL TIME!

Eugène Christophe (pictured here in 1925 on the Parc des Princes velodrome) goes down in history as the first man ever to wear the yellow jersey.

THE 266 YELLOW JERSEYS

IN ALPHABETICAL ORDER

ADRIAENSSENS JAN
(BEL, 1956–1960)

AERTS JEAN
(BEL, 1932)

AIMAR LUCIEN
(FRA, 1966)

ALAVOINE JEAN
(FRA, 1922)

ALTIG RUDI
(GER, 1962, 1964, 1966, 1969)

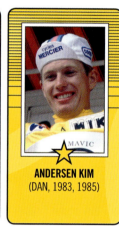

ANDERSEN KIM
(DAN, 1983, 1985)

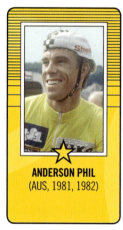

ANDERSON PHIL
(AUS, 1981, 1982)

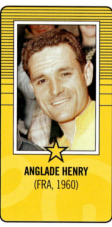

ANGLADE HENRY
(FRA, 1960)

ANQUETIL JACQUES
(FRA, 1957, 1961, 1962, 1963, 1964)

ARCHAMBAUD MAURICE
(FRA, 1933, 1936)

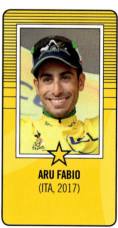

ARU FABIO
(ITA, 2017)

BAHAMONTES FEDERICO
(ESP, 1959, 1963)

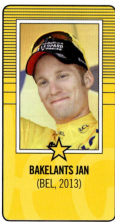

BAKELANTS JAN
(BEL, 2013)

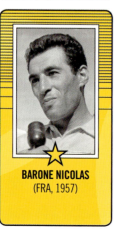

BARONE NICOLAS
(FRA, 1957)

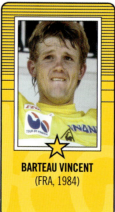

BARTALI GINO
(ITA, 1937, 1938, 1948, 1949)

BARTEAU VINCENT
(FRA, 1984)

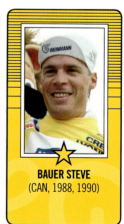

BAUER STEVE
(CAN, 1988, 1990)

BAUTZ ERICH
(GER, 1937)

BAUVIN GILBERT
(FRA, 1951,
1954, 1958)

BELLENGER ROMAIN
(FRA, 1923)

BENOÎT ADELIN
(BEL, 1925)

BERNARD JEAN-FRANÇOIS
(FRA, 1987)

BERNAUDEAU JEAN-RENÉ
(FRA, 1979)

BERTIN YVON
(FRA, 1980)

BERTOGLIATI RUBENS
(SUI, 2002)

BERZIN EVGUENI
(RUS, 1996)

BIAGIONI SERAFINO
(ITA, 1951)

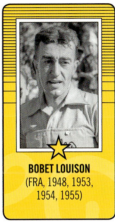
BOARDMAN CHRIS
(GBR, 1994,
1997, 1998)

BOBET LOUISON
(FRA, 1948, 1953,
1954, 1955)

BOONEN TOM
(BEL, 2006)

BONTEMPI GUIDO
(ITA, 1988)

BOSSIS JACQUES
(FRA, 1978)

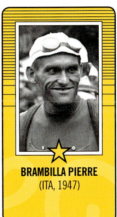
BOTTECCHIA OTTAVIO
(ITA, 1923,
1924, 1925)

BRAMBILLA PIERRE
(ITA, 1947)

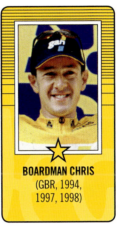
BREUKINK ERIK
(NED, 1989)

BRUYÈRE JOSEPH
(BEL, 1974, 1978)

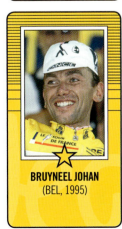
BRUYNEEL JOHAN
(BEL, 1995)

BULLA MAX
(GER, 1931)

BUYSSE JULES
(BEL, 1926)

BUYSSE LUCIEN
(BEL, 1926)

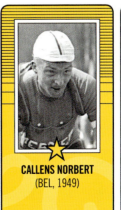
CALLENS NORBERT
(BEL, 1949)

CANCELLARA FABIAN
(SUI, 2004, 2007,
2009, 2010, 2012, 2015)

210

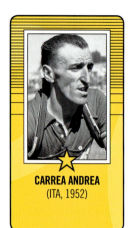
CARREA ANDREA
(ITA, 1952)

CATIEAU JOSÉ
(FRA, 1973)

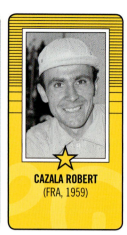
CAVENDISH MARK
(GBR, 2016)

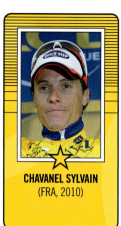
CAZALA ROBERT
(FRA, 1959)

CHAVANEL SYLVAIN
(FRA, 2010)

CHIAPPUCCI CLAUDIO
(ITA, 1990)

CHRISTOPHE EUGÈNE
(FRA, 1919, 1922)

CIPOLLINI MARIO
(ITA, 1993, 1997)

CONTADOR ALBERTO
(ESP, 2007, 2009)

COPPI FAUSTO
(ITA, 1949, 1952)

DARRIGADE ANDRÉ
(FRA, 1956, 1957, 1958,
1959, 1961, 1962)

DA SILVA ACACIO
(POR, 1989)

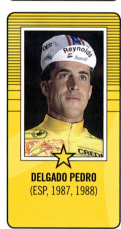
DELGADO PEDRO
(ESP, 1987, 1988)

DELISLE RAYMOND
(FRA, 1976)

DENNIS ROHAN
(AUS, 2015)

DE PRÀ TOMMASO
(ITA, 1966)

DESBIENS LAURENT
(FRA, 1998)

DESMET GILBERT
(BEL, 1956, 1963)

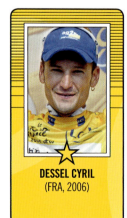
DESSEL CYRIL
(FRA, 2006)

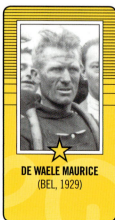
DE WAELE MAURICE
(BEL, 1929)

DIEDERICH JEAN
(LUX, 1951)

DI PACO RAFFAELE
(ITA, 1931)

DOSSCHE AIMÉ
(BEL, 1929)

DURAND JACKY
(FRA, 1995)

DUSSAULT MARCEL
(FRA, 1949)

EGLI PAUL
(SUI, 1936)

ELLI ALBERTO
(ITA, 2000)

ELLIOTT SEAMUS
(IRL, 1963)

ENGELS JAN
(BEL, 1948)

ERRANDONEA JOSÉ-MARIA
(ESP, 1967)

EVANS CADEL
(AUS, 2008, 2010, 2011)

FAVERO VITO
(ITA, 1958)

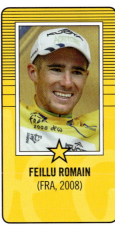
FEILLU ROMAIN
(FRA, 2008)

FIGNON LAURENT
(FRA, 1983, 1984, 1989)

FONTAN VICTOR
(FRA, 1929)

FONTENAY JEAN
(FRA, 1939)

FORESTIER JEAN
(FRA, 1957)

FOURNIER AMÉDÉE
(FRA, 1939)

FRANTZ NICOLAS
(LUX, 1927, 1928, 1929)

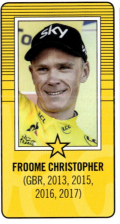
FROOME CHRISTOPHER
(GBR, 2013, 2015, 2016, 2017)

GAIGNE DOMINIQUE
(FRA, 1986)

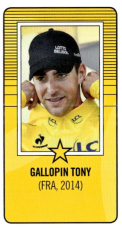
GALLOPIN TONY
(FRA, 2014)

GAUL CHARLY
(LUX, 1958)

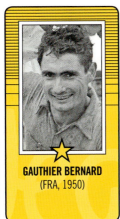
GAUTHIER BERNARD
(FRA, 1950)

GAUTHIER JEAN-LOUIS
(FRA, 1983)

GAVIRIA FERNANDO
(COL, 2018)

GAYANT MARTIAL
(FRA, 1987)

GELDERMANS ALBERTUS
(NED, 1962)

GÉMINIANI RAPHAËL
(FRA, 1958)

GENÊT JEAN-PIERRE
(FRA, 1968)

GERDEMANN LINUS
(GER, 2007)

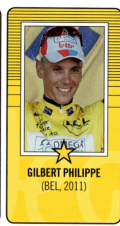

GERRANS SIMON
(AUS, 2013)

GILBERT PHILIPPE
(BEL, 2011)

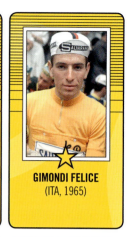

GIMONDI FELICE
(ITA, 1965)

GOLDSCHMIT JEAN
(LUX, 1950)

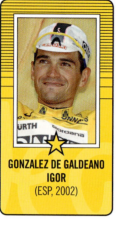

GONZALEZ DE GALDEANO IGOR
(ESP, 2002)

GOTTI IVAN
(ITA, 1995)

GROSSKOST CHARLY
(FRA, 1968)

GROUSSARD GEORGES
(FRA, 1964)

GROUSSARD JOSEPH
(FRA, 1960)

GUERRA LEARCO
(ITA, 1930)

GUIMARD CYRILLE
(FRA, 1972)

HAMBURGER BO
(DAN, 1998)

HAMERLINCK ALFRED
(BEL, 1931)

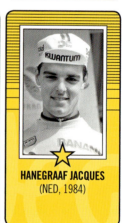

HANEGRAAF JACQUES
(NED, 1984)

HASSENFORDER ROGER
(FRA, 1953)

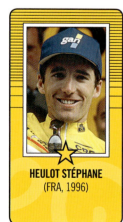

HEULOT STÉPHANE
(FRA, 1996)

HEUSGHEM HECTOR
(BEL, 1922)

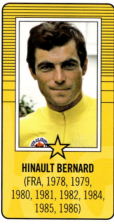

HINAULT BERNARD
(FRA, 1978, 1979, 1980, 1981, 1982, 1984, 1985, 1986)

HOEVENAARS JOS
(BEL, 1958, 1959)

HONCHAR SERGUEÏ
(UKR, 2006)

HUSHOVD THOR
(NOR, 2004, 2006, 2011)

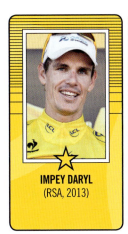

IMPEY DARYL
(RSA, 2013)

INDURAIN MIGUEL
(ESP, 1991, 1992, 1993,
1994, 1995)

JACQUINOT ROBERT
(FRA, 1922, 1923)

JALABERT LAURENT
(FRA, 1995, 2000)

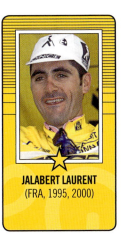

JANSSEN JAN
(NED, 1966, 1968)

KARSTENS GERBEN
(NED, 1974)

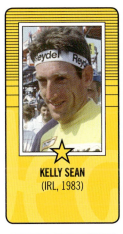

KELLY SEAN
(IRL, 1983)

KINT MARCEL
(BEL, 1937)

KIRCHEN KIM
(LUX, 2008)

KIRSIPUU JAAN
(EST, 1999)

KITTEL MARCEL
(GER,, 2013, 2014)

KNETEMANN GERRIE
(NED, 1978, 1979,
1980, 1981)

KOBLET HUGO
(SUI, 1951)

KÜBLER FERDI
(SUI, 1947, 1950)

KUNDE KARL-HEINZ
(GER, 1966)

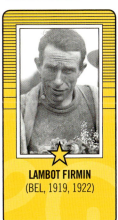

LAMBOT FIRMIN
(BEL, 1919, 1922)

LAMBRECHT ROGER
(BEL, 1948, 1949)

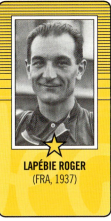

LAPÉBIE ROGER
(FRA, 1937)

LAUREDI NELLO
(FRA, 1952)

LEBAUBE JEAN-CLAUDE
(FRA, 1966)

LEBLANC LUC
(FRA, 1991)

LE CALVEZ LÉON
(FRA, 1931)

LE DROGO FERDINAND
(FRA, 1927)

LEDUCQ ANDRÉ
(FRA, 1929, 1930,
1932, 1938)

214

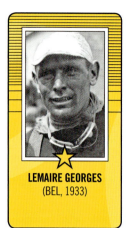
LEMAIRE GEORGES
(BEL, 1933)

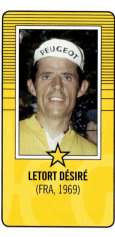
LEMOND GREG
(USA, 1986, 1989, 1990, 1991)

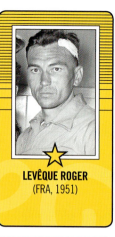
LETORT DÉSIRÉ
(FRA, 1969)

LEVÊQUE ROGER
(FRA, 1951)

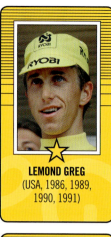
LINO PASCAL
(FRA, 1992)

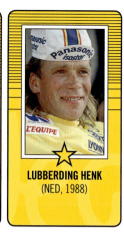
LUBBERDING HENK
(NED, 1988)

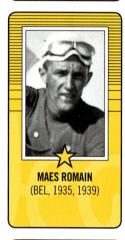
MAES ROMAIN
(BEL, 1935, 1939)

MAES SYLVÈRE
(BEL, 1936, 1937, 1939)

MAECHLER ERICH
(SUI, 1987)

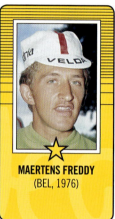
MAERTENS FREDDY
(BEL, 1976)

MAGNE ANTONIN
(FRA, 1931, 1934)

MAGNI FIORENZO
(ITA, 1949, 1950, 1952)

MAHÉ FRANÇOIS
(FRA, 1953)

MAJÉRUS JEAN
(LUX, 1937, 1938)

MALLÉJAC JEAN
(FRA, 1953)

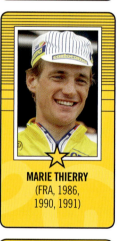
MARIE THIERRY
(FRA, 1986, 1990, 1991)

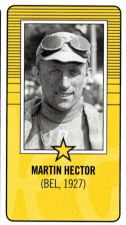
MARINELLI JACQUES
(FRA, 1949)

MARTIN HECTOR
(BEL, 1927)

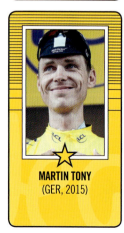
MARTIN TONY
(GER, 2015)

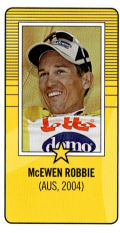
McEWEN ROBBIE
(AUS, 2004)

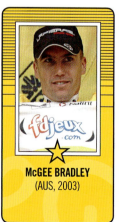
McGEE BRADLEY
(AUS, 2003)

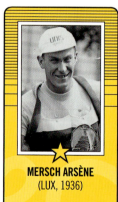
MERCKX EDDY
(BEL, 1969, 1970, 1971, 1972, 1974, 1975)

MERSCH ARSÈNE
(LUX, 1936)

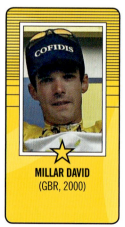
MILLAR DAVID
(GBR, 2000)

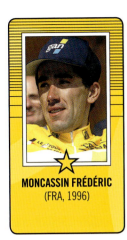

MONCASSIN FRÉDÉRIC
(FRA, 1996)

MOREAU CHRISTOPHE
(FRA, 2001)

MOSER FRANCESCO
(ITA, 1975)

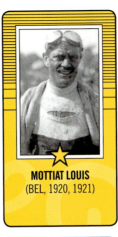

MOTTIAT LOUIS
(BEL, 1920, 1921)

MOTTET CHARLY
(FRA, 1987)

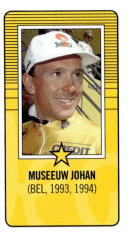

MUSEEUW JOHAN
(BEL, 1993, 1994)

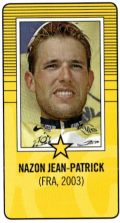

NAZON JEAN-PATRICK
(FRA, 2003)

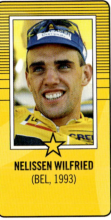

NELISSEN WILFRIED
(BEL, 1993)

NENCINI GASTONE
(ITA, 1960)

NIBALI VINCENZO
(ITA, 2014)

NIJDAM JELLE
(NED, 1987, 1988)

NOCENTINI RINALDO
(ITA, 2009)

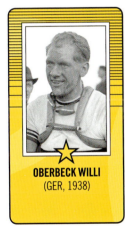

OBERBECK WILLI
(GER, 1938)

OCAÑA LUIS
(ESP, 1971, 1973)

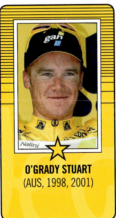

O'GRADY STUART
(AUS, 1998, 2001)

PANTANI MARCO
(ITA, 1998)

PAUWELS EDDY
(BEL, 1959, 1963)

PEDERSEN JÖRGEN-VAGN
(DAN, 1986)

PEETERS LUDO
(BEL, 1982, 1984)

PÉLISSIER CHARLES
(FRA, 1930, 1931)

PÉLISSIER FRANCIS
(FRA, 1927)

PÉLISSIER HENRI
(FRA, 1923)

PEÑA VICTOR-HUGO
(COL, 2003)

PENSEC RONAN
(FRA, 1990)

216

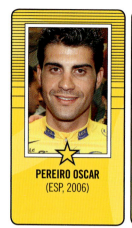 **PEREIRO OSCAR**
(ESP, 2006)

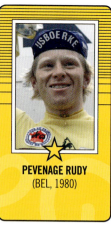 **PEVENAGE RUDY**
(BEL, 1980)

 **PIASECKI LECH**
(POL, 1987)

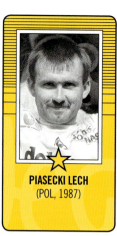 **PINGEON ROGER**
(FRA, 1967)

 **PLANCKAERT JOSEF**
(BEL, 1962)

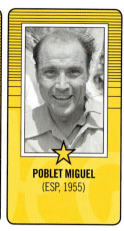 **POBLET MIGUEL**
(ESP, 1955)

 **POLIDORI GIANCARLO**
(ITA, 1967)

 **PRIVAT RENÉ**
(FRA, 1957)

 **RAAS JAN**
(NED, 1978)

 **RASMUSSEN MICHAEL**
(DAN, 2007)

 **REBRY GASTON**
(BEL, 1929)

 **RIIS BJARNE**
(DAN, 1995, 1996)

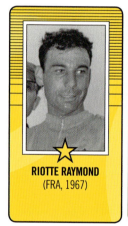 **RIOTTE RAYMOND**
(FRA, 1967)

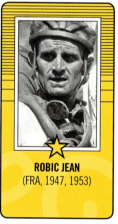 **ROBIC JEAN**
(FRA, 1947, 1953)

 **ROCHE STEPHEN**
(IRL, 1987)

 **ROLLAND ANTONIN**
(FRA, 1955)

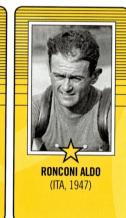 **RONCONI ALDO**
(ITA, 1947)

 **ROSSI GIOVANNI**
(SUI, 1951)

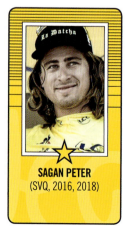 **SAGAN PETER**
(SVQ, 2016, 2018)

 **SAN MIGUEL GREGORIO**
(ESP, 1968)

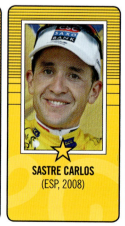 **SASTRE CARLOS**
(ESP, 2008)

 **SCHAER FRITZ**
(SUI, 1953)

 **SCHEPENS JULIEN**
(BEL, 1960)

 **SCHLECK ANDY**
(LUX, 2010, 2011)

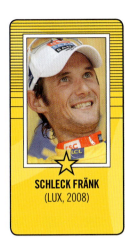

SCHLECK FRÄNK
(LUX, 2008)

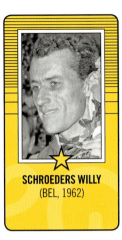

SCHROEDERS WILLY
(BEL, 1962)

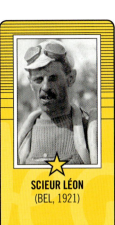

SCIEUR LÉON
(BEL, 1921)

SELS EDWARD
(BEL, 1964)

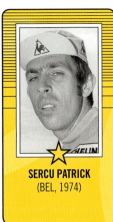

SERCU PATRICK
(BEL, 1974)

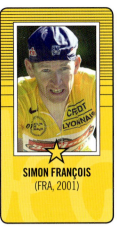

SIMON FRANÇOIS
(FRA, 2001)

SIMON PASCAL
(FRA, 1983)

SIMPSON TOM
(GBR, 1962)

SÖRENSEN ROLF
(DAN, 1991)

SPEICHER GEORGES
(FRA, 1933, 1934)

SPRUYT JOSEPH
(BEL, 1967)

STEVENS JULIEN
(BEL, 1969)

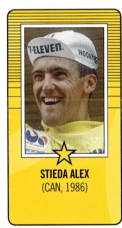

STIEDA ALEX
(CAN, 1986)

STOEPEL KURT
(GER, 1932)

TEIRLINCK WILLY
(BEL, 1973)

THALER KLAUS-PETER
(GER, 1978)

THÉVENET BERNARD
(FRA, 1975, 1977)

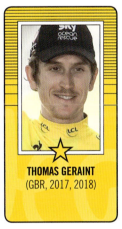

THOMAS GERAINT
(GBR, 2017, 2018)

THURAU DIETRICH
(GER, 1977)

THYS PHILIPPE
(BEL, 1920)

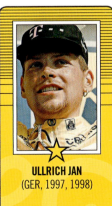

ULLRICH JAN
(GER, 1997, 1998)

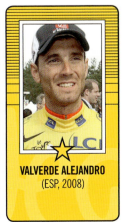

VALVERDE ALEJANDRO
(ESP, 2008)

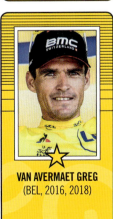

VAN AVERMAET GREG
(BEL, 2016, 2018)

VAN DE KERCKHOVE BERNARD
(BEL, 1964, 1965)

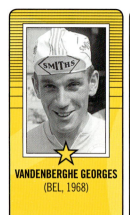

VANDENBERGHE GEORGES
(BEL, 1968)

VANDERAERDEN ERIC
(BEL, 1983, 1985)

VAN DER POEL ADRI
(HOL, 1984)

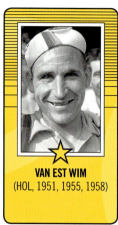

VAN DER VELDE JOHAN
(HOL, 1986)

VAN EST WIM
(HOL, 1951, 1955, 1958)

VAN IMPE LUCIEN
(BEL, 1976)

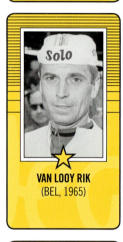

VAN LOOY RIK
(BEL, 1965)

VAN NESTE WILLY
(BEL, 1967)

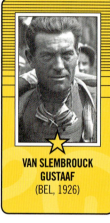

VAN SLEMBROUCK GUSTAAF
(BEL, 1926)

VAN SPRINGEL HERMAN
(BEL, 1968, 1973)

VAN STEENBERGEN RIK
(BEL, 1952)

VAN VLIET TEUN
(HOL, 1988)

VANZELLA FLAVIO
(ITA, 1994)

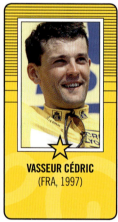

VASSEUR CÉDRIC
(FRA, 1997)

VERMEULIN MICHEL
(FRA, 1959)

VERVAECKE FÉLICIEN
(BEL, 1938)

VIETTO RENÉ
(FRA, 1939, 1947)

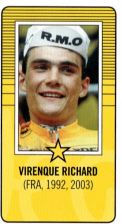

VIRENQUE RICHARD
(FRA, 1992, 2003)

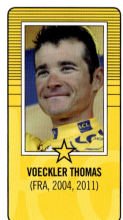

VOECKLER THOMAS
(FRA, 2004, 2011)

VOIGT JENS
(GER, 2001, 2005)

VOORTING GERRIT
(NED, 1956, 1958)

WAGTMANS MARINUS
(HOL, 1971)

WAGTMANS WOUT
(HOL, 1954, 1955, 1956)

WALKOWIAK ROGER
(FRA, 1956)

WAUTERS MARC
(BEL, 2001)

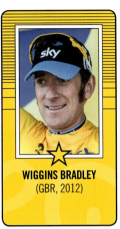

WIGGINS BRADLEY
(GBR, 2012)

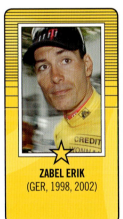

WOLFSHOHL ROLF
(GER, 1968)

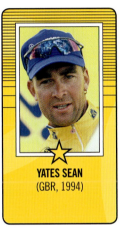

YATES SEAN
(GBR, 1994)

ZABEL ERIK
(GER, 1998, 2002)

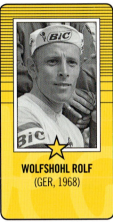

ZILIOLI ITALO
(ITA, 1970)

ZOETEMELK JOOP
(NED, 1971, 1973,
1978, 1979, 1980)

ZÜLLE ALEX
(SUI, 1992, 1996)

WINNERS OF THE TOUR DE FRANCE

(since the creation of the yellow jersey)

1919 : Firmin Lambot (BEL)

1920 : Philippe Thys (BEL)
1921 : Léon Scieur (BEL)
1922 : Firmin Lambot (BEL)
1923 : Henri Pélissier (FRA)
1924 : Ottavio Bottechia (ITA)
1925 : Ottavio Bottechia (ITA)
1926 : Lucien Buysse (BEL)
1927 : Nicolas Frantz (LUX)
1928 : Nicolas Frantz (LUX)
1929 : Maurice De Waele (BEL)

1930 : André Leducq (FRA)
1931 : Antonin Magne (FRA)
1932 : André Leducq (FRA)
1933 : Georges Speicher (FRA)
1934 : Antonin Magne (FRA)
1935 : Romain Maes (BEL)
1936 : Sylvère Maes (BEL)
1937 : Roger Lapébie (FRA)
1938 : Gino Bartali (ITA)
1939 : Sylvère Maes (BEL)

1947 : Jean Robic (FRA)
1948 : Gino Bartali (ITA)
1949 : Fausto Coppi (ITA)

1950 : Ferdi Kübler (SUI)
1951 : Hugo Koblet (SUI)
1952 : Fausto Coppi (ITA)
1953 : Louison Bobet (FRA)
1954 : Louison Bobet (FRA)
1955 : Louison Bobet (FRA)
1956 : Roger Walkowiak (FRA)
1957 : Jacques Anquetil (FRA)
1958 : Charly Gaul (LUX)
1959 : Federico Bahamontes
(ESP)

1960 : Gastone Nencini (ITA)
1961 : Jacques Anquetil (FRA)

1962 : Jacques Anquetil (FRA)
1963 : Jacques Anquetil (FRA)
1964 : Jacques Anquetil (FRA)
1965 : Felice Gimondi (ITA)
1966 : Lucien Aimar (FRA)
1967 : Roger Pingeon (FRA)
1968 : Jan Janssen (NED)
1969 : Eddy Merckx (BEL)

1970 : Eddy Merckx (BEL)
1971 : Eddy Merckx (BEL)
1972 : Eddy Merckx (BEL)
1973 : Luis Ocaña (ESP)
1974 : Eddy Merckx (BEL)
1975 : Bernard Thévenet (FRA)
1976 : Lucien Van Impe (BEL)
1977 : Bernard Thévenet (FRA)
1978 : Bernard Hinault (FRA)
1979 : Bernard Hinault (FRA)

1980 : Joop Zoetemelk (NED)
1981 : Bernard Hinault (FRA)
1982 : Bernard Hinault (FRA)
1983 : Laurent Fignon (FRA)
1984 : Laurent Fignon (FRA)
1985 : Bernard Hinault (FRA)
1986 : Greg LeMond (USA)
1987 : Stephen Roche (IRL)
1988 : Pedro Delgado (ESP)
1989 : Greg LeMond (USA)

1990 : Greg LeMond (USA)
1991 : Miguel Indurain (ESP)
1992 : Miguel Indurain (ESP)
1993 : Miguel Indurain (ESP)
1994 : Miguel Indurain (ESP)
1995 : Miguel Indurain (ESP)
1996 : Bjarne Riis (DAN)
1997 : Jan Ullrich (GER)
1998 : Marco Pantani (ITA)

1999–2005 : No designated
winner
2006 : Oscar Pereiro (ESP)
2007 : Alberto Contador (ESP)
2008 : Carlos Sastre (ESP)
2009 : Alberto Contador (ESP)

2010 : Andy Schleck (LUX)
2011 : Cadel Evans (AUS)
2012 : Bradley Wiggins (GBR)
2013 : Christopher Froome (GBR)
2014 : Vincenzo Nibali (ITA)
2015 : Christopher Froome (GBR)
2016 : Christopher Froome (GBR)
2017 : Christopher Froome (GBR)
2018 : Geraint Thomas (GBR)

AND BEFORE THE YELLOW JERSEY...

1903 : Maurice Garin (FRA)
1904 : Henri Cornet (FRA)
1905 : Louis Trousselier (FRA)
1906 : René Pottier (FRA)
1907 : Lucien Petit-Breton (FRA)
1908 : Lucien Petit-Breton (FRA)
1909 : François Faber (LUX)
1910 : Octave Lapize (FRA)
1911 : Gustave Garrigou (FRA)
1912 : Odile Defraye (BEL)
1913 : Philippe Thys (BEL)
1914 : Philippe Thys (BEL)

A forest ride: Tour de France 2018, Stage 13 from Bourg d'Oisans to Valence.

WHO WORE IT WHEN? COMPLETE DAY-BY-DAY LISTINGS FOR EVERY TOUR

From Eugène Christophe to Geraint Thomas, they have all helped to build the legend that is the Tour de France.

1919
Eugène Christophe (FRA), 3 days ; Firmin Lambot (BEL), 2 days. Before the yellow jersey was introduced, the race leadership was with Jean Rossius (BEL, 1 day), then Henri Pélissier (FRA, 2 days) and Eugène Christophe (FRA, 7 days).

1920
Louis Mottiat (BEL), 1 day ; Philippe Thys (BEL), 14 days

1921
Louis Mottiat (BEL), 1 day ; Léon Scieur (BEL), 14 days.

1922
Robert Jacquinot (FRA), 3 days ; Eugène Christophe (FRA), 3 days ; Jean Alavoine (FRA), 5 days ; Hector Heusghem (BEL), 1 day ; Firmin Lambot (BEL), 3 days

1923
Robert Jacquinot (FRA), 1 day ; Ottavio Bottecchia (ITA), 2 days ; Romain Bellenger (FRA), 2 days ; Ottavio Bottecchia (ITA), 4 days ; Henri Pélissier (FRA), 6 days.

1924
Ottavio Bottecchia (ITA), 15 days

1925
Ottavio Bottecchia (ITA), 2 days ; Adelin Benoît (BEL), 4 days ; Ottavio Bottecchia (ITA), 1 day ; Adelin Benoît (BEL), 1 day ; Ottavio Bottecchia (ITA), 10 days.

1926
Jules Buysse (BEL), 2 days ; Gustaaf Van Slembrouck (BEL), 7 days ; Lucien Buysse (BEL), 8 days.

1927
Francis Pélissier (FRA), 5 days ; Ferdinand Le Drogo (FRA), 1 day ; Hector Martin (BEL), 4 days ; Nicolas Frantz (LUX), 14 days.

1928
Nicolas Frantz (LUX), 22 days.

1929
Aimé Dossche (BEL), 3 days ; Maurice De Waele (BEL), 3 days ; Nicolas Frantz (LUX), 1 day (dead heat with André Leducq and Victor Fontan) ; Gaston Rebry (BEL), 1 day ; Victor Fontan (FRA), 1 day ; Maurice De Waele (BEL), 13 days.

1930
Charles Pélissier (FRA), 1 day ; Learco Guerra (ITA), 7 days ; André Leducq (FRA), 13 days.

1931
Alfred Hamerlinck (BEL), 1 day ; Max Bulla (AUT), 1 day ; Léon Le Calvez (FRA), 1 day ; Raffaele Di Paco (ITA), 4 days (includes a dead heat with Charles Pélissier (FRA) ; Charles Pélissier (FRA), 1 day ; Antonin Magne (FRA), 16 days.

1932
Jean Aerts (BEL), 1 day ; Kurt Stoepel (GER), 1 day ; André Leducq (FRA), 19 days.

1933
Maurice Archambaud (FRA), 8 days ; Georges Lemaire (BEL), 2 days ; Maurice Archambaud (FRA), 1 day ; Georges Speicher (FRA), 12 days.

1934
Georges Speicher (FRA), 1 day ; Antonin Magne (FRA), 22 days (23 times including the half-stages of 27 July).

1935
Romain Maes (BEL), 21 days (27 times including the half-stages of 8, 18, 19, 25 and 27 July)

1936
Paul Egli (SUI), 1 day ; Maurice Archambaud (FRA), 1 day ; Arsène Mersch (LUX), 1 day ; Maurice Archambaud (FRA), 4 days ; Sylvère Maes (BEL), 14 days (20 times with half-stages of 22, 23, 30 July, 1 August, and one-third stage 31 July).

1937
Jean Majérus (LUX), 2 days ; Marcel Kint (BEL), 1 day ; Erich Bautz (GER), 3 days (5 times including the one-third stages of 4 July) ; Gino Bartali (ITA), 2 days ; Sylvère Maes (BEL), 8 days (13 times including the half-stages of 13, 14 and 15 July and the third- stage of 17 July) ; Roger Lapébie (FRA), 4 days (8 times including the one-third stages of 22 July and the half-stages of 23 and 24 July).

1938
Willi Oberbeck (GER), 1 day ; Jean Majérus (LUX), 4½ days (7 times including the one-third stages of 8 July and the loss of a half-stage on 11 July) ;

André Leducq (FRA), 1½ days (including taking the jersey in the half-stage of 11 July) ; Félicien Vervaecke (BEL), 6 days (8 times with the one-third stages of 17 July) ; Gino Bartali (ITA), 8 days (11 times including the half-stages of 26 July and the one-third stages of 30 July).

1939
Amédée Fournier (FRA), 1 day ; Romain Maes (BEL), ½ day (including gaining and losing the jersey In the half-stages of 11 July) ; Jean Fontenay (FRA), 1½ days (gaining the jersey in the half-stage of 11 July) ; René Vietto (FRA), 11 days (16 times including the half-stages of 15, 18, 23 July and the one-third stages of 21 July) ; Sylvère Maes (BEL), 4 days (8 times including one-third stages of 27 July and the half-stages of 29 and 30 July).

1947
Ferdi Kubler (SUI), 1 day ; René Vietto (FRA), 5 days ; Aldo Ronconi (ITA), 2 days ; René Vietto (FRA), 10 days ; Pierre Brambilla (ITA), 2 days ; Jean Robic (FRA), 1 day.

1948
Gino Bartali (ITA), 1 day ; Jan Engels (BEL), 1 day ; Louison Bobet (FRA), 1 day ; Roger Lambrecht (BEL), 2 days ; Louison Bobet (FRA), 8 days ; Gino Bartali (ITA), 8 days.

1949
Marcel Dussault (FRA), 1 day ; Roger Lambrecht (BEL), 1 day ; Norbert Callens (BEL), 1 day ; Jacques Marinelli (FRA), 6 days ; Fiorenzo Magni (ITA), 6 days ; Gino Bartali (ITA), 1 day ; Fausto Coppi (ITA), 5 days.

1950
Jean Goldschmit (LUX), 2 days ; Bernard Gauthier (FRA), 3 days ; Jean Goldschmit (LUX), 1 day ; Bernard Gauthier (FRA), 4 days ; Fiorenzo Magni (ITA), 1 day ; Ferdi Kubler (SUI), 11 days.

1951
Giovanni Rossi (SUI), 1 day ; Jean Diederich (LUX), 3 days ;

Serafino Biagioni (ITA), 1 day ;
Roger Levêque (FRA), 6 days ;
Wim Van Est (NED), 1 day ;
Gilbert Bauvin (FRA), 1 day ;
Hugo Koblet (SUI), 11 days.

1952
Rik Van Steenbergen (BEL), 2 days ;
Nello Lauredi (FRA), 3 days ;
Fiorenzi Magni (ITA), 1 day ;
Nello Lauredi (FRA), 1 day ;
Fiorenzo Magni (ITA), 1 day ;
Andrea Carrea (ITA), 1 day ;
Fausto Coppi (ITA), 14 days.

1953
Fritz Schaer (SUI), 4 days ;
Roger Hassenforder (FRA), 4 days ;
Fritz Schaer (SUI), 2 days ;
Jean Robic (FRA), 1 day ;
François Mahé (FRA), 1 day ;
Jean Malléjac (FRA), 5 days ;
Louison Bobet (FRA), 5 days.

1954
Wout Wagtmans (NED), 3 days ;
Louison Bobet (FRA), 4 days
(5 times including the half-stages
of 11 July) ;
Wout Wagtmans (NED), 4 days ;
Gilbert Bauvin (FRA), 2 days ;
Louison Bobet (FRA), 10 days
(11 times including the half-stages
of 30 July).

1955
Miguel Poblet (ESP), 1 day
(2 times including the half-stages
of 7 July) ;
Wout Wagtmans (NED), 2 days ;
Antonin Rolland (FRA), 3 days ;
Wim Van Est (NED), 1 day ;
Antonin Rolland (FRA), 9 days ;
Louison Bobet (FRA), 6 days.

1956
André Darrigade (FRA), 2 days ;
Gilbert Desmet (BEL), 1½ days
(including the loss of the jersey
in the half-stage of 8 July) ;
André Darrigade (FRA), 3 days ;
Roger Walkowiak (FRA), 3 days ;
Gerrit Voorting (NED), 1 day ;
André Darrigade (FRA), 1 day ;
Jan Adriaenssens (BEL), 3 days ;
Wout Wagtmans (NED), 3 days ;
Roger Walkowiak (FRA), 5 days.

1957
André Darrigade (FRA), 1 day ;
René Privat (FRA), 3 days (4 times
including the half-stages of 29 June) ;
Jacques Anquetil (FRA), 2 days ;
Nicolas Barone (FRA), 1 day ;
Jean Forestier (FRA), 2 days ;
Jacques Anquetil (FRA), 14 days.

1958
André Darrigade (FRA), 1 day ;
Jos Hoevenaars (BEL), 1 day ;
Wim Van Est (NED), 2 days ;

Gilbert Bauvin (FRA), 1 day ;
Gerrit Voorting (NED), 3 days ;
André Darrigade (FRA), 4 days ;
Raphaël Géminiani (FRA), 1 day ;
Vito Favero (ITA), 4 days ;
Raphaël Géminiani (FRA), 3 days ;
Vito Favero (ITA), 2 days ;
Charly Gaul (LUX), 2 days.

1959
André Darrigade (FRA), 2 days ;
Robert Cazala (FRA), 6 days ;
Eddy Pauwels (BEL), 1 day ;
Michel Vermeulin (FRA), 3 days ;
Jos Hoevenaars (BEL), 3 days ;
Eddy Pauwels (BEL), 1 day ;
Federico Bahamontes (ESP), 6 days.

1960
Julien Schepens (BEL), ½ day
(including the loss in the half-stage
of 26 June) ;
Gastone Nencini (ITA), 2 days ;
Joseph Groussard (FRA), 1 day ;
Henry Anglade (FRA), 2 days ;
Jan Adriaenssens (BEL), 4 days ;
Gastone Nencini (ITA), 12 days.

1961
André Darrigade (FRA), ½ day
(including the loss in the half-stage
of 25 June) ;
Jacques Anquetil (FRA), 21 days.

1962
Rudi Altig (GER), 1 day ;
André Darrigade (FRA), 1 day
(2 times including the half-stages
of 25 June) ;
Rudi Altig (GER), 3 days ;
Albertus Geldermans (NED), 2 days ;
André Darrigade (FRA), 1 day (2 times
including the half-stages of 1 July) ;
Willy Schroeders (BEL), 3 days ;
Tom Simpson (GBR), 1 day ;
Josef Planckaert (BEL), 7 days ;
Jacques Anquetil (FRA), 3 days.

1963
Eddy Pauwels (BEL), 2 days
(3 times including the half-stages
of 24 June) ;
Seamus Elliott (IRL), 3½ days
(including the loss of the jersey
in the half-stage of 28 June) ;
Gilbert Desmet (BEL), 10 days ;
Federico Bahamontes (ESP), 1 day ;
Jacques Anquetil (FRA), 5 days.

1964
Edward Sels (BEL), 2 days ;
Bernard Van de Kerckhove (BEL), 2 days
(3 times including the half-stages
of 24 June) ;
Rudi Altig (GER), 3 days ;
Georges Groussard (FRA), 9 days
(10 times including the half-stage
of 1 July) ;

Jacques Anquetil (FRA), 6 days (7 times
including the half-stages of 14 July).

1965
Rik Van Looy (BEL), 1 day (2 times
including the half-stages of 22 June) ;
Bernard Van de Kerckhove (BEL), 1 day ;
Felice Gimondi (ITA), 4 days (5 times
including the half-stages of 26 June) ;
Bernard Van de Kerckhove (BEL), 2 days ;
Felice Gimondi (ITA), 14 days.

1966
Rudi Altig (GER), 9 days (10 times
including the half-stages of 23 June) ;
Tommaso De Pra (ITA), 1 day ;
Jean-Claude Lebaube (FRA), 1 day ;
Karl-Heinz Kunde (GER), 4 days (5 times
including the half-stages of 5 July) ;
Jan Janssen (NED), 1 day ;
Lucien Aimar (FRA), 6 days (7 times
including the half-stages of 14 July).

1967
José Maria Errandonea (ESP), 2 days ;
Willy Van Neste (BEL), 1 day ;
Giancarlo Polidori (ITA), 1 day ;
Joseph Spruyt (BEL), 1 day ;
Roger Pingeon (FRA), 2 days (3 times
including the half-stages of 4 July) ;
Raymond Riotte (FRA), 1 day ;
Roger Pingeon (FRA), 15 days (16 times
including the half-stages of 23 July).

1968
Charly Grosskost (FRA), 3 days ;
Herman Van Springel (BEL), 1 day (2 times
including the half-stages of 30 June) ;
Jean-Pierre Genêt (FRA), 1 day ;
Georges Vandenberghe (BEL), 11 days
(12 times including the half-stages
of 2 July) ;
Rolf Wolfsholl (GER), 2 days ;
Gregorio San Miguel (ESP), 1 day ;
Herman Van Springel (BEL), 3½ days
(including losing the jersey in the
half-stage of 21 July) ;
Jan Janssen (NED), 1 day.

1969
Rudi Altig (GER), 1½ days (including
the loss in the half-stage of 29 June) ;
Eddy Merckx (BEL), 1 day ;
Julien Stevens (BEL), 3 days ;
Désiré Letort (FRA), 1 day ;
Eddy Merckx (BEL), 17 days (19 times
including the half-stages of 6 and 20 July).

1970
Eddy Merckx (BEL), 2 days ;
Italo Zilioli (ITA), 4 days (6 times including
the half-stages of 29 June and 1 July) ;
Eddy Merckx (BEL), 18 days (21 times
including the half-stages of 3, 7 and 16 July).

■■■

1971
Eddy Merckx (BEL), 1 day ;
Marinus Wagtmans (NED), one-third of
a day (with gain and loss of the jersey
in the one-third stages of 27 June) ;
Eddy Merckx (BEL), 9 days (11 times
including the one-third stage of 27 June
and the half-stages of 2 July) ;
Joop Zoetemelk (NED) 1 day ;
Luis Ocaña (ESP), 3 days ;
Eddy Merckx (BEL), 7 days (8 times
including the half-stages of 14 July ;
but he did not wear the yellow jersey on
13 July, after Ocaña crashed out).

1972
Eddy Merckx (BEL), 1 day ;
Cyrille Guimard (FRA), 2½ days
(3 times including losing the jersey in the
half-stage of 4 July) ;
Eddy Merckx (BEL), 1 day ;
Cyrille Guimard (FRA), 4 days
(5 times including the half-stages of 6 July) ;
Eddy Merckx (BEL), 13 days (15 times
including the half-stages of 17 and 23 July).

1973
Joop Zoetemelk (NED), 1 day ;
Willy Teirlinck (BEL), ½ day
(including the loss in the half-stage
of 1 July) ;
Herman Van Springel (BEL), 2 days
(3 times including the half-stages
of 2 July) ;
José Catieau (FRA), 4 days ;
Luis Ocaña (ESP), 14 days
(18 times including the half-stages
of 8, 13, 18 and 22 July).

1974
Eddy Merckx (BEL), 1 day ;
Joseph Bruyère (BEL), 3 days ;
Eddy Merckx (BEL), 1 day ;
Gerben Karstens (NED), 1 day ;
Patrick Sercu (BEL), ½ day (losing
the jersey in the half-stage of 3 July) ;
Gerben Karstens (NED), ½ day ;
Eddy Merckx (BEL), 16 days
(19 times including the half-stages
of 5, 18 and 20 July).

1975
Francesco Moser (ITA), 6 days
(7 times including the half-stages
of 27 June) ;
Eddy Merckx (BEL), 9 days (10 times
including the half-stages of 5 July) ;
Bernard Thévenet (FRA), 8 days.

1976
Freddy Maertens (BEL), 9 days
(10 times including the half-stages of
29 June) ; Lucien Van Impe (BEL), 3 days ;
Raymond Delisle (FRA), 2 days ;
Lucien Van Impe (BEL), 9 days (12 times
including the one-third stages of 14 July
and the half-stages of 18 July).

1977
Dietrich Thurau (GER), 15½ days
(losing jersey in the half-stage of
17 July ;19 times with half-stages
of 5, 8 and 15 July) ;
Bernard Thévenet (FRA), 8 days
(9 times with half-stages of 24 July).

1978
Jan Raas (NED), 3 days (4 times
including the half-stages of 30 June) ;
Jacques Bossis, (FRA) 1 day ;
Klaus-Peter Thaler (GER), 2 days ;
Gerrie Knetemann (NED), 2 days ;
Joseph Bruyère (BEL), 8 days (9 times
including the half-stages of 12 July) ;
Joop Zoetemelk (NED), 4 days ;
Bernard Hinault (FRA), 3 days.

1979
Gerrie Knetemann (NED), 1 day ;
Jean-René Bernaudeau (FRA), 1 day ;
Bernard Hinault (FRA), 7 days ;
Joop Zoetemelk (NED), 6 days ;
Bernard Hinault (FRA), 10 days.

1980
Bernard Hinault (FRA), 1½ days
(losing jersey in half-stage of 27 June) ;
Gerrie Knetemann (NED), 1 day ;
Yvon Bertin (FRA), 1 day ;
Rudi Pevenage (BEL), 8 days
(9 times including the half-stages
of 3 July) ;
Bernard Hinault (FRA), 2 days ;
Joop Zoetemelk (NED), 10 days
(did not wear the yellow jersey on
10 July, following Hinault departure).

1981
Bernard Hinault (FRA), 1½ days
(losing half-stage of 26 June) ;
Gerrie Knetemann (NED), 4 days ;
Phil Anderson (AUS), 1 day ;
Bernard Hinault (FRA), 17 days
(18 times including the half-stages
of 8 July).

1982
Bernard Hinault (FRA), 1 day ;
Ludo Peeters (BEL), 1 day ;
Phil Anderson (AUS), 9 days (10 times
with the half-stages of 12 July and
the cancellation of the 7 July stage) ;
Bernard Hinault (FRA), 11 days.

1983
Eric Vanderaerden (BEL), 2 days ;
Jean-Louis Gauthier (FRA), 1 day ;
Kim Andersen (DAN), 6 days ;
Sean Kelly (IRL), 1 day ;
Pascal Simon (FRA), 7 days ;
Laurent Fignon (FRA), 6 days.

1984
Bernard Hinault (FRA), 1 day ;
Ludo Peeters (BEL), 1 day ;
Jacques Hanegraaf (NED), 1½ days
(losing jersey in the half-stage
of 2 July) ;
Adri Van der Poel (NED), 1 day ;

Vincent Barteau (FRA), 12 days ;
Laurent Fignon (FRA), 7 days.

1985
Bernard Hinault (FRA), 1 day ;
Eric Vanderaerden (BEL), 3 days ;
Kim Andersen (DAN), 4 days ;
Bernard Hinault (FRA), 15 days
(16 times with the half-stages of 17 July).

1986
Thierry Marie (FRA), 1 day ;
Alex Stieda (CAN), ½ day
(includes gaining and losing jersey
in the half-stages of 5 July) ;
Thierry Marie (FRA), 2 days ;
Dominique Gaigne (FRA), 1 day ;
Johan Van der Velde (NED), 2 days ;
Jörgen-Vagn Pedersen (DAN), 5 days ;
Bernard Hinault (FRA), 5 days ;
Greg LeMond (USA), 7 days.

1987
Jelle Nijdam (NED), 1 day ;
Lech Piasecki (POL), 1 day (2 times
including the half-stages of 2 July) ;
Erich Maechler (SUI), 6 days (7 times
including the half-stages of 5 July) ;
Charly Mottet (FRA), 1 day ;
Martial Gayant (FRA), 2 days ;
Charly Mottet (FRA), 5 days ;
Jean-François Bernard (FRA), 1 day ;
Stephen Roche (IRL), 1 day ;
Pedro Delgado (ESP), 4 days ;
Stephen Roche (IRL), 2 days.

1988
Guido Bontempi (ITA), 1 day
(winner of the preface which did not
count for the general classification) ;
Steve Bauer (CAN), ½ day (winning
and losing jersey in the half-stages
of 4 July) ;
Teun Van Vliet (NED), 3 days ;
Henk Lubberding (NED), 1 day ;
Jelle Nijdam (NED), 2 days ;
Steve Bauer (CAN), 4 days ;
Pedro Delgado (ESP), 10 days (11
times including the half-stages of 19 July).

1989
Erik Breukink (NED), 1 day ;
Acacio Da Silva (POR), 3 days (4 times
including the half-stages of 2 July) ;
Greg LeMond (USA), 5 days ;
Laurent Fignon (FRA), 5 days ;
Greg LeMond (USA), 2 days ;
Laurent Fignon (FRA), 4 days ;
Greg LeMond (USA), 1 day.

1990
Thierry Marie (FRA), 1 day ;
Steve Bauer (CAN), 8 days (9 times
including the half-stages of 1 July) ;
Ronan Pensec (FRA), 2 days ;
Claudio Chiappucci (ITA), 8 days ;
Greg LeMond (USA), 2 days.

1991
Thierry Marie (FRA), 1 day ;
Greg LeMond (USA), ½ day
(including winning and losing
jersey in the half stages of 7 July) ;
Rolf Sörensen (DAN), 4 days ;
Thierry Marie (FRA), 2 days ;
Greg LeMond (USA), 4 days ;
Luc Leblanc (FRA), 1 day ;
Miguel Indurain (ESP), 10 days.

1992
Miguel Indurain (ESP), 1 day ;
Alex Zülle (SUI), 1 day ;
Richard Virenque (FRA), 1 day ;
Pascal Lino (FRA), 10 days ;
Miguel Indurain (ESP), 9 days.

1993
Miguel Indurain (ESP), 2 days ;
Wilfried Nelissen (BEL), 2 days ;
Mario Cipollini (ITA), 1 day ;
Wilfried Nelissen (BEL), 1 day ;
Mario Cipollini (ITA), 1 day ;
Johan Museeuw (BEL), 2 days ;
Miguel Indurain (ESP), 12 days.

1994
Chris Boardman (GBR), 3 days ;
Johan Museeuw (BEL), 1 day ;
Flavio Vanzella (ITA), 2 days ;
Sean Yates (GBR), 1 day ;
Johan Museeuw (BEL), 2 days ;
Miguel Indurain (ESP), 13 days.

1995
Jacky Durand (FRA), 2 days ;
Laurent Jalabert (FRA), 2 days ;
Ivan Gotti (ITA), 2 days ;
Bjarne Riis (DAN), 1 day ;
Johann Bruyneel (BEL), 1 day ;
Miguel Indurain (ESP), 13 days.

1996
Alex Zülle (SUI), 3 days ;
Frédéric Moncassin (FRA), 1 day ;
Stéphane Heulot (FRA), 3 days ;
Evgueni Berzin (RUS), 2 days ;
Bjarne Riis (DAN), 13 days.

1997
Chris Boardman (GBR), 1 day ;
Mario Cipollini (ITA), 4 days ;
Cédric Vasseur (FRA), 5 days ;
Jan Ullrich (GER), 12 days.

1998
Chris Boardman (GBR), 2 days ;
Erik Zabel (GER), 1 day ;
Bo Hamburger (DAN), 1 day ;
Stuart O'Grady (AUS), 3 days ;
Jan Ullrich (GER), 1 day ;
Laurent Desbiens (FRA), 2 days ;
Jan Ullrich (GER), 5 days ;
Marco Pantani (ITA), 7 days
(including the nullified stage of 29 July).

1999
Jaan Kirsipuu (EST), 6 days ;
Lance Armstrong (USA), 15 days,
later stripped of his race titles.

2000
David Millar (GBR), 3 days ;
Laurent Jalabert (FRA), 2 days ;
Alberto Elli (ITA), 4 days ;
Lance Armstrong (USA), 12 days,
later stripped of his race titles.

2001
Christophe Moreau (FRA), 2 days ;
Marc Wauters (BEL), 1 day ;
Stuart O'Grady (AUS), 4 days ;
Jens Voigt (GER), 1 day ;
Stuart O'Grady (AUS), 2 days ;
François Simon (FRA), 3 days ;
Lance Armstrong (USA), 8 days,
later stripped of his race titles.

2002
Rubens Bertogliati (SUI), 2 days ;
Erik Zabel (GER), 1 day ;
Igor Gonzalez de Galdeano (ESP), 7 days ;
Lance Armstrong (USA), 11 days,
later stripped of his race titles.

2003
Bradley McGee (AUS), 3 days ;
Jean-Patrick Nazon (FRA), 1 day ;
Victor Hugo Peña (COL), 3 days ;
Richard Virenque (FRA), 1 day ;
Lance Armstrong (USA), 13 days,
later stripped of his race titles.

2004
Fabian Cancellara (SUI), 2 days ;
Thor Hushovd (NOR), 1 day ;
Robbie McEwen (AUS), 1 day ;
Thomas Voeckler (FRA), 10 days ;
Lance Armstrong (USA), 7 days,
later stripped of his race titles.

2005
Jens Voigt (GER), 1 day ;
David Zabriskie (USA), 3 days,
later stripped of race wins;
Lance Armstrong (USA), 17 days,
later stripped of his race titles.

2006
Thor Hushovd (NOR), 1 day ;
George Hincapie (USA), 1 day, disqualified ;
Thor Hushovd (NOR), 1 day ;
Tom Boonen (BEL), 4 days ;
Serguëi Honchar (UKR), 3 days ;
Cyril Dessel (FRA), 1 day ;
Oscar Pereiro (ESP), 2 days + 3 days
(declared winner after the disqualification
of Floyd Landis (USA) + 2 additional
days as leader added retroactively) ;
Floyd Landis (USA), 5 days, disqualified.

2007
Fabian Cancellara (SUI), 7 days ;
Linus Gerdemann (GER), 1 day ;
Michael Rasmussen (DAN), 9 days
(excluded before the start of Stage 17) ;
Alberto Contador (ESP), 4 days.

2008
Alejandro Valverde (ESP), 2 days ;
Romain Feillu (FRA), 1 day ;
Stefan Schumacher (GER), 2 days, ;
Kim Kirchen (LUX), 4 days ;
Cadel Evans (AUS), 5 days ;

Fränk Schleck (LUX), 2 days ;
Carlos Sastre (ESP), 5 days.

2009
Fabian Cancellara (SUI), 6 days ;
Roberto Nocentini (ITA), 8 days ;
Alberto Contador (ESP), 7 days.

2010
Fabian Cancellara (SUI), 2 days ;
Sylvain Chavanel (FRA), 1 day ;
Fabian Cancellara (SUI), 4 days ;
Sylvain Chavanel (FRA), 1 day ;
Cadel Evans (AUS), 1 day ;
Andy Schleck (LUX), 6 days + 6 days
after disqualification of Alberto Contador (ESP).

2011
Philippe Gilbert (BEL), 1 day ;
Thor Hushovd (NOR), 7 days ;
Thomas Voeckler (FRA), 10 days ;
Andy Schleck (LUX), 1 day ;
Cadel Evans (AUS), 2 days.

2012
Fabian Cancellara (SUI), 7 days ;
Bradley Wiggins (GBR), 14 days.

2013
Marcel Kittel (GER), 1 day ;
Jan Bakelants (BEL), 2 days ;
Simon Gerrans (AUS), 2 days ;
Daryl Impey (AFS), 2 days ;
Chris Froome (GBR), 14 days

2014
Marcel Kittel (GER), 1 day ;
Vincenzo Nibali (ITA), 7 days ;
Tony Gallopin (FRA), 1 day ;
Vincenzo Nibali (ITA), 12 days.

2015
Rohan Dennis (AUS), 1 day ;
Fabian Cancellara (SUI), 1 day ;
Chris Froome (GBR), 1 day ;
Tony Martin (GER), 3 days ;
Chris Froome (GBR), 15 days.

2016
Mark Cavendish (GBR), 1 day ;
Peter Sagan (SLQ), 3 days ;
Greg Van Avermaet (BEL), 3 days ;
Chris Froome (GBR), 14 days.

2017
Geraint Thomas (GBR), 4 days ;
Chris Froome (GBR), 7 days ;
Fabio Aru (ITA), 2 days ;
Chris Froome (GBR), 8 days.

2018
Fernando Gaviria (COL), 1 day ;
Peter Sagan (SLQ), 1 day ;
Greg Van Avermaet (BEL), 8 days,
Geraint Thomas (GBR), 11 days.

Joop's done it! Tour de France 1980, Stage 20 time trial at Saint-Étienne.

THE MEN IN YELLOW: BRIEF BIOGRAPHIES

1919

Eugène CHRISTOPHE (FRA) – 3 days
Born 22 January 1885, died 1 February 1970.
A legendary figure, extremely tough but also very unlucky. He never quite managed to win the Tour, but he fully deserved to be the first person ever to win the yellow jersey.

Firmin LAMBOT (BEL) – 2 days
Born 14 March 1886, died 19 January 1964.
At 36 years, 4 months and 9 days he was the oldest ever winner of the Tour in 1922, his second victory.

1920

Louis MOTTIAT (BEL) – 1 day
Born 6 July 1889, died 5 June 1972.
He was the first to take the yellow jersey two years in a row, and won eight Tour stages during a career that spanned the First World War.

Philippe THYS (BEL) – 14 days
Born 8 October 1889, died 17 January 1971.
The first triple winner of the Tour (1913, 1914, 1920). He only wore the 'official' yellow jersey on his final victory, but would appear wearing an alternative yellow pullover before the war.

1921

Louis MOTTIAT (BEL) – 1 day

Léon SCIEUR (BEL) – 14 days
Born 19 March 1888, died 7 October 1969.
Nicknamed 'The Locomotive' for his unfailing power, Scieur won the 1921 Tour and was a prototype for the hard-as-nails Belgian riders of the 1920s.

1922

Robert JACQUINOT (FRA) – 3 days
Born 31 December 1893, died 17 June 1980.
Winner of four Tour stages, Jacquinot took the yellow jersey by winning the opening stage to Le Havre two years in a row.

Eugène CHRISTOPHE (FRA) – 3 days

Jean ALAVOINE (FRA) – 5 days
Born 1 April 1888, died 18 July 1943.
Thirteen years after his Tour debut, he finally put on the yellow jersey from Perpignan to Geneva. He made frequent podium appearances, coming second in 1919 and 1922, and third in 1909 and 1914.

Hector HEUSGHEM (BEL) – 1 day
Born 15 February 1890, died 29 March 1982.
Heusghem never won the Tour but came second twice (in 1920 and 1921) and was fourth in 1922, when he wore the jersey in Strasbourg.

Firmin LAMBOT (BEL) – 3 days

1923

Robert JACQUINOT (FRA) – 1 day

Ottavio BOTTECCHIA (ITA) – 2 days
Born 1 August 1894, died 15 June 1927.
Nicknamed 'The Bricklayer of Frioul' he was the first Italian yellow jersey. Coming second in the 1923 Tour, he excelled in the next two editions, and was end-to-end leader in 1924.

Romain BELLENGER (FRA) – 2 days
Born 18 January 1894, died 25 November 1981.
A specialist in the one-day Classics races, Bellenger finished third in the 1923 Tour, and wore the yellow from Les Sables-d'Olonne to Bayonne.

Ottavio BOTTECCHIA (ITA) – 4 days

Henri PÉLISSIER (FRA) – 6 days
Born 22 January 1889, died 1 May 1935.
One of the first great French champions with a string of victories in the Classics. Some said he was not built for Tour racing: he proved them all wrong.

1924

Ottavio BOTTECCHIA (ITA) – 15 days

1925

Ottavio BOTTECCHIA (ITA) – 2 days

Adelin BENOÎT (BEL) – 4 days
Born 12 May 1900, died 18 June 1954.
Another brilliant Belgian rider from the 1920s, he was the only man to stop Bottecchia from leading the race end-to-end for the second year running.

Ottavio BOTTECCHIA (ITA) – 1 day

Adelin BENOÎT (BEL) – 1 day

Ottavio BOTTECCHIA (ITA) – 10 days

1926

Jules BUYSSE (BEL) – 2 days
Born 13 August 1901, died 31 December 1950.
The younger brother of Lucien, who won the Tour the same year, 1926.

Gustaaf VAN SLEMBROUCK (BEL) 7 days
Born 25 March 1902, died 7 July 1968.
Flemish and proud of it, he won the Metz to Dunkerque stage and kept the yellow jersey for a week.

Lucien BUYSSE (BEL) – 8 days
Born 11 September 1892, died 3 January 1980.
He had only one major victory in his career which was in the longest ever Tour de France (5,745km) and also one of the hardest, notably over the hellish Bayonne to Luchon stage where Buysse guaranteed his victory.

1927

Francis PÉLISSIER (FRA) – 5 days
Born 13 June 1894, died 22 February 1959.
The youngest of the three brothers, and mainly a specialist of one-day races. This did not stop him making his mark on the Tour, with a victory on Stage 1 in 1927.

Ferdinand LE DROGO (FRA) – 1 day
Born 10 October 1903, died 23 April 1976.
Le Drogo, from Pontivy, was the first Breton to wear the yellow jersey on his home ground. Becoming race leader in Brest proved short-lived, and he lost the yellow the next day in Vannes.

Hector MARTIN (BEL) – 4 days
Born 26 December 1898, died 9 August 1972.
A little-known rider who picked up the yellow jersey lost by Ferdinand Le Drogo, without winning the stage.

Nicolas FRANTZ (LUX) – 14 days
Born 4 November 1899, died 8 November 1985.
The successor to François Faber (the winner in 1909), Frantz's cadence was metronomic, especially on the climbs. On his second victory in 1928 he wore the yellow jersey from one end of the race to the other.

1928

Nicolas FRANTZ (LUX) – 22 days

1929

Aimé DOSSCHE (BEL) – 3 days
Born 28 March 1902, died 30 October 1985.
His victory in the first stage allowed the Ghent rider to wear the yellow during the 1929 Tour, which he did not finish.

Maurice DE WAELE (BEL) – 3 days
Born 27 December 1896, died 14 February 1952.
De Waele finished second in the 1927 Tour and third in 1928, but rode to victory in 1929 (the last pre-war Tour contested by commercially sponsored teams). The race was dominated by the Alcyon team.

Nicolas FRANTZ (LUX) – 1 day
At the end of Stage 7 into Bordeaux, Luxembourger Frantz had to share the yellow jersey with André Leducq and Victor Fontan.

Gaston REBRY (BEL) – 1 day
Born 29 January 1905, died 3 July 1953.
Nicknamed 'The Bulldog', Rebry was a triple winner of the Paris–Roubaix, and a specialist on cobblestones. Of his four stage wins on the Tour, two were in the north, from Charleville to Malo-les-Bains.

Victor FONTAN (FRA) – 1 day
Born 18 June 1892, died 2 January 1982.
One of the best climbers of his era, Fontan dominated in the Pyrenees. He had his share of bad luck too, as in 1929 when he broke his bike and had to drop out wearing the yellow jersey.

Maurice DE WAELE (BEL) – 13 days

1930

Charles PÉLISSIER (FRA) – 1 day
Born 20 February 1903, died 28 May 1959.
The youngest of the three brothers was a road and sprint specialist, which helped win him no less than 16 Tour stages, and several days in yellow in 1930 and 1931.

Learco GUERRA (ITA) – 7 days
Born 14 October 1902, died 7 December 1963.
Nicknamed 'The Human Locomotive' he was a popular rider, becoming World Champion in 1931, the year that he also became the first to wear the pink jersey of the Italian Giro.

André LEDUCQ (FRA) – 13 days
Born 27 February 1904, died 18 June 1980.
Cocky, chipper, cheeky – the young Parisian from the Saint-Ouen suburbs became a huge figure in French cycling in the inter-war period. Along with Antonin Magne, he contributed some of the highlights of the France national team.

1931

Alfred HAMERLINCK (BEL) – 1 day
Born 27 September 1905, died 10 July 1933.
An out-and-out hardman of the Northern Classics, Hamerlinck won the first stage in Caen and with it the first yellow jersey of the 1931 Tour.

Max BULLA (AUT) – 1 day
Born 26 September 1905, died 1 March 1990.
To this day, Bulla is the only Austrian rider ever to have worn the yellow jersey. What's more, he did it on his own, riding as a 'tourist' competitor without the assistance of a supporting team.

Léon LE CALVEZ (FRA) – 1 day
Born 14 March 1909, died 7 July 1995.
One of the best Breton riders of his era, he was picked for the France national team. He was the father-in-law of another yellow jersey, François Mahé, and ran the West France team from 1952 to 1956.

Rafaele DI PACO (ITA) – 4 days
Born 7 June 1908, died 21 May 1996.
One of the best sprinters of his day, his duels with Charles Pélissier delighted the crowds. He won 11 Tour stages in all, including five in 1931.

Charles PÉLISSIER (FRA) – 1 day

Antonin MAGNE (FRA) – 16 days
Born 15 February 1904, died 8 September 1983.
One of the greatest French champions in history, Magne was committed, methodical and disciplined, going on to win two Tours and then the World Championship in 1936. Later in his career he became team boss of Mercier, whose racers included both Bobet and Poulidor.

1932

Jean AERTS (BEL) – 1 day
Born 8 September 1907, died 15 June 1992.
The Brussels rider won no fewer than a dozen Tour stages, but only wore the yellow jersey on one occasion, at the end of Stage 1 on the 1932 Tour. He was World Champion in 1935.

Kurt STOEPEL (GER) – 1 day
Born 12 March 1908, died 11 June 1997.
Steopel, from Berlin, was the first German to win a Tour stage and wear the yellow jersey.

André LEDUCQ (FRA) – 19 days

1933

Maurice ARCHAMBAUD (FRA) – 8 days
Born 30 August 1906, died 3 December 1955.
Like Leducq and Speicher, Archambaud was another popular Parisian rider, nicknamed 'The Midget' for his small stature. But he was a giant on a bike, and held the world hour record in 1937 with an average speed of 45.84km/h.

Georges LEMAIRE (BEL) – 2 days
Born 3 April 1905, died 29 September 1933.
Lemaire died young, the same year he took the yellow jersey. In his all too short career, he also became Belgian Champion.

Maurice ARCHAMBAUD (FRA) – 1 day

Georges SPEICHER (FRA) – 12 days
Born 8 June 1907, died 24 January 1978.
Speicher was an exceptional rider, untouchable on the fast mountain descents. His big year was in 1933 when he won both the Tour de France and the World Championship in the same season.

1934

Georges SPEICHER (FRA) – 1 day

Antonin MAGNE (FRA) – 22 days

1935

Romain MAES (BEL) – 21 days
Born 10 August 1913, died 22 February 1983.
Unshowy, but a highly effective rider, Maes made his mark by winning the first stage from Paris to Lille, and then holding on to the yellow jersey for the rest of the Tour and winning the final stage into Parc des Princes.

1936

Paul EGLI (SUI) – 1 day
Born 18 August 1911, died 23 January 1997.
Winner of Stage 1 from Paris to Lille in 1936, Egli was the first Swiss to wear the yellow jersey. He was one of the best riders in his country at the time, and a three-times winner of the gruelling Championnat de Zurich.

Maurice ARCHAMBAUD (FRA) – 1 day

Arsène MERSCH (LUX) – 1 day
Born 14 December 1913, died 12 July 1980.
Mersch had a great Tour this year, with a day in the yellow jersey towards the start, and then won the final stage into the Parc des Princes where he finished in fifth place.

Maurice ARCHAMBAUD (FRA) – 4 days

Sylvère MAES (BEL) – 14 days
Born 22 August 1909, died 5 December 1966.
No relation to Romain Maes, Sylvère was the second 'Maes' in two years to become the Tour champion. After this, there would be no Belgian winners of the Tour until Eddy Merckx, some 30 years later.

1937

Jean MAJERUS (LUX) – 2 days
Born 6 February 1914, died 16 June 1983.
Majerus mainly found success racing in Luxembourg or in Eastern France, but he did win two Tour stages and wore the yellow jersey for two consecutive years.

Marcel KINT (BEL) – 1 day
Born 20 September 1914, died 23 February 2002.
Nicknamed 'The Black Eagle', he was one of the great Belgian champions of his time, winning the World Championship in 1938. He was a one-day Classics specialist (Tour of Flanders, Paris–Roubaix, Flèche Wallonne) and wore the yellow jersey for a day.

Erich BAUTZ (GER) – 3 days
Born 26 May 1913, died 17 September 1986.
Winner of the Vosges stage, he took the yellow jersey before giving it up to Bartali in the Alps. He finished ninth in the 1937 Tour.

Gino BARTALI (ITA) – 2 days
Born 18 July 1914, died 5 July 2000.
A legendary figure, and one of the best climbers in cycling history. He was forced to abandon the race after a crash in 1937, but won in 1938. He is the only rider to have won the Tour twice with a ten-year interval, either side of the Second World War.

Sylvère MAES (BEL) – 14 days

Roger LAPÉBIE (FRA) – 4 days
Born 16 January 1911, died 12 October 1996.
Victory made Roger Lapébie enormously popular among the French supporters, but there was so much bad feeling directed towards his Belgian rivals that Sylvère Maes and the entire Belgian national team felt forced to abandon the race. Lapébie was

unexceptional as a climber, but he was unmatched on the descents.

1938

Willi OBERBECK (GER) – 1 day
Born 21 February 1910, died 9 July 1979.
Oberbeck's was a modest career, with just two Tours completed (he failed to finish two others). However, a victory in Caen on Stage 1 of the 1938 Tour gave him a yellow jersey.

Jean MAJERUS (LUX) – 4½ days

André LEDUCQ (FRA) – 1½ days

Félicien VERVAECKE (BEL) – 6 days
Born 11 March 1907, died 31 October 1986.
Vervaecke put his stamp on the Tour, twice winning the mountain classification (1935 and 1937) and making three podium appearances: second in 1938 and third in 1935 and 1936. He took the yellow jersey in the Pyrenees, but Bartali proved to be the stronger rider in the Alps.

Gino BARTALI (ITA) – 8 days

1939

Amédée FOURNIER (FRA) – 1 day
Born 7 February 1912, died 30 March 1992.
Brought up in the North of France, Fournier was a strong road racer and won the first stage of his one and only Tour de France in 1939. He then lost the leadership to Romain Maes in the following day's time trial.

Romain MAES (BEL) – Half a day

Jean FONTENAY (FRA) – 1½ days
Born 23 July 1911, died 21 May 1975.
Fontenay, from the bay of Mont-Saint-Michel, was another rider to have his cycling career cut short by the war. He took the yellow jersey in Rennes, and wore it for two days as he crossed his native Brittany.

René VIETTO (FRA) – 11 days
Born 17 February 1914, died 14 October 1988.
From his lowly job in a Cannes hotel, the young Vietto became one of the most gifted climbers of his era, and a man marked by a spirit of self-sacrifice for his team – notably offering his wheel to Antonin Magne in 1934. He kept hold of the yellow jersey during his Tours both before and after the war, and earned second place in Paris on the 1939 Tour.

Sylvère MAES (BEL) – 4 days

1947

Ferdi KUBLER (SUI) – 1 day
Born 24 July 1919, died 29 December 2016.
A great champion who won the first stage of the first post-war Tour, and went on to win the 1950 Tour. Four years later, he returned to the podium in second place.

René VIETTO (FRA) – 5 days

Aldo RONCONI (ITA) – 2 days
Born 20 September 1918, died 12 June 2012.
Winner of the stage in Luxembourg, Ronconi finally took the yellow jersey in Grenoble. He finished in fourth place in the 1947 Tour.

René VIETTO (FRA) – 10 days

Pierre BRAMBILLA (ITA) – 2 days
Born 12 May 1919, died 13 February 1984.
The French national (with an Italian background) was wearing the yellow jersey at the start of the final stage from Caen to Paris when Jean Robic created a major upset by gaining 13 minutes on Brambilla and winning the Tour. Brambilla took third place overall (and won the mountain prize).

Jean ROBIC (FRA) – 1 day
Born 10 June 1921, died 6 October 1980.
A legendary figure, nicknamed 'The Kid' or sometimes 'Leather Head'. He became popular after his victory in the first post-war Tour, winning on the final day having never worn the yellow jersey – except for his victory lap in the Parc des Princes.

1948

Gino BARTALI (ITA) – 1 day

Jan ENGELS (BEL) – 1 day
Born 11 May 1922, died 17 April 1972.
Engels, from Brussels, was winner of the Liège–Bastogne–Liège in 1945, and briefly took the yellow jersey at the end of Stage 2, from Trouville to Dinard.

Louison BOBET (FRA) – 1 day
Born 12 March 1925, died 13 March 1983.
One of the greatest French cycling champions of all time, along with Hinault and Anquetil, and with a vast array of victories to his name. The Breton was as courageous as he was ambitious, making his debut in 1948, but only seeing his career really taking off in the mid-1950s.

Roger LAMBRECHT (BEL) – 2 days
Born 1 January 1916, died 4 August 1979.
Lambrecht was a Belgian based in Brittany, and made his mark on the Tour two years running, winning a stage and picking up the yellow jersey in each. The second of these took place back in his homeland, on the stage into Brussels.

Louison BOBET (FRA) – 8 days

Gino BARTALI (ITA) – 8 days

1949

- **Marcel DUSSAULT (FRA) – 1 day**
Born 14 May 1926, died 19 September 2014.
Winner of Stage 1 of the 1949 Tour from Paris to Reims, Dussault also appeared as a film extra (riding a bicycle, of course) in the Jacques Tati comedy *The Big Day*.

- **Roger LAMBRECHT (BEL) – 1 day**

- **Norbert CALLENS (BEL) – 1 day**
Born 22 June 1924, died 12 March 2005.
Callens had a modest career in cycling, which should have been boosted by his one day wearing the yellow jersey – except his team forgot to bring it over to him on the morning of the departure the next day…

- **Jacques MARINELLI (FRA) – 6 days**
Born 15 December 1925.
His six-day escapade with the yellow jersey, from Normandy through to the Pyrenees, kept the whole of France on tenterhooks. Nicknamed 'The Budgie', Marinelli hung on through the rest of the race to a creditable third place podium finish alongside two giants of the sport, Coppa and Bartali.

- **Fiorenzo MAGNI (ITA) – 6 days**
Born 7 December 1920, died 19 October 2012.
Magni was one of the great Italian racers who could stand up to the likes of Coppi and Bartali. In 1950, he had to quit the Tour with the yellow jersey when the Italian teams, led by Bartali, walked out.

- **Gino BARTALI (ITA) – 1 day**

- **Fausto COPPI (ITA) – 5 days**
Born 15 September 1919, died 2 January 1960.
Coppi was a huge presence on the Tour, with his two Tours leading to two victories. In 1949 he overcame a crash which cost him a 20-minute delay, and in 1952 his dominance was total. There was no competition.

1950

- **Jean GOLDSCHMIT (LUX) – 2 days**
Born 20 February 1924, died 14 February 1994. Capable of putting in a strong performance on the stages, he took the yellow on the opening stage of the 1950 Tour, and then got it back a second time (from Bernard Gauthier).

- **Bernard GAUTHIER (FRA) – 3 days**
Born 22 September 1924, died 23 November 2018.
Gauthier, from Grenoble, was one of the best French racers of his era, and picked up the nickname of 'Mr Bordeaux–Paris' on account of his four victories in that race. He excelled in the Northern stages of the Tour, taking the yellow jersey in Lille and wearing it three days, and then a further four into the Pyrenees.

- **Jean GOLDSCHMIT (LUX) – 1 day**

- **Bernard GAUTHIER (FRA) – 4 days**

- **Fiorenzo MAGNI (ITA) – 1 day**

- **Ferdi KUBLER (SUI) – 11 days**

1951

- **Giovanni ROSSI (SUI) – 1 day**
Born 7 May 1926, died 17 September 1983.
Rossi only took part in the Tour once, and did not finish the race. But his win over the first stage in Reims gave him the yellow jersey for the day.

- **Jean DIEDERICH (LUX) – 3 days**
Born 20 February 1922, died 6 December 2012.
Better known by his nickname 'Bim', he won Tour stages three years running (from 1950 to 1952), but it was his solo success on Stage 2 to Ghent that won him the yellow jersey, which he kept for three days.

- **Serafino BIAGIONI (ITA) – 1 day**
Born 12 March 1920, died 13 February 1983.
Biagioni won a GP in Tuscany, three stage wins in the Giro d'Italia, and two stages in the Tour de France in 1951 in Caen (earning the yellow jersey) and later in Tarbes.

- **Roger LEVÊQUE (FRA) – 6 days**
Born 5 December 1920, died 30 June 2002.
In eight years of professional cycling, he scored just one win: Stage 4 of the Tour between Le Tréport and Paris, with a yellow jersey at the end of it too.

- **Wim VAN EST (NED) – 1 day**
Born 23 March 1923, died 1 May 2003.
The first Dutchman to wear the yellow jersey did not have long to enjoy it, as the following day he crashed off the road and into a ravine while coming down the Aubisque. Miraculously, he was back with the yellow jersey four years later.

- **Gilbert BAUVIN (FRA) – 1 day**
Born 4 August 1927.
Bauvin was a typical Tour all-rounder, strong on the flat stages and a good climber. He also wore the yellow jersey on three different Tours from 1951 to 1958, and finished the 1956 on the podium, in second place.

- **Hugo KOBLET (SUI) – 11 days**
Born 21 March 1925, died 6 November 1964.
An outstanding champion, even though his glory was short-lived. He is most famous for an incredible breakaway of 115km between Brive and Agen, despite having big names like Coppi, Bartali, Robic, and Géminiani breathing down his neck. Koblet would have to wait for another stage victory at Luchon before getting hold of the yellow jersey and going on to win the Tour.

1952

- **Rik VAN STEENBERGEN (BEL) – 2 days**
Born 9 September 1924, died 15 May 2003.
Another of cycling's superstars, Steenbergen was a triple World Champion, and consistently excelled in one-day Classics and on the track. He had less success on the Tour, but picked up the yellow jersey two days after winning the first stage from Brest to Rennes.

- **Nello LAURÉDI (FRA) – 3 days**
Born 5 October 1924, died 8 April 2001.
Naturalized as a French citizen after the war, Laurédi was originally Italian, and was a talented enough climber to win two Critériums du Dauphiné. In the Tour, he won three stages between 1950 and 1953, and his success at Rouen also gave him the yellow jersey in 1952.

- **Fiorenzo MAGNI (ITA) – 1 day**

- **Nello LAURéDI (FRA) – 1 day**

- **Fiorenzo MAGNI (ITA) – 1 day**

- **Andrea CARREA (ITA) – 1 day**
Born 14 August 1924, died 13 January 2013.
Carrea was a typical 'gregario', devoting his career to serve team leader Fausto Coppi. He felt somewhat guilty taking the yellow jersey at Lausanne, and was quick to return it to Coppi the next day on the Alpe d'Huez.

- **Fausto COPPI (ITA) – 14 days**

1953

- **Fritz SCHAER (SUI) – 4 days**
Born 13 March 1926, died 29 September 1997.
Behind Kubler and Koblet, Schaer was one of the best in his country during this great era of Swiss cycling. Third placed in the Tour of 1954, he took the yellow jersey in 1953 where he was also the first rider to take the green jersey.

- **Roger HASSENFORDER (FRA) – 4 days**
Born 23 July 1930.
The journalist Pierre Chany saw Hassenforder as somewhere between Louison Bobet and French stand-up comic Fernand Raynaud. Winner of eight Tour stages in all, Hassenforder was a classy rider but also a great joker.

- **Fritz SCHAER (SUI) – 2 days**

- **Jean ROBIC (FRA) – 1 day**

François MAHÉ (FRA) – 1 day
Born 2 September 1930, died 31 May 2015.
His wins don't quite do justice to his qualities as a rider. The Breton was a Tour stalwart, finishing three Tours within the top ten riders (fifth in 1959, and tenth in 1953 and 1955). He became the son-in-law of another yellow jersey, Léon Le Calvez.

Jean MALLÉJAC (FRA) – 5 days
Born 19 July 1929, died 24 September 2000.
The 1953 Tour was dominated by Bretons, with François Mahé, Louison Bobet and Jean Malléjac, who finished second on the podium in Paris. His name has also become synonymous with his collapse in 1955 on the slopes of Mont Ventoux.

Louison BOBET (FRA) – 5 days

1954

Wout WAGTMANS (NED) – 3 days
Born 10 November 1929, died 15 August 1994.
One of the first major players in Dutch cycling to compete on the Tour, Wagtmans took four stage victories between 1953 and 1955.

Louison BOBET (FRA) – 4 days

Wout WAGTMANS (NED) – 4 days

Gilbert BAUVIN (FRA) – 2 days

Louison BOBET (FRA) – 10 days

1955

Miguel POBLET (ESP) – 1 day
Born 18 March 1928, died 6 April 2013.
One of the rare examples of a world-class Spanish sprinter at the time, Poblet was twice winner of Milan–San Remo, and won no fewer than 20 stages of the Giro. Thanks to his win on the first stage of the 1955 Tour in Dieppe, he became the first Spaniard to wear the yellow jersey.

Wout WAGTMANS (NED) – 2 days

Antonin ROLLAND (FRA) – 3 days
Born 3 September 1924.
Winner of the final stage at Parc des Princes in 1952, and then at Roubaix in 1955, Rolland wore the yellow jersey for 12 days in total. He finished fifth in 1955.

Wim VAN EST (NED) – 1 day

Antonin ROLLAND (FRA) – 9 days

Louison BOBET (FRA) – 6 days

1956

André DARRIGADE (FRA) – 2 days
Born 24 April 1929.
World Champion in 1959, Darrigade was a yellow jersey specialist, wearing it in six separate Tours, and sometimes several times within the same Tour (three times in 1956, for example). He was both a talented rider and sprinter, and also road captain, and was a five-times winner of Stage 1 of the Tour.

Gilbert DESMET (BEL) – 1½ days
Born 3 February 1931.
Desmet picked up the yellow twice, adding it to his other titles: Paris–Tours in 1958, second in the Paris–Roubaix, and the Grand Prix des Nations.

André DARRIGADE (FRA) – 3 days

Roger WALKOWIAK (FRA) – 3 days
Born 2 March 1927, died 6 February 2017.
A talented and tenacious rider who could follow the best climbers on the mountain. His constant presence in the breakaways earned him victory in what Jacques Goddet described as one of the 'most beautiful' Tours.

Gerrit VOORTING (NED) – 1 day
Born 18 January 1923, died 30 January 2015.
One of the Dutch riders who made their mark over the first part of the Tour, Voorting had a stage victory in 1953, took the yellow jersey for a day in 1956 in Bayonne, and for rather longer in 1958.

André DARRIGADE (FRA) – 1 day

Jan ADRIAENSSENS (BEL) – 3 days
Born 6 June 1932.
A consistently strong rider, he got into the top ten finishers over seven successive Tours from 1956 to 1961. He finished in third place in 1956 and 1960.

Wout WAGTMANS (NED) – 3 days

Roger WALKOWIAK (FRA) – 5 days

1957

André DARRIGADE (FRA) – 1 day

René PRIVAT (FRA) – 3 days
Born 4 December 1930, died 19 July 1995.
Privat was a great attacker, and won the Milan–San Remo in 1960. In the 1957 Tour, dominated by one of the best France teams ever, Privat won three stages and kept the yellow jersey from Caen through to Charleroi, where he gave it up to Anquetil.

Jacques ANQUETIL (FRA) – 2 days
Born 8 January 1934, died 18 November 1987.
One of the definitive French cycling champions, and possibly the greatest cycle racer of all times. Anquetil was the first five-times winner of the Tour. He had a reputation for low-key pragmatism, calculating exactly what was needed to win, and well able to defend his lead once he hit the mountain stages.

Nicolas BARONE (FRA) – 1 day
Born 6 March 1931, died 31 May 2003.
Barone was in the regional Ile-de-France team, and his presence in a breakaway on the road to Colmar rewarded him with a day in the yellow jersey.

Jean FORESTIER (FRA) – 2 days
Born 7 October 1930.
A great rider who excelled in the Classics. He won Paris-Roubaix in 1955, followed by the Tour of Flanders in 1956. On the 1957 Tour he finished fourth.

Jacques ANQUETIL (FRA) – 14 days

1958

André DARRIGADE (FRA) – 1 day

Jos HOEVENAERS (BEL) – 1 day
Born 30 November 1932, died 14 June 1995.
Hoevenaers's career was relatively short but pretty full too. He won the Flèche Wallonne in 1959, and appeared twice in the top ten finishers of the Tour: tenth in 1958 and eighth in 1959.

Wim VAN EST (NED) – 2 days

Gilbert Bauvin (FRA) – 1 day

Gerrit VOORTING (NED) – 3 days

André DARRIGADE (FRA) – 4 days

Raphaël GÉMINIANI (FRA) – 1 day
Born 12 June 1925.
A colourful character on the Tour, Géminiani took part 11 times in all. He was in second behind Koblet in 1951 (winning the mountains classification), and third in 1958, where he saw his chances of victory evaporate with Charly Gaul's attack.

Vito FAVERO (ITA) – 4 days
Born 21 October 1932, died 16 May 2014.
Favero took second place behind Charly Gaul in the 1958 Tour with a hugely consistent performance. It was Favero who took the yellow on the day that Gaul left Géminiani for dust in the Chartreuse, and he gave it up only on the final time trial in Dijon.

Raphaël GÉMINIANI (FRA) – 3 days

Vito FAVERO (ITA) – 2 days

Charly GAUL (LUX) – 2 days
Born 8 December 1932, died 6 December 2005.
One of the greatest climbers of all time, and especially in the worst weather, with a career highlight being his attack in the Chartreuse mountains. He won the Giro in 1956 and 1959, and was King of the Mountains in 1955 and 1956.

1959

André DARRIGADE (FRA) – 2 days

Robert CAZALA (FRA) – 6 days
Born 7 January 1934.
A great Tour competitor, winning four stages in total, including the final stage into Paris in 1961. Two years earlier he wore the yellow from Roubaix to the Pyrenees but gave it up in Bayonne, disappointing his home supporters in nearby Béarn.

Eddy PAUWELS (BEL) – 1 day
Born 2 May 1935, died 6 March 2017.

Pauwels won four stages in total, including two in Pau, prompting Jacques Goddet to decry the 'passive approach' of the top riders on the 1961 Tour. Pauwels also took the first yellow of the 1963 Tour in Epernay.

Michel VERMEULIN (FRA) – 3 days
Born 6 September 1934.
His promising amateur career was marked by an Olympic gold medal in the team time trial in 1956. His professional career was less successful, but he took the yellow jersey for three days in 1959 between the Pyrenees and the Massif Central.

Jos HOEVENAERS (BEL) – 3 days

Eddy PAUWELS (BEL) – 1 day

Federico BAHAMONTES (ESP) – 6 days
Born 9 July 1928.
Bahamontes was THE legendary climber. The first Spaniard to win the Tour (in 1959), he also took second place in 1963 and was third in 1964. His was capable of blistering acceleration on the climbs where no one could touch him, but he was cautious on the descents and constantly struggled with time trials. He was six-times King of the Mountains between 1954 and 1964

1960

Julien SCHEPENS (BEL) – 1 half-day
Born 19 December 1935, died 16 August 2006.
The Flemish rider picked up several podium places in the Classics, and took the yellow for half a day thanks to his victory in the Lille to Brussels half-stage that opened the 1960 Tour.

Gastone NENCINI (ITA) – 2 days
Born 1 March 1930, died 1 February 1980.
Winner of the Giro in 1957. A strong climber, he was above all a virtuoso of the fast descents. The career-ending crash of Roger Rivière on the Col de Perjuret allowed Nencini to go on to win the 1960 Tour.

Joseph GROUSSARD (FRA) – 1 day
Born 2 March 1934.
An electrifying sprinter, Groussard took the yellow for a day between Dieppe and Caen, but his most notable success was winning the Milan–San Remo in 1963. His younger brother Georges was yellow jersey in 1964

Henry ANGLADE (FRA) – 2 days
Born 6 July 1933.
Anglade was in the French Centre-Midi regional team in 1959, and despite looking a likely winner, was hindered by lack of support from the national team riders. The following year he took the yellow at the start of the Tour.

Jan ADRIAENSSENS (BEL) – 4 days

Gastone NENCINI (ITA) – 12 days

1961

André DARRIGADE (FRA) – 1 half-day

Jacques ANQUETIL (FRA) – 21 days

1962

Rudi ALTIG (GER) – 1 day
Born 18 March 1937, died 11 June 2016.
World Champion in 1966, he also shone in the Tour de France, notably in 1962 with three stage wins and four days with the yellow jersey. He was the most successful German Tour cyclist until Jan Ullrich, three decades later.

André DARRIGADE (FRA) – 1 day

Rudi ALTIG (GER) – 3 days

Albertus GELDERMANS (NED) – 2 days
Born 17 March 1935.
A Saint-Raphaël teammate of Anquetil, Geldermans finished in fifth place in the 1962 Tour.

André DARRIGADE (FRA) – 1 day

Willy SCHROEDERS (BEL) – 3 days
Born 9 December 1932, died 28 October 2017.
His breakaway between La Rochelle and Bordeaux gave him a four-minute lead, and a full three days in the yellow jersey through to Pau.

Tom SIMPSON (GBR) – 1 day
Born 30 November 1937, died 13 July 1967.
Simpson's name is immortalized in the tragic drama that unfolded on the slopes of Mont Ventoux in 1967. He also remains the first British rider to take the yellow jersey, which he did in 1962 at the end of Stage 12 from Pau to Saint-Gaudens.

Josef PLANCKAERT (BEL) – 7 days
Born 4 May 1934, died 22 May 2007.
He won the Liège–Bastogne–Liège in 1962, and also finished second on the Tour (though without posing any major threat to Anquetil). He took the yellow jersey for a week, from Superbagnères through to Lyon.

Jacques ANQUETIL (FRA) – 3 days

1963

Eddy PAUWELS (BEL) – 2 days

Seamus ELLIOTT (IRL) – 3½ days
Born 4 June 1934, died 4 May 1971.
The first Irish rider to join the continental cycling circuit, he was also the first Irish cyclist to wear the yellow jersey. A breakaway on the Jambes to Roubaix stage gave him a big enough lead to keep it for four days.

Gilbert DESMET (BEL) – 10 days

Federico BAHAMONTES (ESP) – 1 day

Jacques ANQUETIL (FRA) – 5 days

1964

Edward SELS (BEL) – 2 days
Born 27 August 1941.

The Belgian champion took no less than four stage wins in the 1964 Tour (and a total of seven through to 1970).

Bernard VAN DE KERCKHOVE (BEL) – 2 days
Born 8 July 1941, died 15 September 2015.
An adept of Belgium's short-distance Kermesse races, he also picked up two stage victories, each one with a yellow jersey too, and three further yellows in 1965

Rudi ALTIG (GER) – 3 days

Georges GROUSSARD (FRA) – 9 days
Born 22 March 1937.
Groussard's trophy cabinet was fairly modest, but he was a very decent climber and managed to hang on to the yellow jersey for a full nine days, from Briançon through to the time trial to Bayonne, and finished in fifth place in Paris. He is the brother of Joseph.

Jacques ANQUETIL (FRA) – 6 days

1965

Rik VAN LOOY (BEL) – 1 day
Born 20 December 1933.
Winner of all the major Classics races, Van Looy was nicknamed 'The Emperor' and was a giant of the one-day racing world. On the Tour, he managed to worry Anquetil, though his climbing powers were limited. He won the green jersey in Paris in 1963.

Bernard VAN DE KERCKHOVE (BEL) – 1 day

Felice GIMONDI (ITA) – 4 days
Born 29 September 1942.
The young Gimondi won the 1965 Tour in his debut year, largely at the expense of Poulidor in the mountain stages. In subsequent years he did less well as Merckx dominated, but he managed a second place in 1972.

Bernard VAN DE KERCKHOVE (BEL) – 2 days

Felice GIMONDI (ITA) – 14 days

1966

- **Rudi ALTIG (GER) – 9 days**

- **Tommaso DE PRA (ITA) – 1 day**
Born 16 December 1938.
A Molteni team mate of Rudi Altig, he effectively took Altig's yellow jersey after winning the stage at Pau following a long breakaway, which also allowed Lucien Aimar to put more than seven minutes into Poulidor.

- **Jean-Claude LEBAUBE (FRA) – 1 day**
Born 22 July 1937, died 2 May 1977.
Lebaube, from Normandy, briefly took the yellow in Luchon after a breakaway between Bayonne and Pau. He was a top five Tour finisher in 1963 and 1965.

- **Karl-Heinz KUNDE (GER) – 4 days**
Born 6 August 1938, died 15 January 2018.
A compact cyclist (1.59m) and a great climber, he was another member of the Bayonne to Pau breakaway.

- **Jan JANSSEN (NED) – 1 day**
Born 19 May 1940.
Known as a sprinter with his eyes set mainly on the green jersey (in 1964, 1965 and 1967), he also picked up a podium position (second) in the 1966 Tour and became the first ever Dutch Tour winner in 1968.

- **Lucien AIMAR (FRA) – 6 days**
Born 28 April 1941.
Aimar's exceptional tactical sense and his fast and skilful descents gave him a unique opportunity, and he took it: he was winner in Paris, while Poulidor was busy fighting his battles with Anquetil.

1967

- **José Maria ERRANDONEA (ESP) – 2 days**
Born 12 December 1940.
The Basque cyclist stunned the crowd and devastated Poulidor (who lost by just six seconds) in the Tour's first prologue at Angers. He crashed out later.

- **Willy VAN NESTE (BEL) – 1 day**
Born 10 March 1944.
Not to be confused with Wim Van Est, the first Dutch yellow jersey. The Belgian Van Neste had success in the Classics, and won in Caen to take the jersey.

- **Giancarlo POLIDORI (ITA) – 1 day**
Born 30 October 1943.
While Raymond Poulidor never wore the yellow jersey, his Italian near-namesake Giancarlo Polidori certainly did, albeit for just one day.

- **Joseph SPRUYT (BEL) – 1 day**
Born 25 February 1943.
A quintessential team rider, he began his career with Mercier before becoming one of Merckx's most faithful assistants. His yellow jersey came at Roubaix.

- **Roger PINGEON (FRA) – 2 days**
Born 28 August 1940, died 19 March 2017.
At his best, Pingeon was untouchable. His epic 110km breakaway during the stage from Roubaix to Jambes gave him a six-minute lead over his rivals and set him up for victory in Paris.

- **Raymond RIOTTE (FRA) – 1 day**
Born 16 February 1940.
Part of the France national team, Riotte was a likeable rider who was in strong form in 1967, winning the stage in Marseille and, four days earlier, snatching the yellow jersey for just 24 hours before passing it on, definitively, to Pingeon.

- **Roger PINGEON (FRA) – 15 days**

1968

- **Charly GROSSKOST (FRA) – 3 days**
Born 5 March 1944, died 19 June 2004.
The France national pursuit champion benefitted from the new prologue format, both in the Giro and in the Tour. In 1968 he won the prologue to Vittel, as well as the following day's stage at Esch-sur-Alzette in Luxembourg.

- **Herman VAN SPRINGEL (BEL) – 1 day**
Born 14 August 1943.
One of the best racers of his generation across a wide range of competitive cycling, he won the Bordeaux–Paris seven times. He gave up the yellow jersey to Jan Janssen in the final half-stage time trial, and finished second on the podium in Paris by just 38 seconds.

- **Jean-Pierre GENET (FRA) – 1 day**
Born 24 October 1940, died 16 March 2005.
A Mercier team cyclist and supporter of Poulidor, Genet finished the 1967 Tour in last place, but came back in 1968 to wear the yellow jersey for the day. He had three stage wins to his name between 1968 and 1974.

- **Georges VANDENBERGHE (BEL) – 11 days**
Born 28 December 1941, died 23 September 1983.
The Belgian rider in the national 'B' team took the jersey at Bagnoles-de-l'Orne in Normandy and only gave it up in Aurillac, some 11 days later.

- **Rolf WOLFSHOHL (GER) – 2 days**
Born 27 December 1938.
A world cyclo-cross champion and a competent climber who took the Tour of Spain in 1965. He finished sixth in the 1968 Tour, and held the yellow jersey for two days.

- **Gregorio SAN MIGUEL (ESP) – 1 day**
Born 2 December 1940.
The Spanish climbing specialist took the yellow jersey briefly in the Alps, and stayed in contention through to the end of a close-fought race, finishing fourth.

- **Herman VAN SPRINGEL (BEL) – 3½ days**

- **Jan JANSSEN (NED) – 1 day**

1969

- **Rudi ALTIG (GER) – 1½ days**

- **Eddy MERCKX (BEL) – 1 day**
Born 17 June 1945.
The greatest champion of all time, Merckx has practically won every race out there. With his virtuosity across every discipline, he exercised

absolute power over the Tour: 34 stage wins and 97 days with the yellow jersey, received a total of 111 times!

- **Julien STEVENS (BEL) – 3 days**
Born 25 February 1943.
Part of Merckx's tightly organized guard, Stevens took the yellow following his stage victory in Maastricht.

- **Désiré LETORT (FRA) – 1 day**
Born 29 July 1943, died 9 September 2012.
A Breton tough guy who was also capable of moments of brilliance. He was Champion of France in 1967, but lost his title for doping offences. He wore the yellow from Mulhouse to Belfort.

- **Eddy MERCKX (BEL) – 17 days**

1970

- **Eddy MERCKX (BEL) – 2 days**

- **Italo ZILIOLI (ITA) – 4 days**
Born 24 September 1941.
One of Merckx's lieutenants in the Faemino team, the Italian delivered a double whammy in Angers where he won the stage and took the yellow from Merckx for four days. On a temporary basis, of course.

- **Eddy MERCKX (BEL) – 18 days**

1971

- **Eddy MERCKX (BEL) – 1 day**

- **Marinus WAGTMANS (NED) – One third of a day**
Born 25 December 1946.
The victory of Merckx's Molteni team in the prologue time trial pushed Wagtmans into the race leadership the next morning, but only for a part-stage time trial between Bâle and Fribourg. Accordingly, Wagtmans holds the yellow for the shortest time in history.

- Eddy MERCKX (BEL) – 9 days

- Joop ZOETEMELK (NED) – 1 day
  Born 3 December 1946.
  One of the best racers of all time, and with a long career (he was World Champion aged 40). He holds the record for participating in the Tour (16 times) and took on both Merckx and Hinault over the years. He finished in second place six times, and won the Tour when Hinault was forced to retire at Pau in 1980.

- Luis OCAÑA (ESP) – 3 days
  Born 9 June 1945, died 20 May 1994.
  A gutsy, stylish rider who made it his mission to beat Eddy Merckx. He would have succeeded in 1971 had he not crashed out on the Col de Menté. He eventually won the Tour two years later, when Merckx was not competing.

- Eddy MERCKX (BEL) – 7 days

1972

- Eddy MERCKX (BEL) – 1 day

- Cyrille GUIMARD (FRA) – 2½ days
  Born 20 January 1947.
  Quick in the sprints, tenacious and gung-ho, Guimard took the yellow jersey for a day at Saint-Brieuc, and then again on the Atlantic coast, before battling with Merckx until the summit of Mont Revard. Knee pain forced Guimard to drop out just two days from Paris.

- Eddy MERCKX (BEL) – 1 day

- Cyrille GUIMARD (FRA) – 4½ days

- Eddy MERCKX (BEL) – 13 days

1973

- Joop ZOETEMELK (NED) – 1 day

- Willy TEIRLINCK (BEL) – 1 half-day
  Born 10 August 1948.
  A formidable finisher and a specialist in last-minute attacks in the final kilometre. He took five stage wins, including the half-stage in Rotterdam which gave him an afternoon with the yellow jersey.

- Herman VAN SPRINGEL (BEL) – 2 days

- José CATIEAU (FRA) – 4 days
  Born 17 July 1946.
  Catieau was part of the well-oiled Bic machine. Already a winner of a half-stage in Belgium, his attack between Roubaix and Reims gave Catieau the yellow jersey through to the Alps.

- Luis OCAÑA (ESP) – 14 days

1974

- Eddy MERCKX (BEL) – 1 day

- Joseph BRUYÈRE (BEL) – 3 days
  Born 5 October 1948.
  A great all-round racer, and a double winner of the

Liège–Bastogne–Liège in 1976 and 1978. He was also one of Merckx's lieutenants within the Molteni team.

- Eddy MERCKX (BEL) – 1 day

- Gerben KARSTENS (NED) – 1 day
  Born 14 January 1942.
  An amazing character with a wicked sense of humour, Karstens was also a top level racer. He picked up six stage victories between 1965 and 1976.

- Patrick SERCU (BEL) – Half a day
  Born 27 June 1944, died 19 April 2019.
  Better known as a top rank track sprinter, he exerted a 'Merckx-like' grip on the track-based Six Day events. He had less success in road races.

- Gerben KARSTENS (NED) – 1 half-day

- Eddy MERCKX (BEL) – 16 days

1975

- Francesco MOSER (ITA) – 6 days
  Born 19 June 1951.
  He made a thundering debut on the Tour, taking the yellow jersey on his very first prologue in Charleroi. The Tour was not his ideal race format, and he built his reputation in other areas of competitive cycling.

- Eddy MERCKX (BEL) – 9 days

- Bernard THÉVENET (FRA) – 8 days
  Born 10 January 1948.
  He had already won some impressive mountain stages on the Tour (La Mongie in 1970, and Ventoux in 1972) but the best was yet to come. He was as good on the flat stages as he was in the mountains, and became the man who toppled Merckx in 1975 on the stage to Pra-Loup. Two years later he beat Kuiper and Van Impe to win the 1977 Tour.

1976

- Freddy MAERTENS (BEL) – 9 days
  Born 13 February 1952.
  Maertens was dynamite on the Tour. He won eight stages in 1976, and 13 in the Tour of Spain the following year. A fine sprinter, he had immense stamina, taking the yellow in the prologue at Saint-Jean-de-Monts and keeping it through to the Alps, with a resounding victory in the Le Touquet time trial.

- Lucien VAN IMPE (BEL) – 3 days
  Born 20 October 1946.
  Van Impe made the polka dot jersey his very own, winning the mountain classification six times to equal the tally of Bahamontès. Cyrille Guimard, the new team manager of Gitane-Campagnolo, realized that Van Impe had it in him to win the Tour, and he did.

- Raymond DELISLE (FRA) – 2 days
  Born 11 March 1943, died 11 August 2013.
  The Normandy rider picked up a big lead during the first Pyrenean stage and looked capable of winning the Tour, but an attack from Van Impe, supported by

Ocaña, led him to lose the jersey at Saint-Lary-Sou-lan.

- Lucien VAN IMPE (BEL) – 9 days

1977

- Dietrich THURAU (GER) – 15½ days
  Born 9 November 1954.
  A talented rider both in track events and on the road, Thurau led the 1977 Tour from the prologue and held onto the yellow jersey for two-thirds of the entire race. He finished in fifth place.

- Bernard THÉVENET (FRA) – 8 days

1978

- Jan RAAS (NED) – 3 days
  Born 8 November 1952.
  A major figure in the one-day Classics, Raas won the prologue in Leiden in the Netherlands but the results did not count for the general classification. He had to win the half-stage the following day to eventually pick up the yellow jersey.

- Jacques BOSSIS (FRA) – 1 day
  Born 22 December 1952.
  Effective on the attack, Bossis was among the best of the French riders of the 1970s. A late attack into Saint-Germain-en-Laye gave him the yellow jersey for a day.

- Klaus-Peter THALER (GER) – 2 days
  Born 14 May 1949.
  Thaler was a cyclo-cross World Champion and formidable climber. Winning the stage into Saint-Ger-mainen-Laye gave him two days as race leader.

- Gerrie KNETEMANN (NED) – 2 days
  Born 6 March 1951, died 2 November 2004.
  One of the best road racers of his era, Knetemann was one of Hinault's great rivals. He took 18 podium places in time trials on the Tour, and won the prologue in Fleurance on the 1979 Tour. A great finisher, he took the yellow jersey in the early part of the Tour four years in a row.

- Joseph BRUYÈRE (BEL) – 8 days

- Joop ZOETEMELK (NED) – 4 days

- Bernard HINAULT (FRA) – 3 days
  Born 14 November 1954.
  A legend of the Tour. After Eddy Merckx, Hinault was, without doubt, the greatest Tour champion. Few of his rivals could match him, with the exception of Fignon and LeMond, and nobody else managed to wear the yellow jersey in eight separate Tours de France.

1979

- Gerrie KNETEMANN (NED) – 1 day

- Jean-René BERNAUDEAU (FRA) – 1 day
Born 8 July 1956.
The Vendée rider was seen as a potential challenger to Hinault, but wasn't able to match him. Nonetheless, he made the most of the start of the 1979 Tour in the Pyrenees to take the yellow jersey after first stage.

- Bernard HINAULT (FRA) – 7 days

- Joop ZOETEMELK (NED) – 6 days

- Bernard HINAULT (FRA) – 10 days

1980

- Bernard HINAULT (FRA) – 1½ days

- Gerrie KNETEMANN (NED) – 1 day

- Yvon BERTIN (FRA) – 1 day
Born 9 April 1953.
Bertin was a useful sprinter, though it was a long breakaway towards Metz in driving rain that got him a ten-minute lead and the yellow jersey.

- Rudy PEVENAGE (BEL) – 8 days
Born15 June 1954.
Thanks to the Metz breakaway (with Bertin), he used the ten-minute lead to keep the yellow jersey for one-third of the entire Tour, from Liège through to the time trial in Laplume. He later became team manager for Jan Ullrich.

- Bernard HINAULT (FRA) – 2 days

- Joop ZOETEMELK (NED) – 10 days

1981

- Bernard HINAULT (FRA) – 1½ days

- Gerrie KNETEMANN (NED) – 4 days

- Phil ANDERSON (AUS) – 1 day
Born 12 March 1958.
Way before Anderson there were Australians on the Tour de France, but he would be the first from his country to wear the yellow jersey, for one day in the Pyrenees in 1981, and nine days in 1982. The Tour de France was going global.

- Bernard HINAULT (FRA) – 17 days

1982

- Bernard HINAULT (FRA) – 1 day

- Ludo PEETERS (BEL) – 1 day
Born 9 August 1953.
A regular on the one-day Classics circuit, winning a Paris–Brussels and also a Grand Prix d'Automne. He won three tour stages in all, two of which came with a yellow jersey too. He finished in eighth place.

- Phil ANDERSON (AUS) – 9 days

- Bernard HINAULT (FRA) – 11 days

1983

- Eric VANDERAERDEN (BEL) – 2 days
Born 11 February 1962.
A rider of enormous potential (partially unfulfilled) who won the 1985 Tour of Flanders in apocalyptic weather conditions, as well as winning the 1987 Paris–Roubaix. He was a formidable time trialist and did well in the prologues, taking the first yellow jersey in the 1983 Tour, and again two years later.

- Jean-Louis GAUTHIER (FRA) – 1 day
Born 22 December 1955, died 11 July 2014.
Gauthier was a tenacious and hard-working rider. Already a stage winner in 1980, he cashed in on the success of Coop-Mercier in the team time trial at Fontaine-au-Pire in 1983 to take the yellow jersey.

- Kim ANDERSEN (DAN) – 6 days
Born 2 October 1958.
The first Danish rider to take race leadership, he took the yellow jersey from Roubaix to Bordeaux in 1983, and from Pont-Audemer to Nancy in 1985.

- Sean KELLY (IRL) – 1 day
Born 24 May 1956.
A tough, hard-working champion with 11 victories on the Classics circuit to his name, and ranking high in the general classification (fifth in 1984 and fourth in 1985).

- Pascal SIMON (FRA) – 7 days
Born 27 September 1956.
Simon's luck ran out when he put on the yellow jersey, fracturing his shoulder in a crash. He struggled on for a further six days before dropping out.

- Laurent FIGNON (FRA) – 6 days
Born 12 August 1960, died 31 August 2010.
The young blond rider in the gold-rimmed glasses was a feature of the Tour in the 1980s, and Pascal Simon's bad luck opened the way for him in 1983. The following year he dominated the Tour, winning five stages and crushing Hinault. In 1989 his luck ran out, narrowly losing in Paris to Greg LeMond.

1984

- Bernard HINAULT (FRA) – 1 day

- Ludo PEETERS (BEL) – 1 day

- Jacques HANEGRAAF (NED) – 1 day
Born 14 December 1960.
The Dutch rider counted a Paris–Brussels and the Amstel-Gold Race among his victories, and took yellow for a day in 1984.

- Adri VAN DER POEL (NED) – ½ day
Born 17 June 1959.
Before becoming Poulidor's son-in-law, Van Der Poel himself took the yellow jersey. He was a great rider, specializing in the Classics and in cyclo-cross.

- Vincent BARTEAU (FRA) – 12 days
Born 18 March 1962.
A talented rider who made the most of a mass breakaway along with Maurice Le Guilloux and the Portuguese rider Ferreira to create a 17-minute lead over the peloton at Cergy-Pontoise. He went on to hold the yellow jersey for 12 days.

- Laurent FIGNON (FRA) – 7 days

1985

- Bernard HINAULT (FRA) – 1 day

- Eric VANDERAERDEN (BEL) – 3 days

- Kim ANDERSEN (DAN) – 4 days

- Bernard HINAULT (FRA) – 15 days

1986

- Thierry MARIE (FRA) – 1 day
Born 25 June 1963.
A powerful figure in the prologues, Marie wore the first yellow jersey in 1986 in Boulogne-Billancourt as well as at Futuroscope in 1990 and Lyon in 1991, where he also led the race after a big breakaway on the road to Le Havre.

- Alex STIEDA (CAN) – ½ day
Born 13 April 1961.
Stieda made a grand entrance to his first Tour, winning the initial half-stage (85km) and racing in a skinsuit (as was usual in the American Criterium races). He became the first North American to wear the yellow jersey.

- **Thierry MARIE (FRA) – 2 days**

- **Dominique GAIGNE (FRA) – 1 day**
Born 3 July 1961.
Part of Cyrille Guimard's Système U team, he took the lead from team mate Thierry Marie with an intermediate sprint bonus.

- **Johan VAN DER VELDE (NED) – 2 days**
Born 12 December 1956.
The Dutch rider made a promising start (best young rider in 1980, and a third place finish in 1982) and waited until 1986 for his first taste of the yellow jersey.

- **Jörgen-Vagn PEDERSEN (DAN) – 5 days**
Born 8 October 1959.
After a stage win in 1985, the Carrera rider did better the following year after a lucrative breakaway on Stage 7 from Cherbourg to Saint-Hilaire-du-Harcouët.

- **Bernard HINAULT (FRA) – 5 days**

- **Greg LEMOND (USA) – 7 days**
Born 26 June 1961.
A pioneer of American road cycling, Hinault had picked LeMond as his successor in 1985. But the 1986 Tour was largely a duel between the two men in which LeMond finally prevailed. Their arrival together, beaming, and hand in hand at Alpe d'Huez remains one of the great moments of Tour history.

1987

- **Jelle NIJDAM (NED) – 1 day**
Born 16 August 1963.
The son of a former World Champion pursuit rider, Nijdam was won the Berlin prologue on the 1987 Tour and re-took the yellow jersey the following year after the Wasquehal time trial.

- **Lech PIASECKI (POL) – 1 day**
Born 13 November 1961.
The first (and only, to this day) Polish yellow jersey, Piasecki was also the first East European tour leader, taking the yellow in Berlin two years before the wall fell.

- **Erich MAECHLER (SUI) – 6 days**
Born 24 September 1960.
A Swiss all-rounder who shone on the Tour over several seasons. He also won the stage to Puy de Dôme in 1986 and won the Milan–San Remo in 1987.

- **Charly MOTTET (FRA) – 1 day**
Born 16 December 1962.
A great Tour racer, despite his small stature, Mottet was sharp on the attack and powerful on the flat, but the Tour was perhaps a bit too long for him.

- **Martial GAYANT (FRA) – 2 days**
Born 16 November 1962.
A better cyclist than his collection of career wins would suggest, Gayant took the yellow jersey at Chaumeil in 1987, vindicating his formidable performance on the Tour.

- **Charly MOTTET (FRA) – 5 days**

- **Jean-François BERNARD (FRA) – 1 day**
Born 2 May 1962.

After a blistering performance in the time trial from Carpentras to Mont Ventoux, Bernard took the yellow jersey, but his Tour hopes were dashed by a puncture.

- **Stephen ROCHE (IRL) – 1 day**
Born 28 November 1959.
Roche's best year was 1987, winning the Giro, the Tour de France and the World Championships, just as Merckx had done in 1974.

- **Pedro DELGADO (ESP) – 4 days**
Born 15 April 1960.
A climbing specialist who developed into an all-rounder, winning the Tour in 1988. His victory was marred by a positive doping control test, but no sanction was given.

- **Stephen ROCHE (IRL) – 2 days**

1988

- **Guido BONTEMPI (ITA) – 1 day**
Born 12 January 1960.
Bontempi won the 'one-off' prologue format involving a team time trial where the final kilometre was contested by each team's best rider. The experiment was not repeated.

- **Steve BAUER (CAN) – 1 half-day**
Born 12 June 1959.
The best Canadian rider in history, Bauer took the yellow jersey twice in 1988, and again in 1990.

- **Teun VAN VLIET (NED) – 3 days**
Born 22 March 1962.
The victory of the Panasonic team in the team time trial propelled the punchy Dutch rider to a comfortable race leadership for the next three days.

- **Henk LUBBERDING (NED) – 1 day**
Born 4 August 1953.
A lynchpin of the TI-Raleigh team (which became Panasonic), Lubberding's record of race wins is a scant reflection of his commitment and generosity.

- **Jelle NIJDAM (NED) – 2 days**

- **Steve BAUER (CAN) – 4 days**

- **Pedro DELGADO (ESP) – 10 days**

1989

- **Erik BREUKINK (NED) – 1 day**
Born 1 April 1964.
A great stage racer who took a podium position (third place) in 1990. He was particularly sharp in the time trials, and won the 1989 prologue in Luxembourg to take his one and only yellow jersey.

- **Acacio DA SILVA (POR) – 3 days**
Born 2 January 1961.
That iconic figure of Portuguese cycling Joaquim Agostinho never won the yellow jersey, but Da Silva did, and on his home turf. His family lived in Luxembourg.

- **Greg LEMOND (USA) – 5 days**

- **Laurent FIGNON (FRA) – 5 days**

- **Greg LEMOND (USA) – 2 days**

- **Laurent FIGNON (FRA) – 4 days**

- **Greg LEMOND (USA) – 1 day**

1990

- **Thierry MARIE (FRA) – 1 day**

- **Steve BAUER (CAN) – 8 days**

- **Ronan PENSEC (FRA) – 2 days**
Born 10 July 1963.
Pensec's desire to succeed made up for relative gaps in his athletic repertoire. A good climber, at Saint-Gervais he took the yellow from Bauer, thanks to his part in the previous day's breakaway.

- **Claudio CHIAPPUCCI (ITA) – 8 days**
Born 28 February 1963.
He chalked up some resounding performances during this era before all the doping scandals began to emerge. In 1990 he was defending the ten-minute lead since his breakaway at Futuroscope on the first day. He still had five seconds on LeMond before the final time trial at Vassivière, but it wasn't enough. He finished the Tour in second place.

- **Greg LEMOND (USA) – 2 days**

1991

- **Thierry MARIE (FRA) – 1 day**

- **Greg LEMOND (USA) – 1 half day**

- **Rolf SÖRENSEN (DAN) – 4 days**
Born 20 April 1965.
Another great attacker who was as good on the Classics (Tour de Flandres, Liège–Bastogne–Liège, Paris–Tours) as he was in 'Grand Tour' stage races, where only the mountain stages got in his way. In 1991 he crashed out in the yellow jersey.

- **Thierry MARIE (FRA) – 2 days**

- **Greg LEMOND (USA) – 4 days**

● **Luc LEBLANC (FRA) – 1 day**
Born 4 August 1966.
Leblanc was a specialist on the most difficult routes, and had a patchy Tour record – nonetheless finishing in the top five on twice (fifth in 1991 and fourth in 1994).

● **Miguel INDURAIN (ESP) – 10 days**
Born 16 July 1964.
The first man ever to take five Tour victories in a row. One of the best riders of all time, he could also demolish the time trials and control his rivals on the mountain stages. Metronomic and self-contained, his quiet power created total domination of the race.

1992

● **Miguel INDURAIN (ESP) – 1 day**

● **Alex ZÜLLE (SUI) – 1 day**
Born 5 July 1968.
Almost as good a climber as a racer on the flat stages, he actually took his first yellow jersey from Indurain through a sprint bonus. He came second on Indurain's final victory in 1995, and again in 1999.

● **Richard VIRENQUE (SUI) – 1 day**
Born 19 November 1969.
Virenque took the King of the Mountains seven times (an unbeaten record) and took his first yellow jersey (briefly) following a long breakaway in the Pyrenees. He again wore yellow for a day in 2003, thus becoming one of just two riders (with Bartali) to have held the yellow jersey after an interval of 11 years.

● **Pascal LINO (FRA) – 10 days**
Born 13 August 1966.
Known for his elegant riding style, Lino took the yellow from his team mate Virenque after an easy breakaway in the Landes giving him a lead of seven minutes. This was enough to keep the yellow for half the Tour, from Bordeaux through to Sestrières.

● **Miguel INDURAIN (ESP) – 9 days**

1993

● **Miguel INDURAIN (ESP) – 2 days**

● **Wilfried NELISSEN (BEL) – 2 days**
Born 5 May 1970.
Nicknamed 'The Bulldog', Nelissen took the yellow after a sprint at Vannes, followed by a back-and-forth with Mario Cipollini as they each picked up a series of sprint bonuses.

● **Mario CIPOLLINI (ITA) – 1 day**
Born 23 March 1967.
A sprinting legend on the Tour, he won 12 stages but never finished any of his eight Tours. He picked up the yellow jersey from a team time trial.

● **Wilfried NELISSEN (BEL) – 1 day**

● **Mario CIPOLLINI (ITA) – 1 day**

● **Johan MUSEEUW (BEL) – 2 days**
Born 13 October 1965.

He marked up some stage wins and also a yellow jersey (though not the green jersey), two years running.

● **Miguel INDURAIN (ESP) – 12 days**

1994

● **Chris BOARDMAN (GBR) – 3 days**
Born 26 August 1968.
A prologue specialist, winning three in all. In 1994 in Lille he put in the fastest average speed (55.152km/h) but lost the yellow jersey before the Tour crossed over to England. Nor could he bring the yellow back from Ireland in 1998, where he had to abandon the race after a crash.

● **Johan MUSEEUW (BEL) – 1 day**

● **Flavio VANZELLA (ITA) – 2 days**
Born 4 March 1964.
A powerful racer, he had been an amateur World Champion team time trialist. Winning a stage in 1994 with the GB-MG team also brought him the yellow jersey

● **Sean YATES (GBR) – 1 day**
Born 18 May 1960.
Another great rider and winner of the Wasquehal time trial in the 1988 Tour. The yellow jersey would only come six years later in Rennes, thanks to a successful breakaway.

● **Johan MUSEEUW (BEL) – 2 days**

● **Miguel INDURAIN (ESP) – 13 days**

1995

● **Jacky DURAND (FRA) – 2 days**
Born 10 February 1967.
A tough rider who excelled in the breakaways. He picked up his yellow jersey in the prologue at Saint-Brieuc, where he set off early and avoided a gathering storm.

● **Laurent JALABERT (FRA) – 2 days**
Born 30 November 1968.
Towards the end of his career Jalabert found his niche with two polka dot jerseys to reward for his attacking spirit. His best year, though, was 1995.

● **Ivan GOTTI (ITA) – 2 days**
Born 28 March 1969.
Twice the winner of the Giro (in 1997 and 1999) during a scandal-hit period in Italian cycling, Gotti was in the Gewiss team and took yellow at Le Havre.

● **Bjarne RIIS (DAN) – 1 day**
Born 3 April 1964.
The following year, Riis became the first Dane to win the 1996 Tour, ending Indurain's run of victories (he finished 11th). In 2007, however, Riis admitted to doping offences.

● **Johan BRUYNEEL (BEL) – 1 day**
Born 23 August 1964.
He was the only rider able to keep up with Indurain during his offensive in the Ardennes, and at Liège both won the stage and took the yellow jersey.

● **Miguel INDURAIN (ESP) – 13 days**

1996

● **Alex ZÜLLE (SUI) – 3 days**

● **Frédéric MONCASSIN (FRA) – 1 day**
A good French sprinter and stage winner on two occasions, he took the yellow at Nogent-sur-Oise. He failed to keep it the next day, caught out by the breakaway of his Gan team mate Stéphane Heulot.

● **Stéphane HEULOT (FRA) – 3 days**
Born 20 March 1971.
Just crowned the French Champion, Heulot picked up the yellow after a long five-man breakaway towards the Lac de Madine, but was later held up by knee problems.

● **Evgeni BERZIN (RUS) – 2 days**
Born 3 June 1970.
The first Russian to wear the yellow jersey, Berzin was a good enough all-rounder to win both the Giro and the Liège–Bastogne–Liège in 1994. Riding for the controversial Gewiss team, he took the yellow at Arcs, and won the time trial on the way up to Val-d'Isère.

● **Bjarne RIIS (DAN) – 13 days**

1997

● **Chris BOARDMAN (GBR) – 1 day**

● **Mario CIPOLLINI (ITA) – 4 days**

● **Cédric VASSEUR (FRA) – 5 days**
Born 18 August 1970.
A long breakaway along the highways of the Indre gave Vasseur the yellow jersey at La Châtre. The son of Alain Vasseur (a stage winner in 1970), Cédric managed to defend the jersey for the next five days, giving it up to Ullrich at Arcalis in the Pyrenees.

● **Jan ULLRICH (GER) – 12 days**
Born 2 December 1973.
After his stunning second place in the 1996 Tour (at the age of just 23) great things were expected of Ullrich. But he won the Tour only once, in 1997,

but took second place on five occasions (including to Pantini in 1998 and Armstrong in 2000, 2001 and 2003). With his third place in 2005, Ullrich managed seven podium finishes out of eight Tours, a record just behind that of Armstrong and Poulidor. His career was shattered by Operation Puerto in 2006, which brought to light a network of systematic blood doping.

1998

● **Chris BOARDMAN (GBR) – 2 days**

● **Erik ZABEL (GER) – 1 day**
Born 7 July 1970.
A highly successful rider on the Tour with 12 stage wins and six consecutive green jerseys between 1996 and 2001, an unbeaten record to this day. More adaptable to harsher racing conditions than most sprinters, he earned two brief spells in yellow.

● **Bo HAMBURGER (DAN) – 1 day**
Born 24 May 1970.
A great Danish all-rounder, but a man who later confessed in his book *Confessions Of A Cyclist* to have been the product of systematic and widespread doping.

● **Stuart O'GRADY (AUS) – 3 days**
Born 6 August 1973.
A great rider on the flat stages with a background in Australian track cycling. He came second four times in the green jersey classification.

● **Jan ULLRICH (GER) – 1 day**

● **Laurent DESBIENS (FRA) – 2 days**
Born 16 September 1969.
With a limited haul of wins, Desbiens was a racer whose career was also marked by a doping scandal.

● **Jan ULLRICH (GER) – 5 days**

● **Marco PANTANI (ITA) – 7 days**
Born 13 January 1970, died 14 February 2004.
Italy had been waiting for a Tour winner since Gimondi in 1965, and Pantani was the man, winning the double Giro-Tour in 1998. One of the best climbers of all time, he was eliminated from the 1999 Giro for blood abnormalities, and died from an overdose in 2004.

1999

● **Lance ARMSTRONG (USA) – stripped of his race wins.**

● **Jaan KIRSIPUU (EST) – 6 days**
Born 17 July 1969.
Kirsipuu was a prolific sprinter with 130 victories to his name, who spent much of his professional career in France. He was the first rider from the Baltic states to wear the yellow jersey, picking it up after a sprint victory at Challans.

2000

● **David MILLAR (GBR) – 3 days**
Born 4 January 1977.
No relation to Robert Millar, David Millar won King of the Mountains on the 1984 Tour and was also a great all-round rider. He won the yellow jersey in the initial time trial (16.5km) at Futuroscope, and would go on to win three further Tour stages (in 2002, 2003 and 2011 in the team time trial).

● **Laurent JALABERT (FRA) – 2 days**

● **Alberto ELLI (ITA) – 4 days**
Born 9 March 1964.
Elli won the yellow after a breakaway at Tours, and kept it through to the Pyrenees.

● **Lance ARMSTRONG (USA) – stripped of his race wins.**

2001

● **Christophe MOREAU (FRA) – 2 days**
Born 12 April 1971.
Another great all-rounder who competed in 15 Tours de France from 1996 to 2010. Moreau lived through the 1998 Festina affair and just missed out on a podium position in 2000 (fourth place). He was Champion de France in 2007, and won the Critérium du Dauphiné twice.

● **Marc WAUTERS (BEL) – 1 day**
Born 23 February 1969.
A solid team rider with 15 professional seasons to his name. Riding with Rabobank, he won both the stage and the yellow jersey at Anvers, with the Tour running through his home village of Lummen.

● **Stuart O'GRADY (AUS) – 4 days**

● **Jens VOIGT (GER) – 1 day**
Born 17 September 1971.
Mentally and physically tough, and a great performer on all kinds of terrain, Voigt won his yellow jersey with a team time trial for Crédit Agricole and a breakaway. He would pick up another yellow jersey in 2005.

● **Stuart O'GRADY (AUS) – 2 days**

● **François SIMON (FRA) – 3 days**
Born 28 October 1968.
Eighteen years after Pascal Simon, François became the second Simon to wear the yellow jersey after a huge breakaway. He finished in sixth place in Paris.

● **Lance ARMSTRONG (USA) – stripped of his race wins.**

2002

● **Rubens BERTOGLIATI (SUI) – 2 days**
Born 9 May 1979.
Bertogliati surprised everyone by winning the yellow (from Lance Armstrong) on Stage 1, and keeping it for a further day from Luxembourg to Saarbrucken.

● **Erik ZABEL (GER) – 1 day**

● **Igor GONZALEZ DE GALDEANO (ESP) – 7 days**
Born 1 November 1973.
A great rider on the flat stages with a metronomic stamina, De Galdeano found himself leader thanks to Once's performance in the team time trial.

● **Lance ARMSTRONG (USA) – stripped of his race wins.**

2003

● **Bradley McGEE (AUS) – 3 days**
Born 24 February 1976.
Another rider from the Australian track competitions, McGee was an Olympic Champion and World Champion in team pursuit. When David Millar's chain failed, McGee won the prologue of the Centenary Tour de France at the foot of the Eiffel Tower.

● **Jean-Patrick NAZON (FRA) – 1 day**
Born 18 January 1977.
A sprint specialist from Eastern France whose winnings maybe fall a little short of his potential, Nazon hit a career high in 2003. He took the yellow jersey at Saint-Dizier, and later won the sprint in the Champs-Elysées.

● **Victor-Hugo PEÑA (COL) – 3 days**
Born 10 July 1974.
His great Colombian predecessors Lucho Herrera and Fabio Parra failed to get the yellow jersey, but Victor-Hugo succeeded: the first Colombian rider in yellow.

● **Richard VIRENQUE (FRA) – 1 day**

● **Lance ARMSTRONG (USA) – stripped of his race wins.**

2004

● **Fabian CANCELLARA (SUI) – 2 days**
Born 18 March 1981.
A strong and skilful rider and a specialist on the cobbles, Cancellara was a triple winner of Paris–Roubaix and the Tour of Flanders. He picked up many yellow jerseys in the prologues, including Liège (in 2004 and 2012), London (in 2007), Monaco (in 2009) and Rotterdam (in 2010). He has the most yellow jerseys among riders who have never won the Tour.

● **Thor HUSHOVD (NOR) – 1 day**
Born 18 January 1978.
The only Norwegian to wear the yellow jersey, Hushovd was known as a sprinter, but was a competent all-rounder. He won his yellow jerseys from time bonuses in 2004, a prologue victory in 2006 and a team time trial in 2011.

Robbie McEWEN (AUS) – 1 day
Born 24 June 1972.
One of the best sprinters of his era, even if he constantly had to take on quicker rivals such as Cipollini and Petacchi.

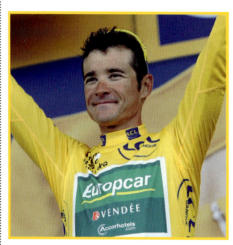

Thomas VOECKLER (FRA) – 10 days
Born 22 June 1979.
He became a popular figure on the Tour, and wore the yellow jersey for a total of 20 days, matching the tally of two-times Tour winner Bartali.

Lance ARMSTRONG (USA) – stripped of his race victories.

2005

Jens VOIGT (GER) – 1 day

Lance ARMSTRONG (USA) – stripped of his race victories.

2006

Thor HUSHOVD (NOR) – 2 days

Tom BOONEN (BEL) – 4 days
Born 15 October 1980.
A top sprinter, he has one of the biggest collections of wins in the Classics, with two Tours of Flanders, and three Paris–Roubaix wins, but with less luck in July.

Serguei HONCHAR (UKR) – 3 days
Born 3 July 1970.
The only Ukrainian to wear the yellow jersey, Honchar was World Champion in time trials in 2000, but was later found to be involved in doping.

Cyril DESSEL (FRA) – 1 day
Born 29 November 1974.
A great stage racer who won the yellow thanks to a breakaway in the Basque mountains along with the Spanish rider Mercado, who won at Pau.

Oscar PEREIRO (ESP) – 2 days
Born 3 August 1977.
He lost the Tour in the final time trial, but then won it after Landis was disqualified. Pereiro received his winner's jersey some time later, as did Andy Schleck.

Oscar PEREIRO (ESP) – 5 days

2007

Fabian CANCELLARA (SUI) – 7 days

Linus GERDEMANN (GER) – 1 day
Born 16 September 1982.
A promising German rider who won the Tour of Germany in 2008, and the Tour of Luxembourg in 2011 and 2015.

Michael RASMUSSEN (DAN) – 9 days
Born 1 June 1974.
One of the most notorious of all yellow jerseys, Rasmussen took the lead after winning in Tignes in the Alps, and then dominated in the Aubisque, seeming to have the race in the bag just four days from the finish. But he was then dismissed from the race by his team for 'lack of ethics' and later found to have traces of EPO in his blood, leading to a two-year suspension.

Alberto CONTADOR (ESP) – 4 days
Born 6 December 1982.
One of the great climbers, as well as an electrifying rider in the time trials, he took his first Tour victory following Rasmussen's exclusion from the race. He won again in 2009 despite tough competition from Armstrong, but was stripped of his 2010 title after a positive doping test.

2008

Alejandro VALVERDE (ESP) – 2 days
Born 25 April 1980.
An attacking cyclist, and winner of the first stage. He later had a two-year suspension for doping offences.

Romain FEILLU (FRA) – 1 day
Born 16 April 1984.
A small rider with big ambition, Feillu was a sprint specialist who lost the yellow jersey after a long breakaway. The time trial the next day would not be enough to win it back.

Kim KIRCHEN (LUX) – 4 days
Born 3 July 1978.
The son of Erny Kirchen, Kim was a decent rider on the flat but a great attacker on the climbs, and was the yellow jersey successor to Charly Gaul 50 years earlier.

Cadel EVANS (AUS) – 5 days
Born 14 February 1977.
Evans crashed out with the yellow jersey in 2008 and fractured an elbow in 2010, but was talented in all cycling disciplines, becoming the first Australian to win the Tour in 2011.

Fränk SCHLECK (LUX) – 2 days
Born 15 April 1980.
The older brother of Andy. A great climber, he won on the Alpe d'Huez in 2006, where he would later lose his first yellow jersey two years later.

Carlos SASTRE (ESP) – 5 days
Born 22 April 1975.
The unshowy Spanish climber was strong across all disciplines, featuring in the top ten finishers over five Tours de France. In 2008 he took the yellow jersey from Cadel Evans in the final time trial, and went on to win the Tour.

2009

Fabian CANCELLARA (SUI) – 6 days

Roberto NOCENTINI (ITA) – 8 days
A great attacker on the climbs, Nocentini took the yellow after an eight-man breakaway, capitalizing on the top riders' teams holding each other back in the peloton behind. He took the yellow in Andorra and held it through to Eastern France.

Alberto CONTADOR (ESP) – 7 days

2010

Fabian CANCELLARA (SUI) – 2 days

Sylvain CHAVANEL (FRA) – 1 day
Born 30 June 1979.
One of the best attacking French riders of the 2000s, he was best known for his success in the one-day Classics. His Tour really took off in 2010, taking the yellow at Spa (but losing it the next day on the cobbles) then retaking the lead in the Jura for a day.

Fabian CANCELLARA (SUI) – 4 days

Sylvain CHAVANEL (FRA) – 1 day

Cadel EVANS (AUS) – 1 day

Andy SCHLECK (LUX) – 12 days
Born 10 June 1985.
A great climber, but hampered by some tactical and technical shortcomings, notably in time trials and on mountain descents. Placed second to Contador in 2009, he won the Tour in 2010 after Contador's positive doping test. He looked to be the favourite for the 2011 Tour, but was let down by his time trial performances.

2011

Philippe GILBERT (BEL) – 1 day
Born 5 July 1982.
Gilbert generally gave the Tour a miss to concentrate on the Classics races. In 2011 he won all three Ardennes Classics, and building on this Grand Slam, he went for the yellow jersey on Stage 1 of the Tour.

Thor HUSHOVD (NOR) – 7 days

Thomas VOECKLER (FRA) – 10 days

- Andy SCHLECK (LUX) – 1 day
- Cadel EVANS (AUS) – 2 days

2012

- Fabian CANCELLARA (SUI) – 7 days
- Bradley WIGGINS (GBR) – 14 days
Born 28 April 1980.
A specialist in time trials and individual and team pursuit, (with five Olympic gold medals from 2008 to 2016), Wiggins came third in the 2009 Tour but felt that he could win it in 2012. Racing with the Sky team, he became the first English winner of the Tour de France, the only Grand Tour win of his career. He went on to hold the hour distance record.

2013

- Marcel KITTEL (GER) – 1 day.
Born 11 May 1988.
Kittel took 14 stage victories during the Tour from 2013 to 2017, excelling on the flat sprints, often against his persistent rival Mark Cavendish. He took the first yellow jersey in the Centenary Tour at Bastia.
- Jan BAKELANTS (BEL) – 2 days
Born 14 February 1986.
A strong Tour debut, winning the stage in Ajaccio with a late attack, and picking up the yellow jersey.
- Simon GERRANS (AUS) – 2 days
Born 16 May 1980.
Gerrans won two Tour stages (in 2008 and 2013), but it was the success of his Orica-GreenEDGE team in the time trial at Nice that brought him the yellow jersey.
- Daryl IMPEY (RSA) – 2 days
Born 6 December 1984.
Strong on sprints and time trials, and first African to take the yellow jersey.
- Christopher FROOME (GBR) – 14 days
Born 20 May 1985.
Born in Kenya to British parents, he had already indicated that he could be at least as good as Wiggins in 2012 (where Froome came second). His talent both as climber and as a road racer has ensured him a succession of Tour wins.

2014

- Marcel KITTEL (GER) – 1 day
- Vincenzo NIBALI (ITA) – 7 days
Born 14 November 1984.
Nibali had already taken the yellow jersey in England when Froome crashed out before the race returned to France. Race favourite Contador's subsequent crash and exit in Stage 10 left the race wide open, and Nibali made the most of it.
- Tony GALLOPIN (FRA) – 1 day
Born 24 May 1988.
His participation in a breakaway in the Vosges earned Gallopin his 24 hours in the yellow jersey.
- Vincenzo NIBALI (ITA) – 12 days

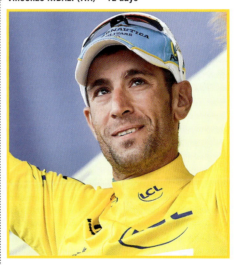

2015

- Rohan DENNIS (AUS) – 1 day.
Born 28 May 1990.
Dennis briefly held the hour distance record at the start of 2015, and won the inaugural time trial at Rotterdam.
- Fabian CANCELLARA (SUI) – 1 day.
- Christopher FROOME (GBR) – 1 day
- Tony MARTIN (GER) – 3 days
Born 23 April 1985.
A powerful road racer, Martin made his breakaway towards the end of the cobbles stage to Arras, and took the yellow jersey for his efforts. He gave it up three days later after a crash near Le Havre.
- Christopher FROOME (GBR) – 15 days

2016

- Mark CAVENDISH (GBR) – 1 day
Born 21 May 1985.
A sprint phenomenon and winner of 30 stages in the Tour de France, he finally took the yellow jersey at the end of the first stage, right alongside the famous Utah Beach of the Normandy landings.

- Peter SAGAN (SVK) – 3 days
Born 26 January 1990.
Supreme sprinter Sagan had missed out on stage wins for the past three years. But on the sharp hill previous Cherbourg the reigning UCI World Champion won both the stage and the yellow jersey.
- Greg VAN AVERMAET (BEL) – 3 days
Born 17 May 1985.
Avermaet led a lucrative breakaway on the Massif Central to become leader as far as the Pyrenees. The same year, he became Olympic Champion in Rio.
- Christopher FROOME (GBR) – 14 days

2017

- Geraint THOMAS (GBR) – 4 days.
Born 25 May 1986.
Thomas took his first yellow jersey in the inaugural time trial in Düsseldorf, which he returned to Chris Froome a few days later. He was still in second place when he crashed out of the race.
- Christopher FROOME (GBR) – 7 days
- Fabio ARU (ITA) – 2 days
Born 3 July 1990.
The Italian climber worked the Pyrenees to create a brief lapse in Chris Froome's domination of the race.
- Christopher FROOME (GBR) – 8 days.

2018

- Fernando GAVIRIA (COL) – 1 day
Born 19 August 1994.
A sprinter from Colombia, land of the climbers, and only the second Colombian to wear the yellow jersey.
- Peter SAGAN (SLK) – 1 day
- Greg VAN AVERMAET (BEL) – 8 days
- Geraint THOMAS (GBR) – 11 days

Luis Ocaña: Tour de France 1973.
Stage 18, from Brive to Puy de Dôme.

NOT ONLY THE YELLOW, BUT ALSO...

MANY YELLOW JERSEY RIDERS HAVE ALSO EXCELLED BEYOND THE GENERAL CLASSIFICATION. HERE'S HOW:

THEY WORE THE YELLOW JERSEY
AND WON THE MOUNTAINS CLASSIFICATION

The mountains classification of the Tour de France was created in 1933 (but the polka dot jersey appeared only in 1975).

René Vietto (FRA, 1934*)
Félicien Vervaecke (BEL, 1935, 1937)
Gino Bartali (ITA, 1938, 1948)
Sylvère Maes (BEL, 1939)
Pierre Brambilla (ITA, 1947)
Fausto Coppi (ITA, 1949, 1952)
Louison Bobet (FRA, 1950)
Raphaël Géminiani (FRA, 1951)
Charly Gaul (LUX, 1955, 1956)
Gastone Nencini (ITA, 1957)
Federico Bahamontes (ESP, 1954, 1958, 1959, 1962, 1963, 1964)
Eddy Merckx (BEL, 1969, 1970)
Lucien Van Impe (BEL, 1971, 1972, 1975, 1977, 1981, 1983)
Bernard Hinault (FRA, 1986)
Richard Virenque (FRA, 1994, 1995, 1996, 1997, 1999, 2003, 2004)
Laurent Jalabert (FRA, 2001, 2002)
Michael Rasmussen (DAN, 2005, 2006)
Carlos Sastre (ESP, 2008)
Thomas Voeckler (FRA, 2012)
Christopher Froome (GBR, 2015).

*The year of their victory in the mountains classification.

THEY WORE THE YELLOW JERSEY
AND WON THE POINTS CLASSIFICATION

Created in 1953.

Fritz Schaer (SUI, 1953*)
Ferdi Kübler (1954)
Jean Forestier (FRA, 1957)
André Darrigade (FRA, 1959, 1960)
Rudi Altig (GER, 1962)
Rik Van Looy (BEL, 1963)
Jan Janssen (1964, 1965, 1967)
Eddy Merckx (1969, 1971, 1972)
Herman Van Springel (BEL, 1973)
Patrick Sercu (BEL, 1974)
Freddy Maertens (BEL, 1976, 1978, 1981)
Bernard Hinault (1979)
Rudy Pevenage (BEL, 1980)
Sean Kelly (IRL, 1982, 1983, 1985, 1989)
Eric Vanderaerden (BEL, 1986)
Laurent Jalabert (FRA, 1992, 1995)
Erik Zabel (GER, 1996, 1997, 1998, 1999, 2000, 2001)
Robbie Mc Ewen (AUS, 2004, 2006)
Thor Hushovd (NOR, 2005, 2009)
Tom Boonen (BEL, 2007)
Mark Cavendish (GBR, 2011)
Peter Sagan (SLQ, 2012, 2013, 2014, 2015, 2016, 2018).

*The year of their victory in the points classification.

THEY WORE THE YELLOW JERSEY
AND WON BEST YOUNG RIDER

Created in 1975.

Francesco Moser (ITA, 1975*)
Dietrich Thurau (GER, 1977)
Henk Lubberding (GER, 1978)
Jean-René Bernaudeau (FRA, 1979)
Johan Van der Velde (NED, 1980)
Phil Anderson (AUS, 1982)
Laurent Fignon (FRA, 1983)
Greg LeMond (USA, 1984)
Erik Breukink (NED, 1988)
Marco Pantani (ITA, 1994, 1995)
Jan Ullrich (GER, 1996, 1997, 1998)
Alberto Contador (ESP, 2007)
Andy Schleck (LUX, 2008, 2009, 2010)

*The year of their victory in the best young rider classification.

TRACK

Chris Boardman (GBR, 1994)
Miguel Indurain (ESP, 1995)
Alex Zülle (SUI, 1996)
Laurent Jalabert (FRA, 1997)
Jan Ullrich (GER, 1999, 2001)
Sergueï Honchar (UKR, 2000)
Fabian Cancellara (2006, 2007, 2009, 2010)
Tony Martin (GER, 2011, 2012, 2013, 2016)
Bradley Wiggins (GBR, 2014)
Rohan Dennis (AUS, 2018).

*Year of their world title.

THEY WORE THE YELLOW JERSEY
AND WERE
WORLD CHAMPION

ROAD

Learco Guerra (ITA, 1931*)
Georges Speicher (FRA, 1933)
Jean Aerts (BEL, 1935)
Antonin Magne (FRA, 1936)
Marcel Kint (BEL, 1938)
Rik Van Steenbergen (BEL, 1949, 1956, 1957)
Ferdi Kübler (SUI, 1951)
Fausto Coppi (ITA, 1953)
Louison Bobet (FRA, 1954)
André Darrigade (FRA, 1959)
Rik Van Looy (BEL, 1960, 1961)
Jan Janssen (NED, 1964)
Tom Simpson (GBR, 1965)
Rudi Altig (GER, 1966)
Eddy Merckx (BEL, 1967, 1971, 1974)
Felice Gimondi (ITA, 1973)
Freddy Maertens (BEL, 1976, 1981)
Francesco Moser (ITA, 1977)
Gerrie Knetemann (NED, 1978)
Jan Raas (NED, 1979)
Bernard Hinault (FRA, 1980)
Greg LeMond (USA, 1983, 1989)
Joop Zootemelk (NED, 1985)
Stephen Roche (IRL,1987)
Luc Leblanc (FRA, 1994)
Johan Museeuw (BEL, 1996)
Mario Cipollini (ITA, 2002)
Tom Boonen (BEL, 2005)
Cadel Evans (AUS, 2009)
Thor Hushovd (NOR, 2010)
Mark Cavendish (GBR, 2011)
Philippe Gilbert (BEL, 2012)
Peter Sagan (SLQ, 2015, 2016, 2017)
Alejandro Valverde (ESP, 2018).

THEY WORE THE YELLOW JERSEY
AND WON THE
VUELTA A ESPAÑA

Rudi Altig (GER, 1962*)
Jacques Anquetil (FRA, 1963)
Jan Janssen (NED, 1967)
Felice Gimondi (ITA, 1968)
Roger Pingeon (FRA, 1969)
Luis Ocaña (ESP, 1970)
Eddy Merckx (BEL, 1973)
Freddy Maertens (BEL, 1977)
Bernard Hinault (FRA, 1978, 1983)
Joop Zoetemelk (NED, 1979)
Pedro Delgado (ESP, 1985, 1989)
Sean Kelly (IRL, 1988)
Laurent Jalabert (FRA, 1995)
Alex Zülle (SUI, 1996, 1997)
Jan Ullrich (GER, 1999)
Alberto Contador (ESP, 2008)
Alejandro Valverde (ESP, 2009)
Vincenzo Nibali (ITA, 2010)
Fabio Aru (ITA, 2015)
Christopher Froome (GBR, 2017).

*Year of their victory in the Vuelta.

THEY WORE THE YELLOW JERSEY
AND WON THE
GIRO D'ITALIA

Learco Guerra (ITA, 1934*)
Gino Bartali (ITA, 1936, 1937, 1946)
Fausto Coppi (ITA, 1940, 1947, 1949, 1952, 1953)
Fiorenzo Magni (ITA, 1948, 1951, 1955)
Hugo Koblet (SUI, 1950)
Charly Gaul (LUX, 1956, 1959)
Gastone Nencini (ITA, 1957)
Jacques Anquetil (FRA, 1960, 1964)
Eddy Merckx (BEL, 1968, 1970, 1972, 1973, 1974)
Felice Gimondi (ITA, 1967, 1969, 1976)
Bernard Hinault (FRA, 1980, 1982, 1985)
Stephen Roche (IRL, 1987)
Laurent Fignon (FRA, 1989)
Miguel Indurain (ESP, 1992, 1993)
Evgueni Berzin (RUS, 1994)
Ivan Gotti (ITA, 1997, 1999)
Marco Pantani (ITA, 1998)
Alberto Contador (ESP, 2008, 2015)
Vincenzo Nibali (ITA, 2013, 2016)
Christopher Froome (GBR, 2018).

*Year of their victory in the Giro.

THEY WORE THE YELLOW JERSEY
AND WON THE
OLYMPIC GAMES

ROAD

Jan Ullrich (GER, 2000*)
Bradley Wiggins (GBR, 2012)
Greg Van Avermaet (BEL, 2016).

TRACK

Miguel Indurain (ESP, 1996)
Fabian Cancellara (SUI, 2008).

*Year of their Olympic title.

THE YELLOW JERSEY
A GLOBAL BILLBOARD

Whether it's made from wool or the most high-tech synthetic textiles, the leader's jersey has become a magnet for sponsors first from within and later from beyond the world of cycling.

From its creation in 1919 through to the beginning of the Second World War, the yellow jersey remained unmarked by any kind of advertising or sponsorship. There was just a discreet map of France on the front pocket – the logo of Uni-Sport (who made the cycling jerseys) which occasionally appeared from around the mid-1930s. Subsequent manufacturers of the yellow jersey (such as Le Coq Sportif or Castelli) have done the same. Commercial sponsorship began in 1948 with the sponsor paying the race leader a bonus fee for each day he wore the jersey. The first brand names visible across the front of the jersey were those of cycle manufacturers or the racing team, and it was only during the Merckx era, starting in 1969, that an advertising space was reserved for the commercial sponsor on the fabric of the jersey itself. It remains to this day a fairly discreet zone on the rider's left chest, just below the collarbone. Virlux became the first commercial partner in 1969. The current sponsor, LCL, has had held this spot for the last 30 years. ∎

Lucien Aimar and Felice Gimondi, yellow jerseys from the 1960s.

1919 – 2018
TOUR WINNERS AND THEIR YELLOW JERSEYS

From Firmin Lambot's yellow jersey in fine wool, to the high-tech breathable polyester worn by Geraint Thomas, here is the definitive gallery of what has become an iconic symbol of victory.

1919
Firmin Lambot
Belgium

1920
Philippe Thys
Belgium

1921
Léon Scieur
Belgium

1922
Firmin Lambot
Belgium

1923
Henri Pélissier
France

1924
Ottavio Bottecchia
Italy

1925
Ottavio Bottecchia
Italy

1926
Lucien Buysse
Belgium

1927
Nicolas Frantz
Luxembourg

1928
Nicolas Frantz
Luxembourg

1929
Maurice De Waele
Belgium

1930
André Leducq
France

1931
Antonin Magne
France

1932
André Leducq
France

1933
Georges Speicher
France

1934
Antonin Magne
France

1935
Romain Maes
Belgium

1936
Sylvère Maes
Belgium

1937
Roger Lapébie
France

1938
Gino Bartali
Italy

1939
Sylvère Maes
Belgium

1947
Jean Robic
France

1948
Gino Bartali
Italy

1949
Fausto Coppi
Italy

1950
Ferdi Kübler
Switzerland

1951
Hugo Koblet
Switzerland

1952
Fausto Coppi
Italy

1953
Louison Bobet
France

1954
Louison Bobet
France

1955
Louison Bobet
France

1956
Roger Walkowiak
France

1957
Jacques Anquetil
France

1958
Charly Gaul
Luxembourg

1959
Federico Bahamontes
Spain

1960
Gastone Nencini
Italy

1961
Jacques Anquetil
France

1962
Jacques Anquetil
France

1963
Jacques Anquetil
France

1964
Jacques Anquetil
France

1965
Felice Gimondi
Italy

1966
Lucien Aimar
France

1967
Roger Pingeon
France

1968
Jan Jansen
The Netherlands

1969
Eddy Merckx
Belgium

1970
Eddy Merckx
Belgium

1971
Eddy Merckx
Belgium

1972
Eddy Merckx
Belgium

1973
Luis Ocaña
Spain

1974
Eddy Merckx
Belgium

1975
Bernard Thévenet
France

1976
Lucien Van Impe
Belgium

1977
Bernard Thévenet
France

1978
Bernard Hinault
France

1979
Bernard Hinault
France

1980
Joop Zoetemelk
The Netherlands

1981
Bernard Hinault
France

1982
Bernard Hinault
France

1983
Laurent Fignon
France

1984
Laurent Fignon
France

1985
Bernard Hinault
France

1986
Greg LeMond
USA

1987
Stephen Roche
Ireland

1988
Pedro Delgado
Spain

1989
Greg LeMond
USA

1990
Greg LeMond
USA

1991
Miguel Indurain
Spain

1992
Miguel Indurain
Spain

1993
Miguel Indurain
Spain

1994
Miguel Indurain
Spain

1995
Miguel Indurain
Spain

1996
Bjarne Riis
Denmark

1997
Jan Ullrich
Germany

1998
Marco Pantani*
Italy

2006
Oscar Pereiro
Spain

2007
Alberto Contador
Spain

2008
Carlos Sastre
Spain

2009
Alberto Contador
Spain

2010
Andy Schleck
Luxembourg

2011
Cadel Evans
Australia

2012
Bradley Wiggins
Great Britain

2013
Christopher Froome
Great Britain

2014
Vincenzo Nibali
Italy

2015
Christopher Froome
Great Britain

2016
Christopher Froome
Great Britain

2017
Christopher Froome
Great Britain

2018
Geraint Thomas
Great Britain

HENRI DESGRANGE AND 'HD'

Henri Desgrange, creator of the Tour de France and director of the race for more than three decades, died in 1940 at the age of 75. It was in his honour that the initials 'HD' appeared on the yellow jersey from 1949 onwards, for the Tour that was won by Fausto Coppi. (The same year, a monument to the Tour was erected at the summit of the Galibier.) Over the following years, the initials 'HD' would adorn either the chest or the shoulders of the race leaders. From the 1980s, the initials were printed alongside the Tour logo, but then they disappeared altogether in 1984, replaced by the 'Le Tour' logo in its various evolving formats. Jean-Marie Leblanc, tour director since 1987 seized on the occasion of the Centenary Tour to bring back the famous initials on the iconic jersey.

YELLOW JERSEY SPONSORS

The leader's jersey has been sponsored since 1948, with the current sponsor, LCL, supporting the jersey for more than 30 years!

1948-1953
SOFIL
(yarn)

Serafino Biagioni (with Gino Bartali and Fausto Coppi)

1954-1955
LA SUZE
(aperitif)

Louison Bobet

1956
CALOR
(electrical appliances

Gerrit Voorting

1958
SOLEIL - L'AIGLE
(insurance)

Vito Favero

1961-1962
SHELL-BERRE
(oil company)

Rudi Altig

1963-1964
LE TORO
(trousers)

Gilbert Desmet (with Louison Bobet and Jacques Anquetil)

1965-1968
CHAMPIGNEULLES
(beer)

Jan Janssen

1969-1970
VIRLUX
(butter)

Désiré Lefort

1971-1983
MIKO
(ice cream)

Luis Ocaña

1984-1986
BANANIA
(breakfast products)

Laurent Fignon

SINCE 1987
CRÉDIT LYONNAIS / LCL
(financial services)

Stephen Roche

Fausto Coppi:
Tour de France, 1952.
Stage 11, Bourg-d'Oisans to Sestrières.

ENCYCLOPEDIA OF
THE YELLOW JERSEY

An Hachette UK Company
www.hachette.co.uk

Originally published in the French language
under the title *L'Encyclopédie du Maillot Jaune*
© 2019, Éditions Solar, an imprint of Edi8,
Paris © 2019, L'Équipe, Paris
Texts: Philippe Bouvet and Frédérique Galametz

This edition first published in Great Britain
in 2019 by Hamlyn, an imprint of
Octopus Publishing Group Ltd
Carmelite House
50 Victoria Embankment
London EC4Y 0DZ
www.octopusbooks.co.uk

English Language Translation © Octopus
Publishing Group 2019

Distributed in the US by
Hachette Book Group
1290 Avenue of the Americas
4th and 5th Floors
New York, NY 10104

Distributed in Canada by
Canadian Manda Group
664 Annette St., Toronto,
Ontario, Canada M6S 2C8

ISBN 978-0-60063-633-5

A CIP catalogue record for this book is
available from the British Library.

Printed and bound in China

10 9 8 7 6 5 4 3 2 1

L'ÉQUIPE

For this edition:
Publishing Director: Trevor Davies
English Translation: Paul Carslake
English Edition Designer: Caroline Guest